PERANAKAN CHINESE IDENTITIES

IN THE GLOBALIZING MALAY ARCHIPELAGO

The **ISEAS – Yusof Ishak Institute** (formerly Institute of Southeast Asian Studies) is an autonomous organization established in 1968. It is a regional centre dedicated to the study of socio-political, security, and economic trends and developments in Southeast Asia and its wider geostrategic and economic environment. The Institute's research programmes are grouped under Regional Economic Studies (RES), Regional Strategic and Political Studies (RSPS), and Regional Social and Cultural Studies (RSCS). The Institute is also home to the ASEAN Studies Centre (ASC), the Singapore APEC Study Centre, and the Temasek History Research Centre (THRC).

ISEAS Publishing, an established academic press, has issued more than 2,000 books and journals. It is the largest scholarly publisher of research about Southeast Asia from within the region. ISEAS Publishing works with many other academic and trade publishers and distributors to disseminate important research and analyses from and about Southeast Asia to the rest of the world.

LEO SURYADINATA

PERANAKAN CHINESE IDENTITIES

IN THE GLOBALIZING MALAY ARCHIPELAGO

ISEAS YUSOF ISHAK
INSTITUTE

First published in Singapore in 2022 by
ISEAS Publishing
30 Heng Mui Keng Terrace
Singapore 119614

E-mail: publish@iseas.edu.sg
Website: <http://bookshop.iseas.edu.sg>

The responsibility for facts and opinions in this publication rests exclusively with the author and his interpretations do not necessarily reflect the views or the policy of the publisher or its supporters.

ISEAS Library Cataloguing-in-Publication Data

Name(s): Suryadinata, Leo, 1941-, author.
Title: Peranakan Chinese identities in the globalizing Malay Archipelago / by
    Leo Suryadinata.
Description: Singapore : ISEAS – Yusof Ishak Institute, 2022. | Includes
    bibliographical references and index.
Identifiers: ISBN 978-981-4951-67-8 (soft cover) | ISBN 978-981-4951-70-8 (pdf)
Subjects: LCSH: Peranakan (Asian people)—Ethnic identity. | Chinese—
    Indonesia. | Chinese—Southeast Asia.
Classification: LCC DS523.4 C5S962

Cover design by Refine Define Pte Ltd
Typesetting by International Typesetters Pte Ltd
Printed in Singapore by Mainland Press Pte Ltd

CONTENTS

Part II: Focusing on Indonesia

PREFACE

In the recent past, there were quite a few studies on the Peranakan Chinese in the Malay Archipelago, particularly in the three countries: Indonesia, Malaysia and Singapore (IMS). I have conducted some bibliographical research and published one article entitled "Selected Publications on Partially Assimilated Chinese in Indonesia, Malaysia and Singapore, 1980–2006" (see Leo Suryadinata, *Understanding the Ethnic Chinese in Southeast Asia* (Singapore: Institute of Southeast Asian Studies, 2007), pp. 173–92). In this article, I have included four categories of the publications: (1) General Studies; (2) Politics, History, Education and Society; (3) Religion; and (4) Memoirs and Biographies.

As the article only covered the publications up to 2006, that means that it did not include publications in the last fourteen years (2007–21). As a matter of fact, after 2006 there were many studies on the Peranakan Chinese in IMS. The Chinese Heritage Centre (NTU) and the Baba House (NUS) had jointly conducted two international conferences on the Peranakan Chinese in the globalizing world. These conference proceedings have also been published in 2010 and 2015 respectively. Apart from the two conference proceedings, there are also many books published, including two books on the Peranakan Chinese in Indonesia during the above period (see Appendix 2).

Peranakan Chinese communities and their "hybrid" culture have fascinated many observers. Some argue that these communities and their culture are still alive while others maintain that they have demised as they have become a museum culture. Apparently, observers are using different perspectives in putting forward their arguments. Who are the Peranakan Chinese? Should they be narrowly or broadly defined? Where are they to be found? What are the Peranakan identity and culture? Do they share identical characteristics throughout the Malay Archipelago? How do the Peranakan communities evolve in the colonial, post-colonial and globalization eras? What is the current status of the Peranakan communities and their culture? How is the future of the Peranakan community being envisioned? These are some of the questions that this book attempts to answer.

In the past, I have edited at least two books on the Peranakan Chinese, published one book on Peranakan politics in Java and many papers on the subject. However, I did not have the opportunity to publish my own studies on the Peranakan Chinese in the Malay Archipelago as a book. This Covid-19 pandemic crisis during which we have to work from home has given me time to look at my past papers on the subject and eventually put them together into a book.

These papers, which were mainly written in the last two decades, addressed issues such as Peranakan identities and culture, society and politics, language and literature in the three countries in the Malay Archipelago, i.e., Indonesia, Malaysia and Singapore. Due to the coverage of the papers, I have divided the book into two parts. Part I is on the regional dimension, which contains nine chapters that discuss the three countries and beyond. Part II consists of five chapters which focus on one country, i.e., Indonesia. This book is far from being comprehensive as it does not include chapters on Peranakan economic activities, Peranakan porcelain, Peranakan cuisine and Peranakan attire, as these require more detailed investigation.

On the regional aspect, I have included one chapter entitled "Prospects of the Peranakan Community: Comments on Dr Tan Ta Sen's Speech", which is in fact my comments on Dr Tan Ta Sen's speech on the same topic. As this is an important issue and worth discussing, I have also included Dr Tan's speech as an appendix.

Many of the chapters were previously published in the *Asian Culture*, a journal of the Singapore Society of Asian Studies, one was specially written for this book, and the rest were derived from various book chapters. However, some have been rewritten or combined to prevent too much repetition.

I hope the publication of this book would further encourage people to look at the Peranakan Chinese phenomena from a regional and even global perspective.

Leo Suryadinata
July 2021
Kota Singa

ACKNOWLEDGEMENTS

We would like to express our thanks to the publishers for permitting us to reproduce fully or partly the following articles:

Chapter 5: "Peranakan Chinese in IMS: The Socio-Political Dimension". First published as "Peranakan Chinese in Indonesia, Malaysia and Singapore: The Socio-Political Dimension", in *Peranakan Chinese in a Globalizing Southeast Asia*, edited by Leo Suryadinata (Singapore: Chinese Heritage Centre and NUS Baba House, 2010), pp. 41–49.

Chapter 6: "Malay/Indonesian Translations of Chinese Literature: Past and Present". First published in *Asian Culture* 34 (June 2010): 24–41.

Chapter 7: "Innovation and Transformation: Peranakan Chinese Literatures/ Publications in IMS". First published as "Innovation and Transformation: Peranakan Chinese Literatures/Publications in Indonesia, Malaysia and Singapore", *Asian Culture* 41 (December 2017): 92–99.

Chapter 9: "Prospects of the Peranakan Community: Comments on Dr Tan Ta Sen's Speech". First published as "Prospects of the Peranakan Community: Comments on Dr. Tan Ta Sen's Speech", *Asian Culture* 40 (December 2017): 130–37.

Chapter 10: "Peranakan Chinese and the Indonesian Press, Language and Literature". The above chapter is based on two of my published articles: "The Contribution of the Indonesian Chinese in the Development of the Indonesian Press, Language and Literature", in *Chinese Studies in the Malay World: A Comparative Approach*, edited by Ding Choo Ming and Ooi Kee Beng (Singapore: Eastern Universities Press, 2003), and "Modern Peranakan Indonesia Literature: Past and Present", in *Peranakan Communities in the Era of Decolonization and Globalization*, edited by Leo Suryadinata (Singapore: Chinese Heritage Centre and NUS Baba House, 2015), pp. 55–65.

Chapter 11: "Muslim Chinese in Indonesia: Between Chinese-ness and Indonesian-ness". First published in *Asian Culture* 32 (June 2008): 32–43.

Chapter 12: "State and 'Chinese Religions' in Indonesia: Confucianism, Tridharma and Buddhism During the Suharto Rule and After". First published in Tan Chee Beng, ed., *After Migration and Religious Affiliation: Religions, Chinese Identities and Transnational Networks* (Singapore: World Scientific Publishing, 2014), pp. 19–42.

Chapter 13: "Peranakan Chinese Politics and Decolonization in Indonesia". First published in Leo Suryadinata, ed., *Peranakan Communities in the Era of Decolonization and Globalization* (Singapore: Chinese Heritage Centre and NUS Baba House, 2015), pp. 3–15.

Chapter 14: "The Integration of Indonesian Chinese into Mainstream Society: A Reflection". First published in *Asian Culture* 36 (August 2012): 9–17.

Appendix 1: Tan Ta Sen, "The Prospects of the Peranakan Community at the Age of Globalization". First published in *Asian Culture* 40 (December 2016): 124–29.

PART I

Regional Dimensions: Indonesia, Malaysia and Singapore (IMS)

1

PERANAKAN AND OTHER RELATED TERMS

At the beginning, it is imperative for us to explain key terms Peranakan and other related terms such as Baba, Nyonya (Nonya), Straits Chinese and Straits-born Chinese to avoid misunderstanding. In fact, the terms are not very straightforward, and the meaning of the terms tended to change from period to period.

Peranakan

Peranakan, a Malay word, is now used as a generic term to refer to the local-born Chinese who speaks Malay or a local language at home. The present meaning of the term is the descendants of the union between indigenous people (*anak negeri*) and foreigners.[1] It is not known when the term first came into existence.[2] In the nineteenth century, *The Hikayat Abdullah*, which was written by Munshi Abdullah, did not mention the term Peranakan but mentioned two Baba in British Malaya.[3]

His son, Mohamed Ibrahim, wrote a book and used the term *peranak awak* to refer to the people in Penang who were born locally to Siamese or Burmese fathers and Chinese mothers.[4] But the meaning is different from our ordinary usage. In fact, in the mid-nineteenth century, the term Peranakan was already quite popular. According to a dictionary published in 1856, the Malays called the "mixed race" of Chinese descendants "Peranakan China" (*Peranakan Cina*, according to the current spelling) during that time.[5] Later, the term Peranakan was used as the abbreviation of *Peranakan Cina*, as if the Peranakan question was a solely Chinese phenomenon.

In fact, there were many types of Peranakan. The term was used to refer to the Indian Peranakan or "Jawi Peranakan", who were the descendants of Indian Muslims and Malay women. Nevertheless, because of the large number of Peranakan Chinese, the term Peranakan has generally been associated with the Chinese community.

The Peranakan phenomenon was not confined to Singapore and Malaysia only. It was quite common to the region as a whole, including Indonesia and the Philippines. While the term Peranakan has been used in Indonesia, Malaysia and Singapore, a different term—"Mestizo"—has been used to refer to a similar group in the Philippines. However, unlike the mestizos in the Philippines, who became Filipino rather than Chinese, the Peranakan Chinese in Singapore, Malaysia, and Indonesia remained largely "Chinese" in terms of their identity. The reasons were complex and religion was definitely an important one.

The emergence of this Peranakan Chinese community is well known. This was due to the fact that earlier Chinese migrants were males who were either bachelors or married men who came to Southeast Asia without their spouses. They married local women,[6] especially those who were nominal Muslim or non-Muslim, and with their children, they formed a new kind of community, which had the sociocultural make-up of both the Chinese and the Malay.

This hybrid culture was distinct from either Chinese culture or Malay culture. The major characteristic was the use of the Malay language. A large number of Peranakan children never developed a command of the Chinese language and could only converse in the Malay language, as was the case with the Peranakans in Batavia (Java), Malacca, and Singapore. Recent studies also confirmed that in the missionary schools where the Chinese language was taught, the medium of instruction was Malay.[7] Their attire was also a mixture of Chinese and local dress. In fact, the female Peranakan wore Malay dress and had Malay hairstyle. The food was also distinct as it included Malay ingredients but pork—the preferred Chinese meat—was retained. These Peranakan Chinese were not only found in Java but also outside Java, and in Peninsular Malaya and Singapore.

Nevertheless, it should be pointed out that during the colonial era, until the nineteenth century, the term Cina Peranakan in Indonesia was used to refer to Chinese Muslims.[8] In fact, it was also the case when the term was first used in British Malaya to refer to the mixed descendants of Indian Muslims (e.g., Jawi Peranakan). Nevertheless, when it was applied to the Chinese in the twentieth-century Dutch Indonesia and British Malaya, it did not have the religious connotation any more. The term Peranakan was used by both the foreign rulers and the Malay speaking local population to refer to the partially "assimilated" local-born Chinese. Subsequently, the Chinese themselves also accepted this term for their "identity". The term is a cultural rather than a political category.

Straits Chinese/Straits-born Chinese

When the British colonized Peninsular Malaya and Singapore, the Peranakan Chinese came to be known as the Straits Chinese. This was due to the fact that they were in the Straits Settlements, which were formed when, in 1826, Penang, Singapore, and Malacca were placed under one administration and came to be known as the British Straits Settlements.

Strictly speaking, the term refers to the birthplace rather than the culture of the Chinese. Therefore, its life is geographically limited and time-sensitive. After independence, there is no more Straits Chinese, and it is anachronistic to use the term to refer to specific Chinese groups. However, as late as the end of the twentieth century, some writers continue to use the term to refer to the Peranakan Chinese. For those who used the term for a cultural group, they often wrongly used "Straits-born Chinese" to refer to the Straits Chinese. This is incorrect. It is true that the Peranakan Chinese were local-born (Straits-born) but not all Straits-born Chinese were Peranakans. Among the Straits-born Chinese, some were still culturally non-Peranakan, or sinkeh (*xinke*, 新客). For instance, the Malacca-born Chen Shengtang (陈省堂, Tan

Seng Tong) was not only Chinese-speaking, but was also a well-known Chinese language writer.[9]

Also, unlike the term Peranakan, which was used by the Malay-speaking population as well as the foreign rulers, the term "Straits Chinese" was used by those who were English-educated, as there is no Malay equivalent for this term. Not surprisingly, in the quarterly English magazine entitled *Straits Chinese Magazine* established by Dr Lim Boon Keng and Song Ong Siang in 1897, the term Straits Chinese or Straits-born Chinese were used interchangeably.[10] During that period, when referring to themselves, they never used the term Peranakan.

The Malays themselves, when referring to these Chinese, used either *Peranakan Cina* or *Baba* (or "Babah"). The Peranakan Chinese also used the term *Baba* to refer to themselves. In fact, initially the local-born Chinese in British Malaya and the Dutch East Indies used the term Baba to refer to themselves, not the Peranakan. This point will be addressed in details when dealing with the individual country.

No one is certain about the origin of the term *Baba*. It might have emerged before the coming of the Dutch or the British, and it was not confined to the Peranakan Chinese in the Straits Settlements. In both northern Sumatra (e.g., Medan) and West Java (e.g., Jakarta and Bogor), this term was known and used by the local "Malay" population and the Peranakan Chinese themselves.[11]

Baba, Nyonya, Nonya and Nona

However, J.D. Vaughan, who wrote a classic on the Straits Chinese (1879) stated: The Chinese born in the Straits are called Baba to distinguish them from those born in China. The term *"Baba* is used by the natives of Bengal to designate the children of Europeans and it is probable that the word was applied by Indian convicts at Penang to Chinese children and so came into general use."[12] It further elaborates that "The word *Baba* is given in Douglas' Hokkien dictionary as meaning a half-caste Chinese from the straits." In the Straits Settlements, however, the term is applied to all Chinese born there, half or not.[13]

The earliest publication that mentioned Baba and Nonya was the Malay (it was called Malayan) dictionary by William Marsden first issued in 1812. The term Baba was used to refer to "an infant son of a person of rank, particularly a European".[14] While Nonya refers to a form of address for "an elderly female who is the daughter of a European by a native woman". However, the term "Peranakan" did not appear in the above-mentioned dictionary, indicating that Peranakan was not used by the Malays during that period.

But the transformation of the terms Baba and Nonya to refer to the Straits-born Chinese only took place towards the end of the nineteenth century. J.D. Vaughan in his book published in 1879 noted that by that time Baba was used "to describe Chinese children".[15]

However, Herbert A. Giles in his Glossary published in 1900 stated clearly that Baba was "a local name for the Chinese born in the Straits Settlements, and for the children of foreigners. Used in India as a respectful form of address towards a man of the lower or middle classes. From the Turki baba father ..."[16] Nevertheless, Giles noted that Nonya was used in Java to refer to a "daughter of a Malay mother and a European father" and it was "an imitation of the Spanish *nona* and the French *nonee* ..."[17] In other words, the term Nonya (Nyonya and Nona in Indonesia) to refer to the female Peranakan Chinese was used even much later.

Since the late nineteenth century, the term Baba has been used to refer to male Peranakan Chinese while female Peranakan Chinese has been called either Nonya in British Malaya but Nyonya (married) and Nona (unmarried) in the Dutch East Indies.[18] In Malaysia, Baba may have emerged before the term Peranakan but in Indonesia, the term Peranakan is likely to exist before Baba.

The current meanings of Baba in Indonesian dictionary and Baba as reflected in the Malay dictionary differ. The Indonesian dictionary states that Baba is an address towards the male Chinese (not necessarily Peranakan Chinese);[19] while in the Malay dictionary, the term is used to mean the Malay-speaking male Peranakan Chinese and is also a form of address towards them.[20] Both dictionaries did not mention that it was a foreign loan word.

It seems that the terms Baba/Nyonya have a relatively wider usage and longer history in Malaysia and Singapore, but not in Indonesia. Some published books in the late twentieth century such as *The Babas*

Revisited, by Felix Chia; *A Nyonya Mosaic: My Mother's Childhood*, by Gwee Thiam Hock; and *Among the White Moonfaces: Memoirs of a Nyonya Feminist*, by Shirley Lim, show that these writers still consider themselves as members of this group.[21] In fact, in Singapore and Malaysia, the terms Baba and Nyonya have a longer lifespan than in Indonesia. I have not come across any Indonesian Peranakan descendants who wrote books and included the words Baba and Nyonya in the titles.[22]

Actually, the terms Baba and Nyonya have been loosely used in the past as well as today. In Singapore and Malaysia, the Babas and Nyonyas are not necessarily those who speak Malay or are culturally Malay. A keen observer of the Baba and Nyonya community scene noted to this author that, so long as a female member of the family dresses herself in a sarong or has a *konde*, they are considered Baba. This kind of definition may be considered too loose but if we use self-identity as the basis of an identity, if the people concerned call themselves Baba/Nyonya, it is difficult to say that they are not, especially if the local Baba community considers these people its members.

Chinese-Speaking Groups and the Peranakan

Chinese-speaking groups in Malaysia, Singapore and Indonesia used slightly different Chinese terms to refer to Peranakan and other related terms.

Chinese-speaking communities in Singapore and Malaysia continue to refer to the Malay-speaking or partially assimilated Chinese as 峇峇 (Baba, a direct transliteration of the term) and more recently, 土生华人 (*tusheng huaren*, local-born Chinese). They also address the Nyonya as 娘惹 (Niangre, which is a direct transliteration of the term). In Indonesia, the Chinese-speaking group more often used 侨生 (*qiaosheng*, local-born Overseas Chinese) instead of 峇峇 to refer to the Baba and Nyonya.

The term *tusheng huaren* means "local-born Chinese"; when used to refer to the Baba and Nyonya, it therefore has a cultural connotation rather than just an indication of birthplace. However, one can argue that this Mandarin term can also be used to refer to the local-born Chinese-speaking Chinese who were locally oriented in politics, although this usage is not common among the Chinese-language writers.

Conclusion

The brief account of the term Peranakan and related terms indicates the complexity of these terms. There are similarities and differences from country to country and from period to period. However, the most popular term to refer to this group of Chinese today is still the Peranakan Chinese.

Notes

1. *Kamus Dewan* (Kuala Lumpur: Dewan Bahasa, 1970), p. 26; *Kamus Besar Bahasa Indonesia*, 3rd ed. (Jakarta: Balai Pustaka, 2005), p. 43.
2. *Sejarah Melayu* (Malay Annals), which was written in the sixteenth century, did not mention the word Peranakan.
3. Abdullah, the contemporary of Sir Stamford Raffles, mentioned "Baba Cheng Lan" and "Baba Hok Guan", see Abdullah bin Abdul Kadir, *The Hikayat Abdullah*, an annotated translation by A.H. Hill (Kuala Lumpur: Oxford University Press, 1970), pp. 75 and 266.
4. He explained that in the course of time, the progeny of such unions with Penang Chinese became more and more numerous. See Abdullah bin Abdul Kadir, *The Voyages of Mohamed Ibrahim Munshi*, translated with an introduction and notes by Amin Sweeney and Nigel Philips (Kuala Lumpur: Oxford University Press, 1975), pp. 90–91.
5. John Crawfurd's *Descriptive Dictionary of the Indian Islands and Adjacent Countries* (London: Bradbury & Evans, 1856), cited in Tan Chee Beng, *Chinese Peranakan Heritage in Malaysia and Singapore* (Kuala Lumpur: Fajar Bhakti, 1993), p. 21.
6. A number of studies on the Chinese in colonial Malaya and Singapore show that indeed many Chinese married non-Chinese (local women); see Chen Jinghe 陈荆和 and Chen Yusong 陈育崧, *Xinjiapo huawen beimingjilu* 新加坡华文碑铭集录 (Hong Kong: Chinese University of Hong Kong, 1972), p. 13; also Zhuang Qinyong (庄钦永, David Chng Khin Yong), *Maliujia, Xinjiapo huawen beiwen jilu* 马六甲, 新加坡华文碑文辑录 (Taipei: Institute of Ethnology, Academia Sinica, 1998), p. 46. On the intermarriages between Chinese men and indigenous women in Indonesia (Java), see Li Minghuan, "Batavia's Chinese Society in Transition: Indications based upon the Tandjoeng Cemetery Archives 1881–1896", *Asian Culture* 24 (June 2000): 90–107.
7. See a recent paper by Zhuang Qinyong (庄钦永, David Chng Khin Yong), "1819–1844 nian Xinjiapo de huawen xuetang 1819–1844年新加坡的华文学堂", unpublished manuscript, Taipei, May 2001.
8. Many Dutch writings mentioned this fact, for instance, F. De Haan, *Oud Batavia*, vol II (Bandoeng, 1935); see also Mona Lohanda, *The Kapitan Cina of Batavia, 1837–1942* (Jakarta: Penerbit Djambatan, 1996), p. 6.

9. See Ye Zhongling (叶钟铃, Yeap Chong Leng), *Chen Shengtang wenji* 陈省堂文集 (Singapore: Singapore Society of Asian Studies, 1994).

10. In the first volume of the magazine, it is noted that the magazine served the Straits-born Chinese community, see p. 2.

11. A well-known Peranakan writer at the end of the nineteenth century and the beginning of the twentieth century, Lie Kim Hok, was often called "Baba Kim Hok" by others. See Tio Ie Soei, *Lie Kim Hok (1853–1912)* (Bandung: Good Luck, 1958).

12. J.D. Vaughan, *The Manners and Customs of the Chinese in the Straits Settlements* (originally published in 1879; reprinted by the Oxford University Press in 1974), p. 2.

13. Ibid.

14. William Marsden, *A Dictionary of the Malayan Language* (New York: Cox and Baylis, 1973, reprinted; originally published in 1812), p. 29.

15. Vaughan, *The Manners and Customs of the Chinese in the Straits Settlements*, p. 2.

16. Herbert A. Giles, *A Glossary of Reference on Subjects Connected with the Far East* (originally published in Shanghai in 1900; reprinted in 1974), p. 10.

17. Ibid., p. 195.

18. The term Nonya cannot be found in the Malay or Indonesian dictionary. In the old edition of *Dewan Bahasa*, Nonya is the equivalent of Nyonya. In Indonesia, Nyonya is also a form of address for a married woman, regardless of ethnic group.

19. *Kamus Besar Bahasa Indonesia*, 3rd ed., p. 82.

20. Ibid., p. 82; *Kamus Dewan*, p. 71.

21. Felix Chia, *The Babas Revisited* (Singapore: Heinemann Asia, 1994); Gwee Thiam Hock, *My Mother's Childhood* (Singapore: Times Book International, 1985); and Shirley Lim, *Among the White Moonfaces: Memoirs of a Nyonya Feminist* (Singapore: Times Books International, 1996).

22. The only exception is probably Queeny Chang's book, *Memories of a Nonya* (Singapore: Eastern Universities Press, 1981). Queeny is the daughter of Tjong A Fie, a tycoon in Sumatra. Her mother is a Penang Nyonya, and the book was published in Singapore, not Indonesia. It is also worth noting that the memoirs was first serialized in *The Star*, a Malaysian newspaper. This perhaps explains why the title uses Nonya.

2

PERANAKAN CHINESE IDENTITIES IN IMS (1): INDONESIA

Part I of this book examines the historical evolution of Peranakan communities in three countries, namely Indonesia, Malaysia, and Singapore (IMS), their development, decline and recent revival in the era of globalization and the rise of China. This chapter focuses on Indonesia. It will be followed by the next chapter on Malaysia and Singapore. A subsequent chapter will address recent developments of these communities provided with a general conclusion.

Introduction

There are a few books on the study of the Peranakan Chinese in Indonesia, one of them was *Peranakan Tionghoa Indonesia: Sebuah Perjalanan Budaya* (The Chinese Peranakan in Indonesia: A Cultural Journey), which was published in 2009. This is a coffee table book, written by a few Indonesian Peranakan scholars such as Mona Lohanda, Myra Sidharta, David Kwa and Handinoto etc. It covers Indonesian Peranakan literature, architecture, clothing, and food.

However, the most comprehensive coverage of the Indonesian Chinese history and culture is *Tionghoa dalam Keindonesiaan: Peran dan Kontribusi dalam Pembangunan Bangsa* (Chinese in the Indonesianess:

Roles and Contributions in Nation-Building). The book consists of three volumes, covering the role and contribution of the Indonesian Chinese in more than ten areas such as language, literature, press, culture, arts, sports, designs, food, real estate, banking, economy, health, medicine, architecture, education, military, and politics. This book is not about Peranakan Chinese per se, but the majority of the chapters are in fact related to them.

Origins of the term Peranakan and Baba

No one is certain about the first appearance of the term Peranakan in Indonesia. However, in Dutch publications, Peranakan was already used during the eighteenth century to refer to the offsprings of mixed marriages between foreign males and Indonesian females on the Java Island. However, the term was specifically used by the Dutch to refer to the locally-born Chinese who were Muslim. The Dutch even appointed the Peranakan Kapitan so that Chinese Muslims could be distinguish from the "indigenous Muslims". However, since 1832 the Peranakan Kapitan in Jakarta was abolished, as the Muslim Chinese were assimilated into the indigenous population. The meaning of Peranakan had also changed. Since then the term was more frequently used to refer to the offsprings of mixed marriages without any religious connotation.[1]

In Kalimantan, however, the Dutch used the term "Peranakan" differently. In the nineteenth century, it was used to refer to the local population who were born in Kalimantan and were considered to be Dutch subjects.[2] These Peranakans, unlike Java's Peranakans who had lost the command of the Chinese language and used a local language or Malay as their medium of communication, still spoke Chinese dialect (especially Hakka). Even the female Peranakans wore Chinese dress rather than the "nyonya dress" known as the "typical" Peranakan women dress. Only in the twentieth century, "many Chinese women in Borneo had adopted sarong kebaya, but they retained Chinese as their first language".[3]

When did the Chinese in Indonesia begin to use the term "Peranakan" to refer to their own community? It seems that it began with the formation of the *totok* community in the twentieth century, especially during the rise of Indonesian nationalism in the post-1926 Communist Uprisings.

Before this, it appears that the term Baba was more commonly used by the locally-born and partially assimilated Chinese. This is reflected in the literary works (such as novels) produced in the early 1900s. For instance, the two earliest Peranakan Chinese novels "Lo Fen Koei" (1903) and "Oeij (Oey) See" (1903) refer to the local-born Chinese as "Baba". During this period, Baba was used more as a term of address rather than as a group identity. For instance, Baba Lo Fen Koei,[4] Bah (Babah) Gede.[5] However, later in the 1930s, the term Baba was also used to refer to the Peranakan Chinese community in the Dutch East Indies,[6] but its usage had gradually ceased. On the contrary, the term Baba in Malaya (especially in Melaka and Singapore) have been used to refer to the Peranakan community until today. (See the next chapter on the Peranakans in Singapore and Malaysia).

The popular use of the term Tionghoa rather than Cina

It should be noted that in the Malay world, the term Cina was popularly used to refer to the Chinese without any derogatory meaning. However, beginning in 1900 with the establishment of the Tiong Hoa Hwe Koan (THHK 中华会馆) in Batavia (Jakarta), the term Cina became out of date and it was gradually replaced by Tionghoa. But in British Malaya/Malaysia and Singapore, Tionghoa was seldom used as Cina was and is still widely used.

Before the establishment of the Republic of China in 1912 when referring to themselves, the local-born and Indonesian-speaking Chinese used the term *bangsa Cina* and *bangsa Tionghoa* (Chinese nation; Chinese race) interchangeably. After 1912, they mainly used the term *bangsa Tionghoa* to refer to themselves. However, they did not differentiate *totok* (*singkeh* 新客) from the peranakan as the Indies Chinese preferred the term *bangsa Tionghoa* that includes these two subgroups. Nevertheless, when they referred to a specific subgroup within the Indies Chinese community, the terms *totok* and peranakan were used. For instance, when they discussed the participation of the Indies Chinese in local politics, the Peranakan dailies—*Perniagaan, Sin Po* and *Djawa Tengah*—mentioned that the Dutch colonial law considered the Peranakan Tionghoa as their subjects (*rahajat*) and not the totok Tionghoa. Those Peranakan Chinese who professed to Chinese nationalism rejected any participation in Dutch political institutions as this would split *bangsa Tionghoa* (Chinese nation), i.e. the peranakan from the *totok*.[7]

In the book *Doea Kapala Batoe* (Two Stubborn Persons, published in 1921) by Kwee Hing Tjiat, the former editor of *Sin Po*, which gives an account of Indonesian Chinese leaders and their society, he only used the term *bangsa Tionghoa* and never mentioned the word Peranakan. Throughout the whole book, he only used the term *totok* once (p. 44) to refer to a rich Chinese in Surabaya where a party was held. Even in the two classics by Peranakan Chinese writers, namely *Riwajat Semarang* (The History of Semarang, published in 1933) by Liem Thian Joe, and *Orang-Orang Tionghoa jang Terkemoeka di Java* (Prominent Chinese in Java, published in 1935) by Tan Hong Boen, the term Peranakan is almost absent. The Chinese in the Dutch East Indies continued to refer to themselves as merely Tionghoa, not Peranakan Tionghoa. This is understandable as many of them were still China-oriented and perceived themselves as a part of the Chinese nation.

In fact, in 1917 when the Dutch colonial government wanted to involve the local-born Chinese in the so-called Volksraad ("People's Assembly"), many local-born Chinese represented by the Sin Po Group organized the masses to oppose ethnic Chinese participation in Dutch colonial institutions as they belonged to the Chinese nation. In their view, the involvement in Dutch colonial institutions would only divide *bangsa Tionghoa*. Understandably, the local-born Chinese did not use the term Peranakan to refer to themselves.

The situation changed only in the 1920s, especially after the Indonesian Communist Uprisings in 1926–27, during which the Indonesian nationalism proper emerged. This was marked by the birth of the Chung Hwa Hui-Java (CHH, 1928), and the Partai Tionghoa Indonesia (PTI, 1932). The former was dominated by the Dutch educated well-to-do local born Chinese who were Dutch Indies oriented and were sympathetic to the Dutch colonial rule, while the latter dominated by both Dutch-educated and Malay-educated Chinese, but they were sympathetic to Indonesian nationalism. The latter appeared to have a lower economic status than the former.

As time passed, with the increase in the number of local-born Chinese involved in local institutions and politics, the term Peranakan began to gain traction in the local-born Chinese community. As only local-born Chinese were allowed to participate in local politics, the Chinese in the Dutch East Indies started to differentiate the Chinese community into peranakan and *totok* (*singkeh*). Some local-born Chinese felt that their economic position had been undermined by the *totok* group and began to be resentful towards the *totok*. Their different perceptions toward the position of China and Indonesia further divided the peranakan and *totok*. It is not surprising that when Liem Koen Hian founded the PTI he wanted to accept only the peranakan, and not the *totok*. While Ko Kwat Tiong, a lawyer who was also a leftist, would like to include the *totok* into the party as well.[8]

In the writings of Peranakan intellectuals and writers (such as Kwee Tek Hoay and Liem Koen Hian) published between 1927 and 1932, one can see that they made a clear distinction between the *totok* and peranakan and they identified themselves as Peranakan Chinese.[9] Even Kwee Hing Tjiat, who had abandoned his Chinese nationalist view in 1934, wrote about the "mature Baba" (*Baba Dewasa*) who considered Indonesia as their home country.[10] Apparently, both the terms Peranakan and Baba tended to be used interchangeably.

Peranakan, hence, began to be used by Peranakan Chinese themselves as their own cultural identity but did not replace the term Tionghoa as the latter has a broader meaning and not all Chinese in colonial Indonesia are Peranakan. Even when referring to the language used and literary works produced by the Peranakan Chinese, they are often branded as "Melayu-Tionghoa" (Chinese-Malay) rather than Melayu Peranakan (Peranakan Malay).

Melayu-Betawi, Melayu Rendah and Melayu-Tionghoa

The Peranakan Chinese themselves initially did not refer to the language that they used as "Melayu-Tionghoa" either, they simply called it Bahasa Melayu (Malay language) or Melayu-Betawi (Batavian Malay, 1884).[11] Please note that Betawi is the Malay equivalent of Batavia. This was precisely why Lie Kim Hok's grammar book was entitled "Melayu-

Betawi", not "Melayu-Tionghoa", as the Peranakan Chinese used the language spoken by indigenous Indonesians in urban areas.[12]

After the rise of Indonesian nationalism proper, there was a distinction between Melayu Rendah (Low Malay) and Melayu Tinggi (High Malay); and the language used by the Peranakan Chinese was often classified as Melayu Rendah while the official language was regarded as Melayu Tinggi. The Peranakan Chinese later also accepted the term "Melayu Rendah" reluctantly. In fact, this was a political move adopted by the colonial government to counter radical nationalist ideas expressed in the populist language, i.e. Melayu-Betawi.

Indigenous Indonesian writers also agreed with the decision to adopt the High Malay as the Indonesian language. Later, the Peranakan writers themselves followed the indigenous Indonesian usage and called the language as Bahasa "Melayu-Tionghoa" (Chinese-Malay) and the literature Sastra "Melayu-Tionghoa" (Chinese-Malay literature). Many contemporary scholars in the West and in Indonesia were of the view that the so-called Melayu-Tionghoa was in fact a type of Indonesian language used by both Peranakan Chinese and non-Chinese as their medium of communication, at least prior to the rise of Indonesian nationalism proper.[13]

The Peranakan community had been firmly established during the colonial period, especially between the eighteenth and early twentieth century. According to William Skinner,[14] new Chinese migrants (*totoks*) were few in number and usually were absorbed into the Peranakan community. Understandably the Peranakan Chinese, especially those from Java, were not aware of other segments of the Chinese community.

The situation started to change in the twentieth century when a large number of new Chinese migrants arrived at colonial Indonesia, particularly Java. These new Chinese migrants were no longer absorbed into the Peranakan community, but remained as *totok* who eventually formed their own community.[15] Therefore, two kinds of Chinese communities existed side by side, i.e. the Peranakan Chinese community and the *totok* Chinese community. While the former was culturally mixed, the latter continued to be "pure" and closer to Chinese culture.

The Chinese community leaders in the twentieth century, especially after the rise of Indonesian nationalism proper, began to be aware of the existence of the peranakan and *totok* Chinese communities. They also gradually discovered that the two communities had not only different language and culture, but also different sense of belonging. Nevertheless, within the Peranakan Chinese community, the members were not united in their political views. The three political orientations continued to exist until Indonesia's early independence period in the 1950s.

The Peranakan Chinese as an Indonesian *suku*

Peranakan Chinese, not the *totok* Chinese, were involved in the Preparation Committee for Indonesian Independence during the Japanese occupation of Indonesia. These peranakans were Liem Koen Hian, Oei Tjong Hauw, Oey Tiang Tjoei, Liem Beng Hwa and Yap Tjwan Bing.[16] Soon after the Japanese surrender, Indonesians who were in the Committee declared Indonesia's independence on 17 August 1945.

The Dutch, however, wanted to continue their colonial rule which resulted in the prolonged conflict which lasted for almost five years. The newly declared Republic of Indonesia was eager to gain the support of the Peranakan Chinese for Indonesia's independence. A peranakan leader, Siauw Giok Tjhan, was appointed as the State Minister for Peranakan Affairs (Menteri Negara Urusan Peranakan) between 1947 and 1948 in the Amir Sjarifuddin Cabinet II.[17] This indicates the formal recognition of Peranakan (mainly Chinese) as part of the Indonesian population, if not part of the Indonesian nation.

In fact, the formal recognition of the Peranakan Chinese as part of the Indonesian nation was during the Sukarno's Guided Democracy period. President Sukarno delivered a speech at the Baperki Congress on 14 March 1963 during which he talked about the components of the Indonesian nation (*Bangsa Indonesia*). He said that the Indonesian nation consists of many *sukus* (ethnic groups), namely suku Jawa, suku Sunda, suku Bali, suku Minang and suku Peranakan Tionghoa.[18] However, he did not offer any explanation regarding Peranakan Chinese except that they were already Indonesianized.

Nevertheless, the successor of Sukarno, Suharto, did not recognize the Peranakan Chinese as a *suku* anymore and demanded complete assimilation of all Chinese into the *pribumi* population immediately. We will discuss the Peranakan Chinese community during the Suharto era and post-Suharto era subsequently.

Baperki and Suku Peranakan (Tionghoa)

Baperki was the largest ethnic Chinese organization in Indonesia during 1954–65. It was a fusion of various Peranakan Chinese organizations such as Partai Demokrat Tionghoa Indonesia (PDTI), Perwit and Persatuan Tionghoa Surabaya. The purpose was to combat racial discrimination and to make locally-born Chinese Indonesian democrats. The name of the organization, Badan Permusjawaratan Kewarganegaraan Indonesia or the Consultative Council for Indonesian Citizenship, shows that it emphasized more on citizenship (*kewarganegaraan*) than nationhood (*kebangsaan*, or *nasion*).

In the Baperki constitution, it emphasized the equality of all Indonesian citizens, regardless of their racial origins. It tended to equate citizenship with nationhood. The organization also included the non-Chinese, but they were an absolute minority. The chairman of Baperki, Siauw Giok Tjan (蕭玉灿, 1914–81), was a Peranakan Chinese from Surabaya who was Dutch-educated and influenced by left-wing ideology.

As Siauw mistook the concept of citizenship for nationhood, he did not develop the position of the Chinese in the Indonesian nation. He wanted to unite the Peranakan and the *totok* Chinese. As a result, before 1965 he tended not to use the term Peranakan.

When Sukarno recognized the Peranakan Chinese as one of the Indonesian *sukus*, he was aware of the existence of the *totok* Chinese. He did not acknowledge the Tionghoa as a *suku* (suku Tionghoa) but recognize Peranakan Tionghoa as a *suku* (suku Peranakan Tionghoa). It was obvious that he did not intend to regard all Tionghoa as an Indonesian *suku*.

Siauw did not respond to Sukarno's suggestion of Peranakan Chinese as an Indonesian *suku*. In fact, Siauw continued to talk about Indonesian citizenship. Why did Siauw not respond to the proposal? There were two probable explanations: if Siauw accepted the concept of Peranakan Tionghoa, many totok Tionghoa who had become Indonesian citizens would have been excluded from the Indonesian *suku*. Perhaps Siauw thought that all Indonesian citizens of Chinese descent are members of the Indonesian nation. If he talked about Tionghoa, not Peranakan Tionghoa as a *suku*, it would show that his view differed from that of Sukarno.

The second probable explanation is that he did not want to talk about the division between Peranakan Chinese and *totok* Chinese. He blurred the distinction between these two by using Peranakan Tionghoa and Tionghoa interchangeably.

In the 1950s and 1960s, Indonesian Chinese society was indeed divided between the peranakan and *totok*, but many *totoks*, especially those who were pro-Beijing, were supportive of Baperki, especially Baperki schools and Baperki University. Perhaps Siauw did not want to lose their support. If we look at Siauw's memoirs which was published in 1981 before he passed away, we might be able to get some insights.

There is a chapter entitled "Minoritas Peranakan Tionghoa" (Peranakan Chinese minority) in the book. Although in the title he mentioned about Peranakan Chinese, in the chapter itself he did not use this term but turunan Tionghoa (Chinese descendants) instead. He noted that Indonesia is a plural society with many *sukus*, some are large in numbers while others are small. Apart from these *sukus*, there were a lot of foreign descendants, as they continued to live in Indonesia, eventually they would form new Indonesian *sukus*. It is interesting to note that in this "memoir", Siauw did not mention Sukarno's speech on Peranakan Chinese as an Indonesian *suku*.

It should be noted that many Chinese, especially after the fall of Suharto, wanted to make Tionghoa, not Peranakan Tionghoa, as an Indonesian *suku*. However, it appears that apart from the Chinese community leaders themselves, no indigenous presidents have ever acknowledged Tionghoa as an Indonesian *suku*. President Sukarno only recognized Peranakan Tionghoa (not Tionghoa in general) as an Indonesian *suku*. It is crucial to remember this.

One important development after Suharto stepped down was the inclusion of the Indonesian Chinese Cultural Park (Taman Budaya Tionghoa) in the Taman Mini Indonesia Indah (Beautiful Miniature Park of Indonesia). This park was established by President Suharto (1921–2008) and his wife in 1975 to promote Indonesian cultural heritage, specially for Indonesian *sukus* to have their ethnic culture displayed in the park by setting up a building/museum. However, Suharto who insisted on total and immediate assimilation of all Chinese into the indigenous society during the New Order era,[19] on 6 January 2003 (about five years after he was forced to step down) suddenly agreed to offer a big piece of land to establish a "Chinese Cultural Park" in the Taman Mini Indonesia Indah.[20] The land, which belonged to Suharto's foundation, was offered to the Paguyuban Sosial Marga Tionghoa Indonesia (Indonesian Chinese social clan association) that was led by retired Brigadier General Tedy Yusuf (熊德怡, Him Tek Ie, a Peranakan Hakka).

However, as the land was occupied by forty families, it took eleven years for Tedy Yusuf to obtain the land.[21] The gate of the park was completed on 8 November 2006, and the park was officially opened in April 2008, although it was not completed. The Hakka Museum, which was built within the park, was only completed in 2014.[22] The inclusion of the Chinese Cultural Park in the Taman Mini Indonesia Indah has been interpreted by Indonesian Chinese as an "official recognition" of ethnic Chinese as one of Indonesian *sukus* which constituted the Indonesian nation.[23] Interestingly, so far, I have not found any document in which Suharto mentioned Tionghoa as an Indonesian *suku* in relation to the Taman Mini.

At this juncture, it is important to talk about the popularization of the terms *totok* and *peranakan* in the western academic world. The person who did this is no other than William Skinner who first mentioned the *totok* and peranakan communities in Indonesia (especially Java) since 1958 when he wrote a brief paper on "the Chinese in Java". He later wrote a few articles on the subject. Equally important was Donald Willmott who published a book on the *Chinese in Semarang* (1960). Scholars on the Chinese in Indonesia became aware of the existence of these two Chinese communities and produced more books on these communities.

The Peranakan and *Totok* Chinese Communities

It is worth noting that despite the partially assimilated status of the Peranakan Chinese, the Dutch authorities in their 1920 and 1930 population census still identified these Chinese in accordance with their dialect groups (such as Hokkien, Hakka, Teochew etc.) as if they were still dialect-speaking. But from the 1920 census onwards, about 70 per cent of the Chinese population in Java no longer speak Chinese (dialects) but Malay and local Indonesian dialects.[24]

According to the 1920 census, the ethnic Chinese in Indonesia were divided into the Chinese-speakers (*totoks*) and Indonesian-speakers (Malay and regional languages, and hence classified as "peranakans"). In the Outer Islands, 90 per cent of the Chinese spoke Chinese and 10 per cent spoke Indonesian. However, in Java and Madura, 70 per cent of the Chinese spoke Indonesian while 30 per cent spoke Chinese. It is clear that the Chinese in the Outer Islands were primarily *totoks* while in Java (and Madura) were mainly peranakans.

The 1930 census does not provide any information about the daily language used by the local Chinese, but it does include information on the birthplace of their fathers born in the Netherlands Indies or abroad. Among the Chinese in Java, 79 per cent had fathers born in the Dutch East Indies, only 21 per cent had fathers born abroad.[25] Among the Chinese in the Outer Islands, 48 per cent had fathers born in the Dutch Indies but 52 per cent had fathers born elsewhere. The birthplace of the father is not a reliable indicator for determining peranakan and *totok* Chinese status because it does not reveal their cultural background. It is likely that in 1930, those in Java having fathers born in the Indies, were peranakans, but it is not so with the Chinese in the Outer Islands, because their patterns of settlement and the nature of their society were different.[26]

The censuses of 1961, 1971, 1980 and 1990 provide neither information about the daily language used by the Chinese nor the number of ethnic Chinese. Therefore it is difficult to compute the size of the peranakan and *totok* Chinese communities. What we can do here is to make educated guesses based on the 1920 census and other sketchy information.

In 1920 there were 890,000 Chinese in Indonesia, of which 38.4 per cent were peranakan while 61.6 per cent were *totok*. In 1930, there were 1,233,000 Chinese in Indonesia, of which 34.7 per cent were peranakan and 65.3 per cent were *totok*. In 1961, there were an estimated 2,450,000 Indonesian Chinese, of which 39.1 per cent were peranakan while 60.9 per cent were *totok*. In 1971 about five years after Suharto came to power, there were an estimated 3,293,000 Chinese in Indonesia, of which 43 per cent were peranakan and 57 per cent were *totok*.[27]

However, the 2000 and 2010 population censuses include ethnicity and hence the size of the Chinese communities is known, but not the number of peranakan and *totok*. Nevertheless, in the 2010 census, there is information on the language used by each ethnic group in Indonesia. There were 2,606,701 Chinese Indonesians, of which about 76 per cent speak Indonesian and local Indonesian dialects at home, while only about 24 per cent still speak Chinese at home.[28] In other words, 76 per cent were peranakan while 24 per cent were *totok*.

It should be noted that the 2000 and 2010 population census used "self-identity" as the basis of the census figure. It is believed that many Chinese Indonesians no longer identified themselves as "Chinese" during the census taking and hence were not recorded as "Chinese" anymore. If these Chinese identified themselves as "Chinese", the number of Peranakan Chinese would have been much higher.

Anthony Reid's Concept of "Peranakan"

In 2009, long after the fall of Suharto, Anthony Reid, an Australian scholar, proposed that "Indonesians of some Chinese heritage" need a new label to replace "Chinese" to help them "escape the burdens of Chineseness". He suggested the term Peranakan as it is "the least offensive and most appropriate label now on offer for one Indonesian ethnic group among others". It seems that he wants all Indonesian citizens of Chinese ancestry to be called "Peranakan" without using the word "Chinese".

This argument is based on the assumption that Indonesianess and Chineseness are incompatible, without realizing that within Indonesianess there are a lot of Chinese elements. In fact, a lot of elements which are called "Chinese" have become part of Indonesianess. Therefore, to dichotomize Indonesianess and Chineseness is not only unscientific and misleading but also harmful for the position of the Chinese, including the Peranakan Chinese, in the Republic of Indonesia. It is interesting to note that Reid did not mention that President Sukarno in March 1963 proposed that Peranakan Chinese be accepted as one of the Indonesian *sukus*, but not "Peranakan" alone as the term was not solely used for Chinese descendants.

The Chinese population in Indonesia during the Suharto era has been rapidly peranakanized and Indonesianized. There is no "typical" Indonesian Peranakan Chinese but a wide range of Indonesian Peranakan Chinese. These Peranakan Chinese have been locally-oriented and considered Indonesia as their home country. They have also used local languages, particularly Bahasa Indonesia, as their main language of communication, or even the daily language. In other words, these Chinese can be called Peranakan Chinese.

There is no doubt that the majority of Indonesian Chinese, both *totok* and peranakan, are Indonesian citizens. Many also see themselves as a *suku*, known as suku Tionghoa. This means that once you have become a suku Tionghoa, you do not have to be assimilated into the so-called *pribumi* population. However, Indonesian leader Sukarno only recognized Peranakan Chinese as a *suku*, not Tionghoa per se. Indirectly, one needs to have the characteristics of being a Peranakan Tionghoa before he/she is recognized as a *suku*.

Notes

1. Mona Lohanda, "Menjadi Peranakan Tionghoa", in *Peranakan Tionghoa Indonesia: Sebuah Perjalanan Budaya*, edited by Lily Wibisono and Rusdi Tjahyadi (Jakarta: Intisari dan Komunitas Lintas Budaya, 2009), p. 42.
2. Mary Somers Heidhues, *Golddiggers, Farmers, and Traders in the "Chinese Districts" of West Kalimantan, Indonesia* (Ithaca: Southeast Asia Program Publications, Cornell University, 2003), p. 192.
3. Ibid., p. 193.
4. Marcus A.S. and Pax Benedanto, eds., *Kesastraan Melayu Tionghoa dan Kebangsaan Indonesia*, Jilid 1 (Jakarta: Kepustakaan Populer Gramedia, 2000), p. 125.
5. Ibid., p. 198.
6. Kwee Hing Tjiat, "Baba Dewasa", *Mata Hari*, 1 August 1934.
7. See "Wet Kerahajatan Olanda", *Djawa Tengah*, 2 January 1917; "Samboengan Verslag", *Perniagaan*, 16 November 1917; "Orang Tionghoa dalam Volksraad I", *Sin Po*, 1 November 1917.
8. Leo Suryadinata, *Peranakan Chinese Politics in Java, 1917–1942* (Singapore: Marshall Cavendish, 2005), p. 96.
9. Ibid., pp. 79–94.

10. Ibid., pp. 105–6.
11. Leo Suryadinata, "Lie Kim Hok: Bapak Bahasa 'Melayu Tionghoa'", in *Tionghoa dalam Keindonesiaan: Peran dan Kontribusi Bagi Pembangunan Bangsa*, vol. 1, edited by Leo Suryadinata and Didi Kwartanada (Jakarta: Yayasan Nabil, 2015), pp. 181–83.
12. Claudine Salmon, "Apakah Bahasa 'Melayu Tiongghoa' bisa diterima?", in *Tionghoa dalam Keindonesiaan: Peran dan Kontribusi Bagi Pembangunan Bangsa*, vol. 1, edited by Leo Suryadinata and Didi Kwartanada (Jakarta: Yayasan Nabil, 2016), pp. 171–80.
13. See the articles in *Tionghoa dalam Keindonesiaan*, vol. 1, "Tionghoa dalam Perkembangan Bahasa Indonesia" by Dede Oetomo (pp. 157–68) and "Apakah Bahasa 'Melayu-Tionghoa' bisa diterima?" by Claudine Salmon (pp. 171–80).
14. William Skinner, "The Chinese Minority", in *Indonesia*, edited by Ruth McVey (New Haven: Yale University Press, 1963), p. 105.
15. Ibid., p. 106.
16. See Didi Kwartanada, "Tokoh Tionghoa dalam Lembaga BPUPK dan PPK", in *Tionghoa dalam Keindonesiaan: Peran dan Kontribusi Bagi Pembangunan Bangsa*, vol. 3, edited by Leo Suryadinata and Didi Kwartanada (Jakarta: Yayasan Nabil, 2016), pp. 339–41.
17. "Menteri Etnis Tionghoa", in *Tionghoa dalam Keindonesiaan*, vol. 3, p. 394.
18. Soekarno, *Baperki Supaja Mendjadi Sumbangan Besar terhadap Revolusi Indonesia* (Djakarta: Departemen Penerangan R.I., n.d.).
19. See Soeharto, *Soeharto: Pikiran, Ucapan dan Tindakan Saya: Otobiografi seperti dipaparkan kepada G. Dwipayana dan Ramadhan K.H.* (Jakarta: Citra Lamtoro Gung Persada, 1989), p. 279.
20. Claudine Salmon and Myra Sidharta, "Sino-Insulindian Private History Museums, Chinese Heritage Places, and the (Re)construction of the Past", *Asian Culture* 42 (December 2018), p. 10. For the process of getting a plot of land in Taman Mini, see Tedy Jusuf, *Kacang Mencari Kulitnya*, 2nd ed. (privately published, 2015), pp. 217–20.
21. Jusuf, *Kacang Mencari Kulitnya*, pp. 217–20.
22. Thung Ju Lan, "Peranakan Chinese Community in Indonesia and Globalization", in *Peranakan Communities in the Era of Decolonization and Globalization*, edited by Leo Suryadinata (Singapore: Chinese Heritage Centre and NUS Baba House, 2015), p. 132; "Taman Budaya Tionghoa TMII Rampung 2010", *Kompas*, 7 February 2008, https://nasional.kompas.com/read/2008/02/07/15075732/Taman. Budaya.Tionghoa.TMII.Rampung.2010 (accessed 30 March 2021).
23. Salmon and Sidharta, "Sino-Insulindian Private History Museums, Chinese Heritage Places, and the (Re)construction of the Past", p. 10.
24. Charles A. Coppel, "Mapping the Perankan Chinese in Java", in *Studying Ethnic Chinese in Indonesia*, by Charles A. Coppel (Singapore: Singapore Society of Asian Studies, 2002), p. 115, Table I.

25. *Volkstelling 1930*, vol. VII (Batavia: Department van Economische Zaken, 1935), pp. 32–35.
26. Both William Skinner and Mary Somers made a similar observation. See Skinner, "The Chinese Minority", pp. 104–5; Somers, "Peranakan Chinese Politics in Indonesia", unpublished PhD thesis, Cornell University, 1965, pp. 31–46.
27. Leo Suryadinata, *Pribumi Indonesians, the Chinese Minority and China: A Study of Perceptions and Policies* (Kuala Lumpur and London: Heinemann Publishers, 1978), pp. 95–96.
28. Aris Ananta, Evi Nurvidya Arifin, M. Sairi Hasbullah, Nur Budi Handayani, and Wahyu Pramo, *Demography of Indonesia's Ethnicity* (Singapore: Institute of Southeast Asian Studies, 2015), p. 300, Table 7.25.

3

PERANAKAN CHINESE IDENTITIES IN IMS (2): MALAYSIA AND SINGAPORE*

In recent years, there have been more studies on the ethnic Chinese, especially with regard to their identities. There are a few in-depth studies on the Peranakan Chinese in Malacca (by Tan Chee Beng), Penang (by Ho Eng Seng), and Singapore (by Jurgen Rudolph). These studies are significant and have thrown new light on these Chinese. Tan Chee Beng has also done a general study on the Peranakan Chinese beyond the Straits Settlements.[1]

Benefitting from the above studies, this chapter re-examines the Peranakan identities in Singapore and Malaysia, from the colonial era to the present. Was the Peranakan identity a sociocultural identity or a political identity or both? Was it a self-identity or an identity given by others? Were the Peranakan Chinese confined to the British Straits Settlements? The chapter also discusses the life experiences of the Peranakan Chinese after independence, what the present Peranakan identities are and what the future holds for them.

It is generally known that the ethnic Chinese in Singapore and Malaysia are heterogeneous. One of these groups, known as the Peranakan Chinese or *Cina Peranakan*, is also known as "Straits Chinese", "Straits-born Chinese", and *Baba* (male Peranakan Chinese) and *Nyonya* (female Peranakan Chinese).

It should be pointed out that the earliest term used to call the local Malay and English-speaking Chinese was Straits Chinese or Straits-born Chinese. The term Baba also has early currency among this community, while the term peranakan came into use only in the twentieth century, especially after World War II.

Nowadays, Straits Chinese and Straits-born Chinese are used in the historical context, but Baba remains quite popular. Some writers and the Peranakans themselves use Peranakan and Baba interchangeably, but in fact they are not identical. For a detailed discussion on various definitions of these terms, see the previous chapter.

Typical Peranakan or Baba?

We often assume that the Peranakan or Baba in Malaysia constitute a homogeneous group. In reality, the Peranakan or Baba are heterogeneous. There is no typical Peranakan or Baba. Peranakan Chinese/Baba can be considered as a spectrum ranging from those who are most Malaynized ("localized", as Tan Chee Beng calls it) to the least Malaynized. While the Penang Baba are the least Malaynized, the Malacca Baba are the most Malaynized. Malaynization involves the use of the Malay language and the adoption of Malay dress and cuisine.

It should be pointed out that even within an area (e.g., Malacca or Penang), there are variations. Not all Penang Peranakan or Baba are Hokkien-speaking. Some might be similar to the Malacca Baba but it appears that the majority are Hokkien-speaking. In Malacca, the same can also be said. Some might be similar to those in Penang but the Malay-speaking Peranakans are the majority.

Another characteristic is the small number of Peranakan Chinese in the Straits Settlements. We do not know the number of Peranakan Chinese as such, but we do have the census figures of Straits-born (later, British Malaya-born) Chinese in the late nineteenth century and the first half of the twentieth century. According to the 1881 census (see Table 3.1), the Straits-born Chinese numbered 25,268 and formed 14.5 per cent of the total Chinese population. By 1891, however, the number had increased to 34,757 and constituted 15 per cent of the total Chinese population in the Straits Settlements. Since the nineteenth century, mass Chinese immigration had not taken place; therefore, we can assume that the majority of the Straits-born Chinese were Peranakans. We can safely argue that the Peranakan Chinese did not exceed 15 per cent of the total Chinese population. In other words, the non-Peranakan Chinese formed the absolute majority of the Chinese population in the Straits Settlements. The proportion of the Peranakans would be even smaller if we were to consider the Federation of Malaya as a whole.

In the first half of the twentieth century, the number of local-born Chinese (i.e., born in British Malaya and Singapore) in the Straits Settlements began to grow steadily (see Table 3.2). It should be noted that in the twentieth century, the number of new Chinese immigrants increased tremendously, particularly in Singapore and Penang. These immigrants settled down and raised their families, which explains the significant increase in the number of local-born Chinese. I would like to argue that the offsprings of these newcomers were culturally different from the earlier settlers. They were still Sinkehs rather than Peranakans.

If we assume that 15 per cent of the Chinese in the Straits Settlements were Peranakans, the rest, that is, about 85 per cent of them, would be non-Peranakans.

TABLE 3.1
Number and Percentage of Local-born Chinese
in the Straits Settlements, 1881 and 1891

Year Territory	1881		1891	
	Number	Percentage	Number	Percentage
Penang	10,477	15.5	16,981	19.3
Malacca	5,264	26.7	4,971	27.4
Singapore	9,527	11.0	12,805	10.5
Total	**25,268**	**14.5**	**34,757**	**15.3**

Source: Computed from *Report on the Census of the Straits Settlements, 1891* (Singapore, 1892), pp. 36–37, 46–47, 94–95, 134–35.

The presence of Peranakan and non-Peranakan communities in the Straits Settlements also explained the existence of different Chinese organizations. The organizations were divided along these sociocultural lines. The Babas had their own mutual help associations (e.g., *Qingde hui*,[2] the Straits Chinese British Association (SCBA), and the State Chinese (Penang) Association), while the Sinkehs had their own clan associations, often known as *bang* (based on dialect groups, such as Fujian *huiguan*, Keshu *gonghui*, etc.)[3] and socio-political organizations such as the Kuomintang. The Chinese Chambers of Commerce, which were established under the instruction of the Chinese (Ching) government, were Sinkeh-dominated.[4]

It is also interesting to note that the economic activities of the Peranakans and Sinkehs tended to be quite different. While the Peranakans were mainly involved in shipping, banking and tin mining, the Sinkehs, on the other hand, were farmers and traders. The type of businesses involved was linked to their cultural and language backgrounds. As

TABLE 3.2
Number and Percentage of Local-born Chinese in
Penang, Malacca and Singapore

Year Territory	1901	1911	1921	1931	1947	1957
Penang	23,569	35,529	52,041	76,854	173,261	266,723
	(24%)	(32%)	(38%)	(46%)	(70%)	(72%)
Malacca	4,955	7,366	13,130	22,494	63,028	95,211
	(26%)	(21%)	(29%)	(35%)	(66%)	(79%)
Singapore	15,498	43,833	79,686	150,033	437,243	741,605
	(10%)	(20%)	(24%)	(36%)	(58%)	(68%)
Total	**44,022**	**86,778**	**144,857**	**249,381**	**673,532**	**1,103,539**
	(16%)	**(23%)**	**(29%)**	**(38%)**	**(63%)**	**(72%)**

Sources: Report on the Census of the Straits Settlements, 1901 (Singapore: Government Printing Office, 1902), p. 19; *The Census of British Malaya, 1921* (printed in London, 1922), p. 95; *A Report on the 1947 Population Census* (Kuala Lumpur: Government Printer, 1949); *1957 Population Census of the Federation of Malaya* (Report No. 14) (Kuala Lumpur: Department of Statistics, 1961), computed from Table 1 and Table 7B; and Saw Swee Hock, *The Population of Singapore* (Singapore: Institute of Southeast Asian Studies, 1999), pp. 33–47.

shipping and banking businesses require a knowledge of the English language, naturally the English-educated Babas were more suitable than their Sinkeh counterparts.

The patterns in political activities were also formed along sociocultural lines. The Peranakan elites, being British subjects, were politically oriented towards the colony and the United Kingdom, while the Sinkehs were China-oriented and considered themselves part of the larger Chinese nation. The orientation began to change at the end of World War II with the establishment of the major political Malayan parties. The SCBA, the Baba association which was politically pro-British, was a contrast to the Malayan branch of the Kuomintang, which was a Sinkeh party. The left-wing organization, the Malayan Communist Party (MCP), was politically "international" but still closely linked with China and dominated by the Sinkehs. The situation, of course, was different at the end of World War II. The Chinese in Malaya/Malaysia, both Peranakans and Sinkehs, began to adjust their positions to new developments.

Baba and Peranakan

How significant are the terms Baba, Nyonya and Peranakan in the context of culture and politics? In the past, Baba or Peranakan identity was significant, especially during the colonial era, when the British colonial power tended to use the Baba to serve their political interests. Are the Babas or Peranakans still relevant in the political scene today? In fact, in both Singapore and West Malaysia, it appears that the division is no longer between Peranakan and Sinkeh, or between Baba and non-Baba, but between the different kinds of education received. Among the older-generation Chinese in Singapore, the division was between the Chinese-educated and the English-educated, but among the younger generation, such division is less obvious as they receive a similar type of education. However, in West Malaysia, the division is between the Malay-educated and the Chinese-educated. Nevertheless, the so-called Baba community, or more appropriately, the Peranakan community, still exists today. The community, nonetheless, is in decline and its political significance has also diminished.

Before proceeding further, one has to point out that the term Baba, which has sometimes been used very rigidly—that is, to mean "Malay-speaking Chinese"—is misleading. In fact, there are at least two types of Baba: the Malacca Baba and the Penang Baba. (With regard to the Singapore Baba, they are an offshoot of the Malacca Baba and, hence, do not really present a new category.[5]) The former, who are the Malay-speaking Babas, have been used as the "standard" for the Babas, as if all Babas are Malay-speaking. Many are not aware that the Penang Babas are Hokkien-speaking. Nevertheless, they are still called Baba because of the influence of the Malay culture over them. The Malacca Babas speak Malay (Low Malay) with Hokkien vocabulary while the Penang Babas speak Hokkien using Malay vocabulary. One can argue that the Penang Babas are more Chinese than the Malacca Babas in linguistic terms but both communities consider themselves Baba or Nyonya.

Nevertheless, some writers are of the view that the Peranakans in Penang are not precisely Baba, and that their daily language is Hokkien infused with Malay words. This is due to the fact that Baba is defined in terms of the Peranakan in Malacca. In the 1950s, for instance, Diana Ooi did not use the term Baba to refer to the local-born and English-educated Chinese but the term "English-educated Chinese", as if all Babas in Penang were English-educated.[6] Others continued to feel that the correct way to refer to them was "Straits Chinese".[7] Yet others insisted that they were Baba and Nyonya.[8] Khoo Joo Ee maintains that,

> the term "Baba" has colonial connotations and "straits-born Chinese" is anachronistic insofar as the Straits Settlements no longer exist in a political unit. "Peranakan" is preferably labelled. Yet such definition is irrelevant for the Baba who are absorbed in the larger Chinese community. However, for citizenship and present-day political entities, "Peranakan" becomes mandatory. In private and non-political affairs, "Peranakan" is less used. The "Baba-Nyonya" term is still prevalent among the Malays and [in] the Peninsular community.[9]

This is perhaps true that for the older-generation Baba, the terms Baba and Nyonya are more commonly used than Peranakan among the Peranakan Chinese themselves. Even the books and memoirs by Felix Chia and Shirley Lim use Baba and Nyonya in the title rather than Peranakan.[10] Long after the change of names of Baba organizations to Peranakan organizations, the term Baba for the Peranakan congress is still used. For instance, the Peranakan Association of Singapore in 1993 held the Sixth Baba Convention rather than the "Peranakan Convention".[11] At the convention, apart from the Peranakan Association of Singapore, four other Peranakan organizations were present: they were the Persatuan Peranakan Cina Pulau Pinang; Persatuan Peranakan Cina Melaka; Gunong Sayang Association (Singapore); and Persatuan Peranakan Cina Kelantan.[12] Nevertheless, all of these organizations used Peranakan in their formal/official names. Perhaps this was due to the fact that the term Peranakan is a Malay/Indonesian term, while Baba is a non-Malay term.

The SCBA, Political Identity and Peranakan Identity

However, one has to point out that Baba and Nyonya do not have colonial connotation but "Straits Chinese" does. It is not surprising that the Straits Chinese British Association (SCBA), which was established in 1900, changed its name to "Singapore Chinese Peranakan Association" in November 1964, when Singapore was part of Malaysia, and eventually adopted the name "Peranakan Association" in February 1966. "Straits Chinese" implies pro-British Peranakan Chinese and, hence, was considered anachronistic. The members considered themselves "King's Chinese" or "Queen's Chinese". Their political loyalty, before independence, was to the British.

It is also interesting to note that after the establishment of the SCBA, in Malacca, a similar organization was formed. However, in Penang, the Baba Chinese refused to establish such an organization as it was too exclusive—it tended to differentiate the Babas from the larger Chinese community.[13] Apparently, the Straits Chinese (in a cultural sense) were weak and other existing Chinese organizations such as the Chinese Chamber of Commerce and the Chinese Town Council, both dominated by the Sinkeh Chinese, were strong. Eventually, the Baba Chinese in Penang established the State Chinese (P) Association (SCA—note that the term "Straits Chinese" does not appear in the name). It is again interesting to note that after Malaya's independence, the association came to be known as the Persatuan Peranakan Cina Pulau Pinang. Perhaps this was in accordance with the Babas' fight for their indigenous status.

The Malaysian situation is different from that of Singapore as it is an indigenous state where the indigenous population, or Bumiputra, has more rights than the non-indigenous population. The ethnic Chinese, in general, are trying to gain the indigenous status; hence, some Peranakan Chinese seek to claim the status based on their "unique" status. In Khoo Joo Ee's words:

> The Straits Chinese [sic] combined Chinese, Western and Malay cultures in aspects such as language, dress, cuisine and occupation. This identity is a fragile one, with straits Chinese striving to assert their identity as genuine indigenous people of Malaysia and Singapore. They drew on several ethnic traditions yet transcended them into a new identity. The syncretism achieved by the Baba went beyond the political coalition which exists between the different races in present-day Malaysia.[14]

Khoo Joo Ee is correct when she maintains that some of these Baba Chinese attempted to seek "indigenous" (Bumiputra, or sons of the soil) status because the Malaysian constitution differentiates indigenous people from non-indigenous people and accord them different rights (no. 26).[15] However, their attempt to be recognized as such encountered failure.

Malaysian Peranakan Chinese and the Bumiputera status

However, there has been a renewed attempt on the part of Peranakan Chinese in Malaysia to be recognized as Bumiputera. Before going further, a brief note on Bumiputera is in order.[16] According to the official information, in 2015, 68 per cent of the population in Malaysia are considered Bumiputera. The Malays constitute 54.6 per cent, while others (mainly Orang Asli, Sarawak and Sabah natives) formed 11.5 per cent. They are considered as indigenous groups and hence have special status and rights. Malaysian Peranakan, especially the Malacca Baba, were born and brought up in Malaysia for centuries and adopted local culture. They therefore sought for Bumiputera status after Malaysia's independence was achieved.

In 2014, the president of the Peranakan Chinese Association of Malaysia, Ronald Gan, sought the approval of Malaysia's Federal Government for the Peranakan Chinese to be bestowed with Bumiputra status. The argument was that the Peranakan had settled down in Malaysia since the fourteenth century, used Peranakan Malay as their daily language and was recognized to have a Malay status by the British under the Customary Land Law.[17] The Chief Minister of Malacca Idris Haron and the Minister of Culture Nasri Aziz during the Najib administration supported the proposal. Nevertheless, the Federal Government has not given its green light.

In fact, in Malaysia, many descendants of the Straits Chinese or Babas have rapidly been resincized. This is largely a result of the government policy which is based on "race" and "indigenism". However, the rise of China, the resurgence of ethnicity worldwide, and the spread of democratic ideas are also responsible for the resinicization of the Chinese in Malaysia. Many send their children to Chinese primary schools—which are part of the national education system—to learn the Chinese language.[18] Only after completing six years of primary education in Chinese, do they enrol in the national secondary schools, which use Malay as the medium of instruction. Some continue to study in independent Chinese-medium schools and are resinicized further.[19] One young scholar wrote in 1986 that the Baba Chinese in Penang no longer existed as they had already merged with the Penang Chinese in general. Those Baba Chinese that he could identify were in their seventies![20] Perhaps this was a slight exaggeration, but certainly the number of so-called Babas in Penang was extremely small.[21]

However, after Singapore's separation from Malaysia in 1965, the Babas faced new challenges. The bilingual policy, which defines mother tongue in terms of "racial language", has a tendency to "resinicize" the Baba Chinese. The descendants of the Babas begin to learn Chinese again. However, the emphasis on English permits the Babas to continue maintaining their English-educated Chinese identity rather than the old Baba identity.

English-educated and Chinese-educated

Some observers maintain that after the two countries became independent, when we refer to the socio-political scene of the ethnic Chinese, it is more relevant to discuss the division between the Chinese-educated and the English-educated.

In Malaysia, for instance, it is true that the Malayan Chinese Association (MCA) was first led and controlled by the Babas (e.g., Tan Cheng Lock and Tan Siew Sin). But as time passed by, the non-Baba Chinese began to lead the organization (e.g., Lee San Choon and Tan Koon Suan). The current president, Ling Liong Sik, and his deputy, Lim Ah Lek, may be considered Baba, but more see them as English-educated. In fact, many top leaders in the MCA now are either Chinese-educated (e.g., Chan Kong Choy) or bilingual (e.g., Chua Jui Ming). The rank and file of MCA members are also Chinese-educated.

With regard to Chinese non-governmental organizations (NGOs), these are divided between the Chinese-educated and the English-educated, and not between the Babas and non-Babas. This is due to the small size of the Baba community and the popularity of Chinese education. Many Chinese, including the Babas, have sent their children for primary Chinese education. Some English-educated Chinese politicians have also picked up Chinese and are able to converse in Mandarin, although with rather limited vocabulary. The division between the Chinese-educated and the English-educated is often blurred, but it is still real as the Chinese schools are flourishing.

The situation in Singapore is quite similar. Prior to independence, many Peranakans were in politics, so were non-Peranakans. The first generation of top political leaders in Singapore belonged to the community of the so-called Straits Chinese. They were Peranakans but also English-educated. However, with the passing away of this first generation, there was an emergence of new leaders who were not necessarily Peranakan but were English-educated. Gradually, the leaders have become bilingual, with English as their main language. However, unlike in Malaysia, where Chinese-medium schools are still in operation, in Singapore, the national education system tends to produce one type of leaders.

Peranakan Chinese in Post-Independence Singapore

The term Peranakan Chinese or Peranakan has re-emerged in Indonesia, Malaysia, and Singapore in recent years. Peranakan Chinese associations have been formed in these three countries, and Peranakan museums have also been established. Chinese Indonesians also started to seek for the status of *suku* for the ethnic Chinese community.

However, there was a comparable development in Malaysia, which is the Peranakan Chinese would like to be recognized as Bumiputera (sons of the soil), just like the Malays. Once they are recognized as such, the Peranakan Chinese would enjoy the same privileges as the Malays and other indigenous groups. However, in ethnic Chinese-dominated Singapore, there is no attempt on the part of the Peranakan Chinese to claim their "indigenous people" status comparable to the Malay minority.

Singapore is an "immigrant state" and the Peranakan status does not bring any actual benefit for the Peranakan Chinese. In fact, the national educational system requires each ethnic group to learn their mother tongue as defined by the Singapore state (i.e. the Mandarin Chinese or *Huayu*). In addition, the school system has been based on English, not Malay or Chinese. The Peranakan Chinese in Singapore have been rapidly Westernized, and to a lesser extent, "re-sinicized". But some disagreed with the term re-sinicized as Peranakan Chinese in Singapore (and also in Malaysia) had remained as Chinese, the re-learning of the Chinese language as a subject could not be said as "re-sinicization", but modernization. Peranakan descendants continue to speak English rather than Malay or Mandarin in their daily lives. There is an emergence of a special type of Peranakan in Singapore—the English-speaking Peranakan who speak some Chinese and a little Malay.

Notes

*This chapter is partly based on "Peranakan Chinese Identities in Singapore and Malaysia: A Re-examination", in *Ethnic Chinese in Singapore and Malaysia: A Dialogue between Tradition and Modernity*, edited by Leo Suryadinata (Singapore: Times Academic Press, 2002), pp. 69–84.
1. For instance, the Peranakan Chinese in Trengganu.
2. On *Qingde hui*, see Lin Xiaosheng (Lim How Seng), *Xinjiapo huashe yu huashang* (Singapore: Singapore Society of Asian Studies, 1995), p. 100.
3. Ibid.
4. Yen Ching-hwang, "Ch'ing China and the Singapore Chinese Chamber of Commerce, 1906–1911", in *Southeast Asian Chinese and China: The Politico-*

Economic Dimension, edited by Leo Suryadinata (Singapore: Times Academic Press, 1995), pp. 133–60.

5. Felix Chia, *The Babas Revisited* (Singapore: Heinemann Asia, 1994), p. 11. Chia states that "excepting a few, all families of the Singapore Babas trace their roots to Malacca".

6. Diana Ooi. "The English-educated Chinese in Penang", Master's thesis, University of Malaya, 1957.

7. Khoo Joo Ee, *The Straits Chinese: A Cultural History* (Kuala Lumpur: Papin Press, 1996); Khoo Joo Ee, "The Straits Chinese Today", *Suara Baba: The Voice of the Peranakan Associations in Malaysia and Singapore*, no. 2 (November 1993), p. 2.

8. Ho Eng Seng, "Problems of Identity among the Overseas Chinese: A Historical Examination of the Baba Chinese in Penang", Honours essay for the major in social sciences, Stanford University, Department of Anthropology, June 1986.

9. Khoo Joo Ee, "The Straits Chinese Today".

10. Felix Chia, *The Babas* (Singapore: Times Book International, 1980); Shirley Lim, *Among the White Moonfaces: Memoirs of a Nyonya Feminist* (Singapore: Times Books International, 1996).

11. See the Sixth Baba Convention, 26–27 November 1993.

12. Ibid., contents page. The name of Persatuan Peranakan Cina Kelantan, however, is not listed. I was present at the convention and listened to the presentation of the spokesman of that organization on 26 November 1993.

13. Ho Eng Seng, "Problems of Identity", pp. 55–56.

14. Khoo Joo Ee, "The Straits Chinese Today".

15. Tan Chee Beng in his book (1988) argued that prior to independence, some Peranakan Chinese leaders, for instance Heah Joo Seang, president of SCBA (sic) Penang, had claimed the sons of the soil status for the Peranakan Chinese, but it was dismissed by Tunku Abdul Rahman, then the president of UMNO. Tan Chee Beng, *The Baba of Melaka: Culture and Identity of a Chinese Peranakan Community in Malaysia* (Petaling Jaya: Pelanduk Publications, 1988), p. 227.

16. Trinna Leong, "Who are Malaysia's Bumiputera?", *Straits Times*, 3 August 2017, https://www.straitstimes.com/asia/se-asia/who-are-malaysias-bumiputera (accessed 5 March 2019).

17. R.S.N. Murali, "Nazri: Peranakan Chinese have the Right to pursue Bumiputera Status", *The Star*, 25 August 2017, https://www.thestar.com.my/metro/community/2017/08/25/seeking-recognition-nazri-peranakan-chinese-has-theright-to-pursue-bumiputra-status/ (accessed 26 February 2019).

18. See Tan Chee Beng, *The Baba of Melaka*; Tan Chee Beng, *Chinese Peranakan Heritage in Malaysia and Singapore* (Kuala Lumpur: Fajar Bakti, 1996); John Clammer, *Straits Chinese Society: Studies in Sociology of the Baba Communities of Malaysia and Singapore* (Singapore: Singapore University Press, 1980).

19. There are about sixty such schools in Malaysia, funded by the Chinese community. Tan Liok Ee has published many excellent studies on Chinese education in Malaysia. See, for instance, Tan Liok Ee, "Chinese Independent Schools in West Malaysia: Varying Responses to Changing Demands", in *Changing Identities of the Southeast Asia Chinese since World War II*, edited by Jennifer Cushman and Wang Gungwu (Hong Kong: Hong Kong University Press, 1988), pp. 61–74; Tan Liok Ee, *The Politics of Chinese Education in Malaya, 1945–1961* (Kuala Lumpur: Oxford University Press, 1997); Tan Liok Ee, "Chinese Schools in Malaysia: A Case of Cultural Resilience", in *The Chinese in Malaysia*, edited by Lee Kam Hing and Tan Chee-Beng (Shah Alam, Malaysia: Oxford University Press, 2000), pp. 228–54.

20. See Ho Eng Seng, "Problems of Identity", p. 2.

21. In 2001, I met an ex-Penang woman in Singapore who was in her late forties and claimed to be a Nyonya.

4

PERANAKAN CHINESE IDENTITIES IN IMS (3): THE RESURGENCE OF PERANAKAN ASSOCIATIONS AND PERANAKAN IDENTITIES

The Resurgence of Peranakan Associations

On 24–25 November 2018, I was invited to attend and give a keynote speech at the 31st Peranakan/Baba Nyonya Convention (abbreviated as the 31st Peranakan Convention) in Tangerang, West Java, Indonesia. I also had the opportunity to observe the interactions between the Peranakans from Malaysia, Singapore, Indonesia, Thailand and Australia. There were about 600 participants from these countries, of whom, more than 500 were from outside Indonesia.

To have smooth interactions with the Peranakan participants, English was made the medium of communication. Privately when the Peranakans from different countries communicate, they still use more English than Malay. This is because not all Peranakans are fluent in Indonesian or Malay, with the exception of Indonesian Peranakans who use Indonesian as their daily language. This point is important to remember in order to avoid an impression that the Peranakan Chinese are a homogeneous group. The so-called Peranakan Malay/Indonesian is not used either as this is a dying language and its vocabulary and structure are not sufficient to express complicated matters.

The Convention's programme was rich. Aside from the keynote speech and two paper presentations on the Peranakan Chinese history and hybrid culture in Java, there were musical performances and a series of workshops on things Peranakan Chinese, ranging from food, cuisine, batik and games. In addition, there were visits to Peranakan historical sites in Tangerang, Central and East Java. This was some sort of a Peranakan cultural journey in Indonesia which lasted a few days, coinciding with the theme of the conference entitled "Exploring the Roots of Peranakan".

The roots of the Peranakan are also quite controversial as both Indonesian Peranakan Chinese and Malaysian Peranakan Chinese thought that their Peranakan societies are the oldest, and hence they are the roots of the Peranakan. It is difficult to argue which Peranakan community is the oldest as more studies are needed. However, from the information available, it seems that the Indonesian Peranakan appeared to be older and much larger in number. During the (1405–33) expedition of Zheng He (Cheng Ho), Ma Huan discovered a number of Chinese clusters in Java (namely Gresik, New Village, Surabaya and Majapahit) and Sumatra (Palembang), and many of these Chinese were also Muslims.[1] However, no such Chinese communities in Peninsular Malaya were found and mentioned by Ma Huan.[2]

Nevertheless, the Peranakan communities later grew significantly. At the beginning of the twentieth century, Peranakan Chinese from Penang had interactions with the Peranakan Chinese in Medan, while Peranakan Chinese in Singapore had interactions with their counterparts in Java, especially Jakarta (Batavia).[3] However, these interactions appeared to have been lost. For a period of time, Peranakans from these two countries had not interacted with each other; they tended to live in their own world. It appears that this Peranakan Convention was the first time that the Malaysian and Indonesian Peranakan Chinese came together at such a large scale.

Sixteen Peranakan associations participated, including one Peranakan Indian association:[4]

Malaysia (six in total)

- Persatuan Peranakan Baba Nyonya Malaysia
- State Chinese (Penang) Association (Persatuan Peranakan Cina Pulau Pinang)
- Persatuan Peranakan Cina Melaka
- Persatuan Peranakan Baba Nyonya Kuala Lumpur & Selangor
- Persatuan Peranakan Cina Trengganu, Malaysia
- Kelantan Chinese Peranakan Association

Singapore (three in total)

- The Peranakan Association Singapore
- Gunong Sayang Association, Singapore
- Peranakan Indian (Chitty Melaka) Association Singapore

Indonesia (two in total)

- Asosiasi Peranakan Tionghoa Indonesia (ASPERTINA)
- Persaudaraan "Peranakan Tionghoa Warga Indonesia" (Persaudaraan Pertiwi)

Thailand (one in total)
- Thai Peranakan Association

Malaysia's Overseas Peranakan Associations (four in total)

- Peranakan Community of Western Australia
- Peranakan Baba Nyonya Perth
- Peranakan Association Australia Inc. (Melbourne)
- Peranakan Association Australia NSW Inc.

Of these Peranakan associations in Malaysia and Singapore, some were established during the colonial times but were given new names after Malaya and Singapore gained independence. In the previous chapters, we have mentioned the Peranakan Association of Singapore, which was originated from the Straits Chinese British Association (SCBA); the Persatuan Peranakan Cina Melaka, which was based on the SCBA Malacca branch; and the Persatuan Peranakan Cina Pulau Pinang, which was based on the State Chinese Association (SCA). Those associations in Malacca, Singapore and Penang belonged to this category. However, the rest were established more recently, long after Malaya/Malaysia gained independence. For instance, the Persatuan Peranakan Cina Kelantan, which is not well known.

With regard to Indonesia, there was a Peranakan Chinese party (Partai Tionghoa Indonesia) before World War II and a few Peranakan-based socio-political organizations after World War II, but there was no association which was specifically aimed at promoting Peranakan culture. Even Baperki, a large Peranakan organization, was mainly concerned with nationality issues and anti-racial discrimination. It never explicitly promoted "Peranakan culture" or "Peranakan identity". Also, the term Peranakan was never used in any Peranakan-based socio-political organizations prior to the fall of Suharto.

Only after the fall of New Order, Peranakan Chinese associations were established in Jakarta: Asosiasi Peranakan Tionghoa Indonesia (ASPERTINA) was established on 28 October 2011;[5] and Persaudaraan Peranakan Tionghoa Warga Indonesia (Persaudaraan Pertiwi) was established on 11 November 2011.[6] Apart from organizing meetings and conferences, these associations also organized blood donation drives, charity drives and group discussions. Persaudaraan Pertiwi also has its own Peranakan Museum. Outside Malaysia, Singapore and Indonesia, the Peranakan associations were equally recent. They were established by Peranakan migrants from these countries in recent years, and the membership appeared to be small.

The re-emergence of the Peranakan Chinese associations is partially linked to globalization, when Chinese new migrants, or known as *Xinyimin*, began to move to Southeast Asia and beyond. This was especially the case when the PRC government wanted to blur the distinction between foreigners of Chinese descent and the Chinese new migrants. This is perhaps a reaction of some Peranakan Chinese in Maritime Southeast Asia to show that they are more integrated into the region and are different from the mainland Chinese. This is the impression that I got after I exchanged views with many Peranakan association leaders.

Those Peranakan associations that participated in the Congress are mainly represented by people who are either in their middle ages or belong to the older generation. They were immersed in Indonesian Peranakan food and dances (such as *Ronggeng* and *Joget*). As the travelling and accommodation fees were not cheap, therefore those who participated were likely to come from a middle-class background. The songs sung were mainly Indonesian/Malay songs and the melody played using *Angklung* was Western. A Mandarin song was sung, but the whole atmosphere was definitely hybrid. As it was held in Indonesia, the programmes also tended to have an Indonesian flavour.

As noted earlier, this is the first Peranakan Baba and Nyonya Convention held in Indonesia. The organizer, Persaudaraan Pertiwi, was based in Tangerang and led by Udaya Halim (alias Lim Tjin Pheng 林振鹏), an entrepreneur who runs educational institutions in Tangerang and Western Australia. He only succeeded in bringing the Malaysia/Singapore-based Convention to Indonesia in 2018. Apparently, the Peranakan Chinese in Indonesia had not been aware of their Peranakan counterparts in the neighbouring countries, and hence there were not much interactions between them. They forgot about their interactions at the beginning of the last century. It seems that it was Udaya Halim who took the initiatives to rebuild the bridge between the two Peranakan communities.

The fact that there was an absence of interactions between Peranakan associations in Indonesia and those in Malaysia/Singapore explained why both sides thought that they represent the "typical" Peranakan model. Other models are less Peranakan or not Peranakan at all. Through the big gatherings from different countries, the Peranakans realized their similarities and differences.

From the sixteen Peranakan associations mentioned above, those from Malaysia use the term Peranakan in the name of their organizations, but two still attached the terms Baba and Nyonya after "Peranakan". While in Singapore and Indonesia, only the term Peranakan is used. It is worth noting that the term *Cina* is not derogatory in Malaysia but it is offensive in Indonesia, therefore Peranakan Cina is still used in the name of Malaysia's Peranakan associations, but in Indonesia's associations only Tionghoa is used.

There have been a lot of misunderstandings about Baba and Nyonya and the Peranakan, even the definitions of these terms found in the authoritative dictionaries of Indonesia and Malaysia are problematic. They are often self-centred and only reflect the knowledge that the local Chinese have about their own communities.

Different Interpretations of Various Terms

Peranakan Chinese in the Malay Archipelago have a long history. It existed before the birth of Indonesia and other nations. This can be seen from the existence of the term Peranakan and its counterpart such as Baba.

The term Baba has been used by Indonesian Chinese prior to the twentieth century and it became a form of address for the Peranakan Chinese in Indonesia and also Malaya/Malaysia. However, in the twentieth century, it also became the name/label of this community. Even in Malaysia/Singapore, some older Peranakans today still want to be called Baba instead of Peranakan Chinese.

Nonetheless, Peranakan Chinese is now a more widely used term by both the government and the Peranakan Chinese themselves. In colonial Indonesia, the term was used to refer to the "off spring of intermarriage between a native and foreigner". The Dutch authorities used it to refer to the local-born Chinese who were Dutch subjects in the Outer Islands. But in Java, the term was also used to refer to the local-born Chinese who were Muslims. However, in Malaya and Singapore, the term has never had the Islamic religious connotation. Nevertheless, the religious connotation of Peranakan in Indonesia disappeared only in the latter part of the nineteenth century.

The Peranakan Chinese themselves began to use the term regularly only at the end of the second decade of the twentieth century when the Dutch wanted to involve the local-born Chinese in the political institutions. It became more popular in the third decade when the Peranakan Chinese wanted to get involved in local politics. The indigenous Indonesians began to be aware of the division within the Chinese community after World War II. Even in the Amir Sjarifuddin Cabinet II in 1947–48, a portfolio of Urusan Peranakan (Peranakan affairs) was established and

Siauw Giok Tjhan was appointed as the Minister of State in charge of Peranakan affairs. In fact, this is a recognition of the significance of the Peranakan Chinese in Indonesian society. In 1963, President Sukarno in his speech even proposed that Peranakan Chinese be considered as one of the Indonesian *sukus* (Indonesian ethnic groups) comparable to the Javanese, Batak, Sundanese and others.

As most of the Indonesian Chinese are Peranakan, one can therefore argue that they have become an Indonesian *suku*. In Indonesia, the official term Peranakan has now replaced other terms in reference to the local-born and partially-assimilated Chinese, but in Singapore and Malaysia, the terms Baba and Nyonya continue to be used today. Nonetheless, the identity of the Peranakan Chinese is far from clear. While it is clear that all Peranakan Chinese share the influence of Malay culture, especially language and food, the degree of influence has been uneven.

While Peranakan Chinese and Baba/Nyonya continue to survive today, other terms such as "Straits Chinese", and "Straits-born Chinese" have had shorter lifespans as they are history- and geography-bound. In fact, "Straits Chinese" and "Straits-born Chinese" have become historical terms. With the exception of the older generation who can still be called "Straits Chinese" and "Straits-born Chinese" owing to their birthdates and birthplaces, it is anachronistic to use the terms to refer to the Chinese who were born and brought up in Singapore and Malaysia after independence.

The usage of the terms Baba and Nyonya have also been in decline in Indonesia, while in Singapore and Malaysia they are still being used interchangeably with the term Peranakan Chinese. Nevertheless, younger Peranakan Chinese no longer identify themselves as Baba and Nyonya. In Indonesia where the terms were once widely used, they have gradually fallen into disuse. Few Chinese Indonesians understand the meanings of the terms today. But in Malaysia and Singapore, Baba/Nyonya remain quite popular. Peranakan food and Nyonya food are used interchangeably. It is worth noting that in Malaysia, even the names of Peranakan organizations still included Baba after the word Peranakan, which is quite redundant.

Self-identity and the perception of others are equally important for the perpetuation of "ethnic identity" during the colonial era, hence the terms "Straits Chinese" and "Straits-born Chinese" were preferred. This was because this group of Chinese in British Malaya (including Singapore) appeared to form the upper class of the Chinese community. However, with the end of colonialism, the terms were used less and less as more Chinese came to regard them as anachronistic.

There has been a shift of identities to Baba/Nyonya and Peranakan Chinese, which represent merely cultural rather than socio-political identities. The function of identity is also crucial. During the colonial period, a Straits Chinese carried a higher social and even "superior" status than that of other Chinese. But in Malaysia today, to be a Straits Chinese is anachronistic, and hence, the term has been abandoned.

Nevertheless, Babas and Peranakans can still claim to have links with the Malays—who are the ruling elite. Therefore, it is still useful socially and politically to claim to be linked to the indigenous population. However, with racial and religious polarization, the Peranakan Chinese face new challenges. With globalization and the rise of Chinese culture, many Peranakan children are being exposed to non-Baba cultures, with some eventually becoming more "Chinese" and less "Malay".

The retention of the Baba identity in Singapore does not have social and political "values" since the ruling elite is predominantly Chinese. Although the city-state is located in the so-called Malay seas, the rise of China as an economic giant and globalization continues to "dilute" Baba culture. Nevertheless, some Peranakan individuals still attempt to salvage this culture. But the objective conditions are not favourable and the Peranakan identity is gradually fading from the scene.

The Malay Ancestry of the Peranakan Chinese

The mixed racial ancestry of the Peranakan Chinese has always been a presumption of many people, especially the Peranakan Chinese themselves. This has become a debatable point in recent years. The most recent scientific findings released by a team of researchers from the Agency for Science and Research's (A*STAR) Genome Institute of Singapore (GIS) is worth noting. Their findings have been published in the scientific journal *Molecular Biology and Evolution* on 21 June 2021.[7]

The team of researchers analysed the genomes of 177 Singapore Peranakan Chinese. They discovered that Peranakan Chinese inherited 5.62 per cent Malay ancestry around 190 years ago, a proportion that is significantly higher than that in Singapore Chinese (1.08 per cent Malay ancestry), southern Chinese (0.86 per cent Malay ancestry) and northern Chinese (0.25 Malay ancestry). The findings confirm that the Peranakan Chinese (in Singapore) has 5.62 per cent Malay's genome. The above number is the mean of 4.76 per cent and 6.49 per cent (see Table 4.1). But the percentage is not as high as some people expected, indicating that there has not been much recent mixed marriage with the Malay, otherwise the Malay genome could have been much higher.

It is worth noting that the samples of the Peranakan Chinese for the project are from Singapore. It is not only rather small in number (177) but also not inclusive of the Peranakan Chinese from Indonesia (especially Java) and Malaysia. Therefore, one may question the representativeness of the samples. Nevertheless, these scientific findings are significant for us to understand one of the major issues of Peranakan Chinese racial ancestry.

The findings also show that these Malay DNA came from female Malay rather than male Malay, suggesting that there was indeed

TABLE 4.1
Global Ancestry Fractions of Different Chinese Groups

Chinese Groups	Chinese %	Malay %	Indian %	European %
Peranakan Chinese	93.3 (92.3–94.2)	5.62 (4.76–6.49)	0.92 (0.73–1.11)	0.20 (0.13–0.27)
Singapore Chinese	98.3 (98.3–99.2)	1.08 (0.65–1.51)	0.11 (0.07–0.15)	0.08 (0.06–0.09)
Southern Chinese	98.9 (98.5–99.2)	0.86 (0.50–1.23)	0.06 (0.05–0.07)	0.20 (0.17–0.23)
Northern Chinese	98.9 (98.8–99.0)	98.9 (98.8–99.0)	98.9 (98.8–99.0)	98.9 (98.8–99.0)

Source: Adapted from Table 1, Global Ancestry Fractions of Different Chinese Groups Inferred by RFMix, in "Genetic Admixture in the Culturally Unique Peranakan Chinese Population in Southeast Asia", *Molecular Biology and Evolution*, 21 June 2021, p. 5.

intermarriage between Chinese male and Malay female. However, this occurred only about 190 years ago, not earlier than that year.

There is another revelation, which is not in the report nor in the press release. It was contained in the official website of the Singapore Peranakan Chinese Association, which provided the blood samples from their volunteers and others for the project.[8] It stated that in the Peranakan blood samples, 10 per cent of these 177 self-identified Peranakan Chinese does not have any Malay ancestry at all. In other words, this 10 per cent is 100 per cent Chinese. This revelation shows that the Peranakan identity is also a self-identity (self-identification). A Peranakan Chinese can be an individual who does not possess mixed racial ancestry. Nevertheless, these "pure" Chinese have been integrated into the so-called Peranakan culture and lifestyle.

Evolution of the Peranakan Concept

Peranakan is a Malay term and was used to refer to the offsprings of intermarriages between a Malay and a foreigner. However, as most of these foreigners happened to be Chinese, the term was later developed to refer mainly to the Peranakan Chinese community. Although intermarriage was initially an important element, gradually it was used to refer to local-born and localized Chinese with local citizenship. Subsequently intermarriage is no longer an important element in the Peranakan identity. In the eighteenth and early nineteenth centuries, the Dutch used the term Peranakan Chinese to mean Chinese Muslims in Java and Madura, but later they used this term to refer to localized Chinese to differentiate them from new migrants known as *totok* (*singkeh*) without any Islamic connotation.

The Indonesian Chinese themselves initially did not accept the term Peranakan. They used Baba to refer to themselves and it was used by the non-Chinese to refer to the local-born Chinese. Only in the second quarter of the twentieth century did the localized Chinese begin to use the term to refer to themselves in order to differentiate their group from the *totok* Chinese. One can see this major division in the Indonesian Chinese community in the 1950s and 1960s. During the Suharto era, as a rapid assimilation policy was implemented, a large majority of the Chinese had been Peranakanized. Nonetheless, the internal division continued to exist as there was still cultural division among the Chinese Indonesians.

In Malaysia and Singapore, initially the term Peranakan has an identical meaning as in the Indonesian dictionary. The Peranakan Chinese was initially not used by the local-born and localized Chinese. They preferred Baba and/or Straits Chinese. Those who were born in the Straits Settlements and English educated called themselves either Baba or Straits Chinese. The localization of the Chinese also took place in Kelantan and Terengganu, but they were initially excluded from both the Baba and the Straits Chinese community. After Malaya's independence, with the Malay-dominated government, the term Peranakan became popular. It was also gradually accepted by the Chinese in Malaysia/Singapore as a term to refer to the localized Chinese.

Growing Popularity of Things Peranakan

Apart from the Peranakan associations, it should be noted that in the last decades, there has been growing popularity of things Peranakan, including Peranakan food (also cuisine), dress, movies and tv series, museums, seminars/webinars, books etc.

In Indonesia, Malaysia and Singapore, especially in Singapore, there have been many Peranakan restaurants and food stalls selling Peranakan food. The Peranakan Singapore restaurant has been quite popular, so is Penang Nyonya food. In fact, in many malls and residential areas, you can also encounter many Peranakan food stalls, often called the Nyonya food or with different names. The Peranakan cuisine, the Bengawan Solo, named after the Solo River in Indonesia, has become some sort of a brand name in Singapore. It can be found in almost every major mall in Singapore and appears to be very popular. In fact, Peranakan food are also sold in Indonesia and Malaysia. Sometimes they are mistaken as Malay food/Indonesian food as there are many similarities, except for one thing, Peranakan food includes pork which is *haram* in Malay food.

The Peranakan dress also attracts a lot of attention. The Peranakan sarong kebaya (in Indonesian: *Kain Kebaya*) has been worn by Peranakan females. In order to keep up with the times, the kebaya has been modernized. There have been a number of Peranakan dress exhibitions held to display new styles of kebaya. In Jakarta, for instance, this kind of exhibition is very popular, and many were held in major hotels.[9] In Singapore, a number of Peranakan sarong kebaya exhibitions have been staged and there is a growing interest in things Peranakan, including sarong kebaya.[10] The Peranakan sarong kebaya exhibitions were even exported overseas, including Japan.[11] In Malacca, Kuala Lumpur and Penang, the sarong kebaya exhibitions have been held more frequently.

Peranakan museums have been established in Indonesia, Malaysia and Singapore only after 1985. Before this, the Peranakan exhibits were part of the national museum. After 1985, all of the Peranakan museums were private museums, with the only exception of the Peranakan Museum in Singapore, which was officially opened in 2008. In the same year the Baba House (NUS) was also opened in Singapore. While in Malaysia, there was the Baba and Nyonya Heritage Museum, opened in 1985 and the Penang Peranakan Mansion, opened in 2008.[12] Interestingly, in Indonesia where the largest number of the Peranakans resided, there was no such museum until 2011. This museum, called Benteng Heritage Museum or Museum Warisan Budaya Tionghoa Tangerang (Museum of Chinese Cultural Heritage at Tangerang), was established by a local-born Chinese entrepreneur and educator, Udaya Halim. As there is growing interest in the Peranakan culture, all of the above-mentioned museums attracted many visitors.

TV shows based on the Peranakan theme or story have also been produced both in Singapore and Indonesia. For instance, the Little Nyonya (Xiao Niangre 小娘惹), a Mandarin TV drama series produced by the Singapore Broadcasting Corporation was a great success. Mainland Chinese film makers later remade the Little Nyonya for the audience in China. Unfortunately, it was unable to match the original series as the producers and the actors are not familiar with the Peranakan culture. Peranakan plays in English were also produced in Singapore. The play by Stella Kon, "Emily of the Emerald Hill", was premiered in Singapore in 1985. "It was an unexpected success and hence became an iconic Singapore's play."[13]

In Indonesia, movies such as Ca-bau-kan (2002) which denotes the story of a Peranakan show girl and Gie, which depicts the life story of a Peranakan Chinese student leader in Indonesia Soe Hok Gie (1942–69), were also produced. The film Gie was made in 2005 by a young Indonesian director and won the Citra best award (comparable to American Oscar) for the best picture of 2005.[14]

There have also been a lot of seminars on the Peranakan culture in Indonesia, Malaysia and Singapore. These seminars were held at various academic institutions in Jakarta, Kuala Lumpur and Singapore. During the Covid-19 pandemic, the Peranakan fever appears to be going strong. In Surabaya, a group of Peranakan Chinese, together with native Indonesians, established an association called Roemah Bhinneka Surabaya (Diversity House of Surabaya), and since June 2020 have succeeded in launching a regular webinar every Monday on the Peranakan Chinese in Indonesia.

Some of the seminar papers have been collected and published as a book, for instance the seminar papers by the Chinese Heritage Centre and the NUS Baba House;[15] while other papers have been developed into a major book, such as Peter H. Lee's book on the sarong kebaya.[16]

Conclusion

In recent years, the Peranakan Chinese associations have been active again. In fact, there is a growing interest in things Peranakan such as Peranakan food, dress, seminars/webinars and books.

The Peranakan phenomenon should be seen from a historical perspective. The three interrelated terms, namely Peranakan Chinese, Baba and Nyonya have been widely used in the Malay Archipelago. Nevertheless, their meaning and usage varied from country to country and from period to period. In addition, the Peranakans are not a homogeneous group. Nevertheless, being local-born and possessing a high degree of localization in terms of language/culture are two important elements of being a Peranakan. Some included a third element: a presumption that one is of mixed racial ancestry with the Malays. This point has been substantiated by a recent scientific study that the Peranakan Chinese in Singapore have significantly higher percentage of Malay DNA compared to their non-Peranakan Chinese counterparts. Nevertheless, 10 per cent of the self-proclaimed Peranakans in the study are "pure" Chinese.

The Peranakan and Baba communities played significant roles in the politics, economy and administration during the British Malaya and Dutch East Indies as well as in the initial period of Malaya's and Indonesia's independence.

Later their political and economic significance declined gradually, yet the Peranakan communities continue to survive in the three countries and beyond as evidenced by the presence of Peranakan associations and Peranakan conventions from year to year. Nevertheless, their relevance varies from country to country.

In Malaysia, the group seeks for the indigenous (Bumiputera) status while in Indonesia, it seeks for the indigenous *suku* (ethnic group) status. In Singapore, the Peranakan status appears to be less relevant and less important. Nevertheless, the rise of China and the presence of new Chinese migrants often pose a challenge to the Peranakan identity, especially in Singapore and Malaysia.

In Malaysia and Singapore, the Straits-born Chinese has been in decline while new types of Peranakans are emerging. The old terms for Peranakan such as Baba (for male) and Nyonya (for female) are more popular among the older generation Peranakans in both Malaysia and Singapore, but not in Indonesia.

The Peranakan Chinese in Indonesia appeared to have been more assimilated into their society compared to their counterparts in Malaysia and Singapore.

With the passing away of the older generation Peranakan/Baba, new types of Peranakans are emerging. Nevertheless, in Malaysia and Singapore, they remain a minority among the Chinese communities, but in Indonesia, especially in Java, they form a majority. However, all Peranakans are increasingly "nationalized" in accordance with the country they belong to.

Notes

1. See Chen Dasheng (陈达生, Tan Ta Sen), *Zheng He yu Donyangya Yisilan* 郑和与东南亚伊斯兰 (Beijing: Haiyang Chubanshe, 2008), p. 104, Table 9 for the locations of the Indonesian Chinese in the fifteenth century.
2. "Mahuan also wrote about Melaka but did not mention the Chinese living among the natives." See Tan Chee Beng, *The Baba of Melaka: Culture and*

Identity of a Chinese Peranakan Community in Malaysia (Kuala Lumpur: Pelanduk Publications, 1988), p. 29.

3. In fact, Zhang Bishi of Penang was from Medan; Lim Boon Keng of Singapore was the advisor of Tiong Hoa Hwee Koan in Batavia. He was closely associated with the Confucian movement in Java during the initial stage.

4. In fact, there were three Indonesia's overseas Peranakan associations which were listed but did not send delegates: Chinese Indonesian Heritage Center (CIHC)-Holland, Peranakan Indonesia in USA and Peranakan Indonesia in Australia. See *Suara Baba: Exploring the Roots of PERANAKAN, 31st Peranakan Convention* (published in Tangerang, November 2018), p. 169.

5. See https://www.facebook.com/Aspertina/ (accessed 22 June 2020). According to a report, IPTI (should be ASPERTINA) has 4,000 members in 13 provinces. See Zakir Hussain, "Chinese Indonesians Come Full Circle", *Straits Times*, 8 June 2012, p. A22.

6. *Suara Baba* (Special Issue), November 2018, p. 87.

7. Most of the data on the findings are taken from two sources: "Genomic Analysis of Peranakan Chinese Reveals Insight into Ancestry", *A*STAR Press Release*, 16 July 2021 and "Genetic Admixture in the Culturally Unique Peranakan Chinese Population in Southeast Asia", *Molecular Biology and Evolution*, 21 June 2021, p. 5.

8. "The Singapore Peranakan Genome Project", https://www.peranakan.org.sg/2021/the-singapore-peranakan-genome-project/ (accessed 26 September 2021). The original words are: Out of the 177 blood samples from volunteer donors studied, GIS's analysis determined that 90 per cent had averaged 90 per cent Chinese DNA and 10 per cent Malay DNA. The remaining 10 per cent of the blood samples, a significant segment, showed 100 per cent Chinese DNA.

9. See Thung Ju Lan, "Peranakan Chinese Community in Indonesia and Globalization", in *Peranakan Communities in the Era of Decolonization and Globalization*, edited by Leo Suryadinata (Singapore: Chinese Heritage Centre and NUS Baba House, 2015), pp. 126–39 (particularly pp. 132–33).

10. Peter Lee, "Peranakan Fashion and Its International Sources: Sarong Kebaya", *BeMuse* 4, no. 2 (April–June 2012), https://www.roots.gov.sg/stories-landing/stories/peranakan-fashion-and-its-international-sources/story (accessed 25 April 2021).

11. "Singapore, Sarong Kebaya and Style Exhibition", *Fukuoka Now*, 17 April–12 June 2016, https://www.fukuoka-now.com/en/event/singapore-sarong-kebaya-style-exhibition/ (accessed 25 April 2021).

12. For a brief discussion on the Peranakan museums in Malaysia and Singapore, see Kenson Kuok, "Museum of the Peranakan Culture: Local and Global Impetus", in *Peranakan Communities in the Era of Decolonization and*

Globalization, edited by Leo Suryadinata (Singapore: Chinese Heritage Centre and NUS Baba House, 2015), pp. 115–25.

13. Ibid., p. 119.

14. "Gie Film Terbaik FFI 2005", https://www.liputan6.com/showbiz/read/223007/igiei-film-terbaik-ffi-2005 (accessed 15 April 2021).

15. For instance, Leo Suryadinata's edited book on the *Peranakan Chinese in a Globalizing Southeast Asia* (2010). For the full information, see Bibliography.

16. Lee, Peter H. *Sarong Kebaya: Peranakan Fashion in an Interconnected World 1500-1950* (Singapore: Asian Civilisations Museum, 2014). This book was based on a paper that he read in a conference at the University of Malaya.

5

PERANAKAN CHINESE IN IMS: THE SOCIO-POLITICAL DIMENSION*

The term Peranakan Chinese has had different meanings throughout the history of the Malay world. However, the degree of Malayness is often used as one of the criteria for the use of this term. In this chapter, I use Peranakan Chinese to mean the local-born Chinese who use a local language, usually Malay, as their home language, although the elite in the past were mainly Dutch- or English-educated. This chapter will examine the socio-political position of the Peranakan Chinese community in Indonesia, Malaysia and Singapore during the colonial period and post-independence, including the era of globalization. From this comparative survey, we will be able to see a variety of Peranakan communities and ascertain their future developments.

It should be noted here that the socio-political position of the Peranakan Chinese, to a large degree, has been determined by both the colonial and independent states. The state policy towards the Chinese minority in general, and the Peranakan Chinese in particular, shaped the Chinese society. In colonial society, the social stratification was based on race, and the Chinese were placed under the Europeans but above the indigenous population. In independent Southeast Asia, with the removal of Europeans from the position of power, the indigenous population raised to the top. The Singapore case is unique as it is a

Chinese dominant state and the Chinese are at the top. Nevertheless, as a modern state, Singapore's social stratification is more inclined to "meritocracy" and class rather than race.

Peranakan Chinese in the Colonial Era

Indonesia

Prior to the nineteenth century, most Chinese migrants were easily absorbed into the Peranakan society as they were small in number. But by the end of the nineteenth century, a larger number of Chinese migrants had arrived in Indonesia, especially Java. These later comers did not integrate into the Peranakan group but remained as *totoks* and formed a *totok* Chinese community. The arrival of a large number of *totoks* also coincided with the rise of overseas Chinese nationalism. The Pan-Chinese organization, Tiong Hoa Hwe (Hwee) Koan (THHK, 中华会馆), which was initiated by the Peranakan Chinese with the support of the *totok*, was established. It aimed at promoting Confucianism through the establishment of Chinese-medium schools. This was followed by the emergence of other Chinese organizations. Chinese schools were established throughout Java and the Outer Islands. The Peranakan Chinese society also began to be re-sinicized.

The Dutch authorities felt threatened by the rise of this overseas Chinese nationalism. They realized that this could result in converting the Peranakan Chinese into Chinese nationalists and become a threat to Dutch rule. They decided to win the Peranakan Chinese to their side by promoting Dutch education (HCS), declaring the Peranakan Chinese as Dutch subjects (Nederlandsch Onderdanen), removing discriminative policies towards the Peranakan Chinese and involving them in colonial administration and politics such as Volksraad and Municipal Councils. William Skinner argued that the Dutch fought on the side of the Peranakans, and the Peranakan Chinese community became divided.

Indeed, by the 1920s, the Peranakan Chinese had been divided into the China-oriented group and the Dutch-oriented group, and in the early 1930s, the Indonesia-oriented group also emerged. These were represented by the Sin Po Group, the Chung Hwa Hui and the Partai

Tionghoa Indonesia (PTI), respectively. The two latter groups attempted to weaken the strength of overseas Chinese nationalism. Nevertheless, that did not stop the re-sinicization of the Peranakan Chinese although the Peranakan Chinese community became more fragmented.

In the colonial society, the Peranakan Chinese in Indonesia became a special group. The Kapitan Cina system which was set up in the seventeenth century and lasted until the 1930s can also be seen as a way to get the Peranakan Chinese to serve as Dutch administrators. From the Dutch's point of view, the Peranakan Chinese, especially those who were Dutch-educated, should occupy a higher position compared to the *totoks* who were unable to speak Dutch and Malay. In fact, the economic status of the Peranakans was at one time higher than that of the *totoks* but gradually, the *totoks* surpassed the Peranakans and dominated the business sector.

Malaya and Singapore

Similar to the Dutch East Indies, the Chinese community in British Malaya was also divided into peranakan and *singkeh* (新客), but the number of *singkeh* was much larger than that of the peranakan. As in the situation in colonial Indonesia, the British authorities in Malaya and Singapore also feared the rise of overseas Chinese nationalism. To restrict its growth in strength, the British adopted a similar policy by providing English education to the Peranakan Chinese up to a certain level, declaring the Straits-born Chinese as British subjects, and involving them in the colonial administration and politics. They were included in the British colonial legislative council and civil service, representing the interests of the local Chinese. Benefitting from the policy, some Peranakan Chinese responded well to the British overture. Some members of the Peranakan Chinese elite became Anglicized. They proudly declared themselves the "King's Chinese" and "true British subjects" whose loyalty was to the United Kingdom.[1]

In August 1900, the first Straits Chinese British Association (SCBA) was established in Singapore, then in Malacca (October 1900) and Penang (1920). But the Penang SCBA was not "Straits" Chinese British Association but "State" Chinese British Association, implying that they held a strong position relative to the Straits Chinese (Peranakan Chinese). All of the SCBAs were established by the Peranakan Chinese, especially those who were English-educated, for several reasons: apart from the feeling of having a different identity from the migrant Chinese, they also felt the need to show their loyalty to the British Crown so that they would not be suspected by the British and hence would be able to develop freely.[2]

In the colonial society, the position of the Peranakan Chinese was still lower than the British but was higher than that of the migrant Chinese. Peranakan Chinese were trusted by the British due to their British education and the fact that they were less enthusiastic about, if not against, Chinese nationalism. Nevertheless, culturally, especially taking the Peranakan masses as a whole, they were still very "Chinese".

Peranakan Chinese in the Era of Independence

Indonesia

Indonesia proclaimed its independence in 1945 after a period of protracted armed conflict between the indigenous Indonesians and the Dutch. Indonesia became a sovereign state in 1950. But the policy of Indonesianizing Chinese only started in 1957 with the passing of a regulation to convert Indonesian citizens of Chinese descent (WNI) into Indonesian-speaking Chinese. Chinese Indonesians could no longer attend Chinese-medium schools. (Although a large number of Peranakan Chinese were already in Indonesian-medium schools, yet many attended Chinese-medium schools due to the popularity of Chinese education.) The 1957 regulation may be seen as the most concrete measure to "Indonesianize" the Chinese in Indonesia.

The peranakanization of the *totok* community started when the children of the *totoks* who were Indonesian citizens were compelled to receive Indonesian education. In 1963, two years before his fall from power, President Sukarno introduced the concept of an Indonesian nation (*Bangsa Indonesia*) consisting of many *sukus* (Indonesian ethnic groups), one of which is Peranakan Tionghoa (Peranakan Chinese). This gave a boost to the Peranakan Chinese community at the expense of the *totok* community. Had this concept been accepted by the following regime, Peranakan Chinese could have been a legitimate ethnic group in Indonesia without having to undergo further (total) assimilation.

However, when Suharto came to power after the 30 September 1965 movement, he introduced a total assimilation policy towards the Chinese, thus abandoning Sukarno's proposed policy of accepting the Peranakan Chinese as an Indonesian *suku*. Furthermore, Suharto banned and dissolved the three pillars of the Chinese culture overseas: ethnic Chinese organizations, Chinese medium schools and Chinese language press. He also restricted the development of Chinese religions. These measures resulted in the further Indonesianization of Chinese Indonesians, especially the *totoks*. In fact, the thirty-two years of Suharto's rule witnessed the peranakanization of the *totok* community as those *totok* children who were brought up during this New Order era lost their command of the Chinese language.

As a total assimilation policy was introduced, Peranakan Chinese were forced to become "indigenous" Indonesians. In fact, the Peranakan culture as such was unable to develop. Peranakan Chinese were forced to become *pribumi*, losing its "Peranakan Chinese" characteristics, while *totok* Chinese were rapidly peranakanized. There were laws and regulations to restrict the public celebration of Chinese festivals and the practice of Chinese religions.

After the fall of Suharto, the new authorities introduced the policy of pluralism towards the ethnic groups, including the ethnic Chinese, and the three pillars of Chinese culture were restored; although no Chinese medium school was established, bilingual and trilingual schools have been permitted. Peranakan Chinese identity re-emerged as manifested in the formation of many Peranakan Chinese associations, the re-recognition of the Confucian religion, the organization of the Peranakan beauty contest and publication of Peranakan literary works. Peranakan Chinese identity once again is accepted in Indonesia, at least as part of the official policy.

It should be noted that Peranakan Chinese in Indonesia have long been involved in politics. Prior to World War II, political participation in Indonesia in general was limited and tended to follow the ethnic approach. It began to diversify after Indonesia's independence but the ethnic Chinese approach was still strong. Baperki, a Peranakan-based socio-political organization, was a mass organization for the Peranakan Chinese. During the Suharto era, ethnic politics was prohibited and Chinese Indonesians, especially the Peranakans, were only allowed to participate in politics through indigenous political organizations. Only after the fall of Suharto was there a revival of ethnic Chinese political parties but these were unable to develop and eventually subsided. Chinese Indonesians, both Peranakans and peranakanized *totoks*, have continued to participate in politics through the non-ethnic Chinese political parties. Two major reasons are they realize that Chinese Indonesians are not a homogeneous group, and that as the number of the Chinese is small they are unlikely to be elected into political office if they use ethnic Chinese parties as vehicles.

Malaysia

After Malaya achieved independence in 1957, the government began to "Malayanize" the Chinese school system. However, apart from introducing a national-type school system and requiring non-Malay schools to teach Malay which is the national language, vernacular schools have been permitted to exist. Independent secondary Chinese medium schools, known collectively as *Du Zhong*, are still in operation. In 1967, the government transformed the English medium schools into Malay medium schools. Nevertheless, no assimilation policy such as that of Indonesia was ever introduced.

Malaya/Malaysia began with the adoption of an accommodation model in its educational and language policies. The Malaya/Malaysian constitution recognizes religious freedom and the use of ethnic languages while stipulating Islam as the official religion of the Federation. A multi-ethnic and multi-religious society of Malaya/Malaysia became a fact of life, with the existence of racial/ethnic tensions in varying degrees. However, after the 1969 riot, the Malay dominated government introduced the Bumiputera (indigenous) policy which favours the indigenous (read: Malay) population resulting in the polarization of the Malaysian population. Ethnic nationalism has since run deep and the Peranakan Chinese, many of whom having lost their command of the Chinese language, have been sending their children to Chinese primary schools again. This has been seen as a result of ethnic/racial polarization in Malaysia. The ethnic identity of the Peranakan Chinese—the Chinese identity—has become strong. Some observers have noted that there is a re-sinicization of the Peranakan Chinese in Malaysia.[3]

The pro-Malay policy has alienated many Chinese, especially the Chinese-educated and English-educated Peranakan Chinese, as they are denied positions in the universities and public service due to their ethnic/ racial origin. Many who had the opportunity to go overseas have left Malaysia; however, the majority have stayed and tried to adapt to the situation. They have joined local political parties to defend their rights and improve their socio-political positions. Peranakan Chinese identity is more acceptable to the authorities compared to the "pure" Chinese identity, but it has remained weak as the number of non-Peranakan is much larger and many Peranakan children are being re-sinicized. This is especially so with globalization and the rise of China as an economic and political power.

In the past the Chinese were represented by the Peranakans in the colonial representative councils while the *totoks* were busy with politics in China. As the country became independent, the Peranakan Chinese established their own party: the Malayan (Malaysian) Chinese Association (MCA). Gradually the Peranakan Chinese were joined by the perakanized *singkeh* Chinese. Increasingly, the peranakanized *singkeh* Chinese are taking over from the Peranakan in MCA. Besides MCA, Democratic Action Party (DAP) and Gerakan are also ethnic Chinese-dominated parties. Their leaders are either Peranakan Chinese or peranakanized *singkeh*.

Singapore

The situation in Singapore is different. After its departure from Malaysia in August 1965, Singapore's educational policy chose the English/ American model, gradually replacing Chinese and Tamil with English as the teaching medium. Within one generation Chinese Singaporeans became English-educated. Only when the government realized that English education had caused the loss of the mother tongue (read: Mandarin) and Chinese tradition among the Chinese population that a bilingual policy was implemented.

The Peranakan Chinese in Singapore, especially the elite among the group, were English-educated. Their mother tongue can either be English or Malay, but with the new policy of promoting the (state-defined) mother tongue, Mandarin, Peranakan Chinese were compelled to learn Mandarin as a second language in school. It was reported that many Peranakan Chinese children were unable to cope with Mandarin and were forced to move to the English-speaking world. On the whole, the majority of the Peranakan Chinese appears to stay in Singapore and have adjusted to the new policy.

It is worth noting that although Singapore is a multi-ethnic and multi-cultural society, ethnic Chinese are numerically dominant. To be well-versed in Malay would be less useful in modern Singapore compared to Mandarin. The government, for practical purposes, has encouraged the study of Mandarin, rather than Malay, for the ethnic Chinese. It is therefore interesting to note that if the Peranakan Chinese were defined in terms of their possession of "Malayness" in the past, the Singapore Peranakan Chinese have gradually lost their "Malayness", at least in terms of the command of the Malay language. Increasing they have become English-speaking Chinese with Mandarin as a second language.

The Peranakan Chinese were involved in Singapore politics prior to World War II and they continued to do so after the war. A few political parties were formed by the Peranakan Chinese who were English-educated. Some of them were linked to the SCBA, but no one suggested that the organization be transformed into a political party. The reason was quite obvious as the organization was loyal to the British and would not be popular in an independent Singapore/Malaya. Besides, non-Peranakans who formed a large number of Singapore citizens, would have not been included; it would have been political suicide for the party. It was not surprising that the People's Action Party (PAP) was established by not only Peranakan Chinese but also Chinese-educated Chinese.

Conclusion

Reviewing the socio-political positions of the Peranakan Chinese in the three ASEAN countries—Indonesia, Malaya/Malaysia and Singapore—it is evident that they differ from period to period and from state to state. However, they had more similarities during the colonial era. The Dutch and British colonial rulers introduced the policy of using Peranakan Chinese in the local administration and legislative councils, and offered them higher social status than the new Chinese migrants. As a result, they occupied higher ranks in colonial society compared to the migrant Chinese. However, the Peranakan Chinese who used to enjoy a strong economic position were gradually replaced by the more dynamic *totok/ singkeh* Chinese, creating tensions between these two communities.

During the era of colonial rule, the Peranakan Chinese elite were considered by the colonial authorities as the representatives of the Chinese community, but the arrival of new migrant Chinese in large numbers and the growth of migrant Chinese economic power gradually pushed the Peranakan Chinese out of the economic/business sector. More and more Peranakan Chinese elite came to be concentrated in the professional and administrative sectors where a knowledge of the English and Malay languages was needed. However, the departure of the colonial rulers made the Peranakan Chinese adjust to the changing political situation out of necessity.

During the colonial period, the Peranakan Chinese were not forced to be integrated into local society. In fact, the authorities were afraid that they would integrate and ally with the "indigenous" population to rebel against colonial rule. However, during the post-independence period, the independent governments changed the policy towards the ethnic Chinese (including Peranakan Chinese). They have introduced varying degrees of integration in their policies.

In Indonesia, for instance, the Peranakan identity was initially welcome but when Suharto came to power, a complete assimilation policy was introduced. The Peranakan Chinese were forced to be assimilated into the indigenous population and Peranakan Chinese culture was denied, let alone the "pure" Chinese culture. In fact, prior to the New Order (1945–65), many Peranakan Chinese were appointed as cabinet ministers, but none did so during the thirty-two years of Suharto rule.[4] Nevertheless, the fall of Suharto has given rise to new opportunities for the Peranakan Chinese. Many Peranakan or peranakanized Chinese have moved into the professional sectors while many Chinese-speaking Chinese have consolidated their economic/business positions.

Independent Malaya/Malaysia recognizes the position of the Chinese Malaysians and guarantees their cultural and religious freedom. While the Chinese Malaysians have been expected to learn and master the Malay language as the national language, Chinese education up to the secondary school level has been tolerated. But the pro-Malay policy in various fields has pushed a large number of the Peranakan Chinese to the side of the *singkeh* Chinese. However, similar to the Chinese in Indonesia, the Peranakan Chinese have moved to the professional sectors while the Chinese-speaking Chinese still occupy the economic sector, including the business sector.

Singapore as a nation with a Chinese majority is in a dilemma. It adopts a bilingual policy: English and mother tongue. Mother tongue for the Singapore Chinese is defined as "Mandarin Chinese". As a result, the Peranakan Chinese in Singapore are losing their Malayness. Nevertheless, the Peranakan Chinese are still in a strong position but they are gradually joined by the bilingual Chinese. They are dominant in the professions and in government administration. Non-Peranakan Chinese are still strong in the economic sectors, including in businesses.

The different policies adopted by the three independent governments can be explained in terms of the size of the Chinese community in the country concerned and the proportion of the Peranakan Chinese vis-à-vis the *singkeh* Chinese. The smaller the Chinese community, the more likely the government adopts an assimilation policy. Nevertheless, the outcome of the Chinese communities today is also linked to their different historical developments.

Notes

*This chapter was first published in Leo Suryadinata, ed., *Peranakan Chinese in a Globalizing Southeast Asia* (Singapore: Chinese Heritage Centre and NUS Baba House, 2010).

1. Claudine Salmon, ed. *Literary Migrations: Traditional Chinese Fiction in Asia (17th–20th Centuries)* (Beijing: International Culture Publishing Corporation, 1987), p. 406.

2. C.F. Yong, *Chinese Leadership and Power in Colonial Singapore* (Singapore: Times Academic Press, 1992), pp. 52–61.
3. In fact, this trend has continued until today.
4. In his last cabinet before he was forced to step down, Suharto quickly appointed his crony, Bob Hasan, as the Minister of Trade. He lasted for less than a month.

6

MALAY/INDONESIAN TRANSLATIONS OF CHINESE LITERATURE: PAST AND PRESENT*

Introduction

The Chinese have been in the Malay world, namely Indonesia and Malaya/Malaysia for centuries. Nevertheless, the translation of Chinese works into the local languages, particularly the Malay language, only took place in the late 1880s.[1] The existence of such translations is related to three important developments:

1. There was a rise of Chinese nationalism, or at least cultural nationalism, among the Chinese in the Malay region;
2. There was an emergence of Western-educated Chinese writers and journalists who undertook the translation of Chinese works;
3. With the development of the printing press, often known as print capitalism, the Chinese began to get involved in such a business.

Prior to the 1880s, the above developments were absent in the Malay world, and as a result, no Chinese works were translated into the Malay language.

In fact, towards the end of the nineteenth century, printing presses and newspapers in Malay/Indonesian had begun to emerge, but none was in the Chinese language.[2] The Peranakan and Baba who were no longer fluent in Chinese but equally inadequate in their command of the Western languages needed to read newspapers, magazines and books in the language that they understood. They were also interested in reading more about Chinese culture, and some enterprising Chinese started translating Chinese stories into Malay. In Java, for instance, these Chinese stories were initially published by Dutch printing houses such as H.M. van Dorp and W. Bruining & Co.,[3] but one year later the Peranakan Chinese themselves set up their own printing houses (e.g. Ijap Goan Ho) and published these stories by themselves. In the Straits Settlements of British Malaya, the publishers were Chinese (e.g. Kim Sek Chye Press, Poh Wah Hean Press) from the beginning.[4]

It is imperative to note that the demand for Malay translations of Chinese works did not come from the Malay community but the Chinese themselves, as many Chinese in the Malay world had lost their command of the Chinese language. They were Peranakan Chinese who were well versed in Malay, which was the lingua franca of different ethnic groups in the Malay Archipelago. Among the Peranakan Chinese in colonial Indonesia and British Malaya, Malay, not Chinese, was the medium of communication.

However, the publication of Malay translation of Chinese works, during the later period, also had an impact on the non-Chinese readers; this was particularly true in Indonesia as those translations were read by indigenous Indonesians as well. This was not the case in Malaya.

The Indonesians and the Malays initially adopted the Arabic script rather than the Roman script. However, in Indonesia, with the rise of the Dutch Eurasian and the Peranakan Chinese press, simultaneously with the rise of Indonesian nationalist movement, the Roman script was used and popularized. Nevertheless, the Malays continued to use the Arabic script in the school system. Only much later did they use both the Arabic and Roman scripts, but many Malays still felt more at home with the Arabic script than the Roman script. Since the translation of Chinese works into Malay was in the Roman script, Malay readers were unlikely to read them.

When examining the Malay translations of Chinese works, it appears that the Peranakan Chinese in Indonesia were ahead. According to Claudine Salmon, the earliest translation into Indonesian was a book on *Haij Soeiij* (Hai Rui 海瑞), which was published in 1882,[5] while in Malaya, the first translation that was published was entitled *Gong Kiah Sie* 戇子婿 or Stupid Son-in-Law in 1889. In fact in the same year, another translation entitled *Teong Chiat Ghee* 忠节义 also came into being (translator: Chek Swee Leong).[6] Since then more translations appeared in colonial Indonesia (better known as the Dutch East Indies) and British Malaya.

I. The Peranakan/Baba Community and Pre-War Chinese Works in Translations

The presence of Malay translations of Chinese works is directly linked to the nature of the Chinese communities in colonial Indonesia and British Malaya.

Prior to the influx of the Chinese into Southeast Asia, the Chinese communities in both colonies were small and largely integrated into local societies. In those days, there were difficulties in communications and the Chinese were banned from leaving and re-entering China. Those Chinese who left China did not bring their families with them. They intermarried with local women and settled down in Southeast Asia. Because of the small size of these groups, in Java they tended to integrate into the local communities. These Chinese lost active command of the Chinese language and used Malay—the lingua franca of the Malay Archipelago—to communicate. In the Straits Settlements, especially in Malacca and Singapore, there were also Chinese who intermarried with local women. They too lost command of the Chinese language and used Malay as the medium of communication. These Chinese were usually called either Peranakan or Baba.[7]

It is worth noting that in the late nineteenth and early twentieth centuries, the Chinese in Java were mainly Peranakan while in the Straits Settlements of British Malaya the *totok* (foreign born and Chinese speaking) were predominant. The size of the Peranakan/Baba communities in the two areas had an impact on the development of translation literature in the respective areas. The former had more variety in Malay translations work than the latter. There was also a strong Peranakan press[8] and even creative works which were weak, if not absent, in the Straits Settlements.

It should be pointed out that in Java, initially the term Peranakan was used to refer to the local-born Chinese who were Muslims. However, gradually it lost its religious connotation. It simply refers to the Chinese who had been localized in both language and lifestyle. The mass immigration of the new Chinese, which resulted in the rise of a *totok* community, only took place after the nineteenth century. Nevertheless, these two communities never really merged. In Java, at the beginning of the twentieth century, most of the Chinese were Peranakan. When the first modern pan-Chinese organization, the Tiong Hoa Hwe (Hwee) Koan 中华会馆 (THHK) was established in 1900, its constitution was written in Malay and Dutch. No one was able to translate it into the Chinese language, indicating that the command of the Chinese language among the Chinese in Java was poor.[9] However, it appears to be easier to look for a translator to translate from Chinese to Malay or from English to Malay.

Among the early translators in Indonesia and Malaya, many received some Western education, but a few might not be able to read Chinese. How did these "translators" do their translation? Some might be able to read Western languages such as Dutch and English, and they re-translate the Chinese stories from the Western works. Others collaborated with the Chinese who still understand Chinese but were unable to write in Malay, their collaboration eventually produced the Malay versions of these Chinese stories.

Unfortunately there was no information about the early translators in Indonesia except their names, for instance Ijo Tian Soeij who translated *Boekoe Tjerita Hoen Tjeng Lauw* (Fen Zhuang Lou, 粉粧楼) and Tjong Loen Tat who translated *Song Kang* 宋江 (Song Jiang, one of the 108 heroes in *Water Margin*). But we know a bit about Sie Hian Ling who translated *See Yoe* (Xiyou Ji 西游记, Records of the Journey to the West) in 1886 and Lie In Eng who re-translated *Sam Kok* 三国 (Romance of the Three Kingdoms). The former was a Peranakan journalist while the latter was a "professional" translator who was a second-generation Chinese in Sumatra.[10] The situation in Malaya is slightly better. The most prolific translator was Batu Gantong whose Chinese name is Chan Kim Boon 曾锦文 (Zeng Jinwen, 1851–1920) and his "successor" Panah Pranakan, which was the pen name of Wan Boon Seng 袁文成 (Yuan Wencheng). Chan was educated in an English school in Penang while studying Chinese through private tuition. He also went to China to study but returned because of ill health.[11] However, he recovered after returning to Singapore and completed the translation of the three Chinese classics (*Sam Kok, Song Kang* 宋江 and *See Yoe*) by himself and received praise from his readers. However, his successor Wan, although having published many translations, was not well versed in Chinese. He sought help from his Chinese friends in translating Chinese classics.[12]

Initially, most of the Chinese works "translated" into Malay/Indonesian were from the so-called *yanyi xiaoshuo* 演义小说 (popular classical novels) such as *Sanguo Yanyi* 三国演义 (*Sam Kok*, or the Romance of the Three Kingdoms), *Shuihu Zhuan* 水浒传 (*Song Kang*, Water Margin) and *Xiyou Ji* (*See Yoe*, Records of the Journey to the West). These three novels were written during the Ming dynasty (1368–1644). *Sanguo Yanyi*, which was "written" by Luo Guanzhong 罗贯中 (1330–1400), depicts the struggle of the three kingdoms between 169 and 280 in ancient China. It was this novel which popularizes the figures such as Zhu Geliang 诸葛亮, Guan Gong 关公 and Cao Cao 曹操. Guan Gong, one of the characters, later became a deity worshipped by many ethnic Chinese. *Shuihu Zhuan* which was "written" by Shi Nai'an 施耐庵 (1296–1370), depicts the phenomenon of peasant rebellions during the Northern Song dynasty led by Song Jiang who was supported by over one hundred heroes. Unlike the two novels, *Xiyou Ji*, which was written by Wu Chengen 吴承恩 (1500–82), was a fantasy, which narrates the story of a monk who went to India to study Buddhism. The monk was escorted by Sun Wukong 孙悟空, known as the Monkey King. In fact, the above three novels have been considered to be three of the four Chinese classics.

But the fourth Chinese classic, *Honglou Meng* or *Dream of the Red Chamber*, which was written by Cao Xueqin 曹雪芹 (1715–63), was produced during the Qing dynasty (1644–1911). This book was not translated into Malay/Indonesian until after World War II. It is not clear why no one attempted to translate the novel, perhaps this classical novel is the most difficult to translate as it is complex and full of poems. It is the story of four big traditional families during the Qing dynasty and their complex relationships. It was also a tragic love story of Lin Daiyu 林黛玉 and Jia Baoyu 贾宝玉, the two protagonists of the book.

The early translations of these Chinese novels were often incomplete. Some were partial translations. However, they were published in many volumes, some consisting of thirty to fifty volumes. After World War II, these Chinese classics were re-translated by Peranakan writers using standard Bahasa Indonesia rather than the so-called Peranakan Malay, the pre-war Malay language. It should be noted that the Malay translations of Chinese classics in colonial Indonesia and British Malaya differ. Let me compare the translations of the titles of the three classics:

1 A (Indonesia) *Tjerita dahoeloe kala di benoea Tjina, tersalin dari boekoe tjerita Sam Kok*. Disalin oleh Correspondant Hindia XX, 12 volumes. Batavia: Van Dorp, 1883–85.

1 A (Indonesia) *Sam Kok atawa Peprangan antara tiga negri (terkias gambar) satoe tjerita jang betoel soeda kedjadian di Tiongkok pada djeman dahoeloe kala, jaitoe dari abad ke 2, dari itoengan taon Masehie 175 sampe taon 269. Tersalin ke dalem Melajoe rendah jang banjak terpake, dari boekoe tjerita bahasa Tionghoa, tjitakan jang paling baroe*. Disalin oleh Tjie Tjin Koei. Batavia: Tjiong Koen Bie, 1910–13, 62 jilid.

1 B (Malaya/Singapore) *Chrita dahulu-kala nama-nya Sam Kok atau Tiga Negri Berprang: Siok, Gwi sama Gor, Di jaman "Han Teow"* by Chan Kim Boon, 30 volumes. Singapore: n.p., 1892–96.

2 A (Indonesia) *Song Kang*, serialized in *Pemberita Betawi*, 1885 Disalin oleh Tjong Loen Tat.

2 B (Malaya/Singapore) *Chrita dahulu kala di triak Song Kang atau 108 P'rampok di zaman "Song Teow"*, 19 volumes, by Chan Kim Boon, 1899–1902.

3 A (Indonesia) *Boekoe tjerita dahoeloe kala di benoea negrie Tjina, tersalin dalam boekoe Tjina, "See Yoe" di ambil dari tjeritanya Tong Sam Tjong pegi ka See Thian, tempo karadjaan Lie Sie Bin, merk Tong Tiauw.* Semarang 1886, 1 volume, 5 pages. Translated by Sie Hian Ling.

3 A (Indonesia) *Tjerita dahoeloe di negeri Tjina tersalin dari boekooe Tjina See Ijoe.....* Batavia: Ijap Goan Ho, 1895–96, 24 volumes, possibly translated by Ijap Goan Ho himself. Reprinted in Batavia: Kho Tjeng Bie, 1919, 24 volumes, 1886 pages.

3 B (Malaya/Singapore) *Chrita She Yew pasal Kou Chey Thian zaman tandun dan Tong thye chu pergi ke negeri She thian chu keng.* Singapore: Chan Kim Boon, 1911–13.

The above are only some examples. In fact, there are at least four and five more translations of *Sam Kok* and *See Yoe* in Indonesia but fewer in Singapore/Malaya.[13]

The titles of the translated work in the late nineteenth and early twentieth centuries show that Indonesian translations appeared to be closer to the Malay language used by Indonesians. In Indonesia, the Dutch spelling was used, while in Malaya/Singapore, the English spelling was adopted. Also, there were no Chinese characters in Indonesian translations whereas Chinese characters were inserted after Chinese names or terms in the Malayan translation. Nevertheless, both used the Hokkien (Fujian) dialect to transliterate Chinese names and terms.

In fact, in Indonesia a more popular Chinese story was that of Xue Rengui 薛仁贵 (Sie Djin Koei) of the Tang dynasty, a strong man who later became an army general to lead eastern and western expeditions. It was first translated by Lim Ho Hin under the following title: *Boekoe tjerita merk Tong Tiauw, Hongte Lie Sie Bin, tjerita tatkala tempo Sih Djin Koei Tjeng Tang* (Betawi: Ernst Co., 1884, 766 pages). The translation on *Sie Djin Koei* has at least twelve versions. It was perhaps the most popular story among the Peranakan readers in the Dutch East Indies before World War II.

In the first half of the twentieth century, there was in Java an emergence of translations based on Chinese *kungfu* novels (*cerita silat*). Kuo Lai Yen (the pen name of Tan Tek Ho) translated *Tiga Djago*

Silat (Three Kungfu Heroes) and *Tay Beng Kie Hiap* 大明奇侠 (The extraordinary hero of the Ming dynasty). This genre of Chinese works became extremely popular after Indonesia attained independence. We will return to this point later.

In the early twentieth century, apart from Chinese literary works, Chinese classics relating to Confucianism were also translated into Malay in Indonesia, coinciding with the rise of pan-Chinese movements in general and the revival of Confucianism among the Peranakan Chinese in particular. *Thay Hak* 大学 (Da Xue, Great Learning) and *Tiong Yong* 中庸 (Zhong Yong, the Doctrine of the Mean) were the two Confucian classics which appeared in Chinese-Malay quite early on. However, the first book on Confucius: *Hikajat Khong Hoe Tjoe*, which was published in 1897 by a leading Peranakan writer Lie Kim Hok (1853–1912), was not a translation of a Chinese work. It appears that it was a free translation from Dutch or English publications as Lie Kim Hok often did this with his other works. It appears that this kind of translation work was absent in the Straits Settlements.

The Baba Chinese literature in the Straits Settlements was confined to the translation of Chinese classical novels and did not develop into creative writing like its counterpart in Java. If one compares the translations done in Java and in the Straits Settlements, one gets the impression that not only was the quantity much larger in Java, the language used was also much richer.

There are many reasons for the development of Peranakan Chinese literature in Java and the underdevelopment of Baba literature in Malaya. The size of the Peranakan/Baba communities was definitely a factor. In Java, before World War II, there were more Peranakan than *totok* among the Chinese, but in Malaya, more Chinese were *totok* than Baba (Peranakan). The Baba Chinese tended to congregate in the Straits Settlements where the translations were done and published, but they constituted a minority, only around 15 per cent.[14] It is also illuminating that no Peranakan Malay press was developed in Malaya but the Peranakan press was firmly established in Java which was in fact able to sustain the growth of Peranakan Chinese literature. It is also worth noting that while there were translations of *kungfu* novels in Java, there was none in Malaya.

II. Post-war Translations in Indonesia

After Indonesia gained independence, not only were more *kungfu* novels translated into Indonesian, some serious literary works were also translated. However, the largest number is still in the category of *kungfu* novels and the publication of *kungfu* novels in translations was primarily an Indonesian phenomenon. In Indonesia, *kungfu* novel is now known as *cerita silat* or martial arts story.

Kungfu Novels

After the end of World War II, Malay (or more appropriately, Indonesian) and Chinese newspapers managed by Peranakans usually serialized *kungfu* novels. *Kungfu* novel is known as *wuxia xiaoshuo* 武侠小说, which originally means martial arts and chivalrous novels. Its origins were debatable but it seems that the *chuanqi* 传奇 (legend and romance) produced during the Tang dynasty was the embryonic forms of *kungfu* novels. During the late Qing dynasty and Republican China, this genre of novels rapidly developed. Since 1950, there has been a breakthrough in the development of *kungfu* novels with the publication of a new genre (*xinpai wuxia xiaoshuo* 新派武侠小说) first in Hong Kong, then in Taiwan. They were written in *baihua* 白话 or vernacular Chinese and many have been influenced by modern literature in its techniques.

Kungfu novels were very popular among the readers of both Peranakan and indigenous newspapers. *Sin Po* and *Keng Po*, two major Peranakan dailies in Indonesian published in Jakarta, competed with one another in publishing *kungfu* novels. This was one way of getting more subscribers to the newspapers.[15] Even *Pedoman*, a leading indigenous Indonesian newspaper in Jakarta, also followed suit in serializing *kungfu* novels. Initially, the translations were based on the works of pre-war *kungfu* writers but later, they were based on the works of post-war writers.

Indonesian *kungfu* novels were initially serialized in daily or weekly newspapers. After a while, they were also published in pocketbook form (approximately 100 pages per volume). Because of their interesting plots and lively translation, many Peranakan readers liked to purchase those pocketbooks. Even indigenous readers were also attracted to them. I still remember that one well-known indigenous writer would turn to the *kungfu* novel column the moment the Peranakan newspapers were delivered. The *kungfu* novels also greatly boosted the indigenous Indonesian *cerita silat*, or Indonesian *kungfu* novels, which used Indonesian history as their setting. Beginning in the mid-1960s, indigenous Indonesian writers started producing Indonesian *kungfu* novels using Indonesian kingdoms such as Singhasari, Majapahit, Mataram and Demak as the background gained popularity. These indigenous *silat* novels emerged complementing, if not competing, with the *kungfu* novels. Many well-known indigenous *silat* writers include Singgih Hadi Mintardja, Herman Pratikto, and Arswendo Atmowiloto. There is no doubt that these silat novels have a lot of similarities with the Chinese *kungfu* novels.

The impact of *kungfu* novels was not confined to the indigenous Indonesian writers, but also Indonesian readers. Even Indonesian politicians often cited the plots or language of the *kungfu* novels to make their points in informal meetings. Greater impact came with the screening of *kungfu* movies or TV serials in the post-1980s. Many TV stations showed Hong Kong-made *kungfu* serials, which captured a very high percentage of viewers. It is reasonable to say that movies and TV shows have further popularized *kungfu* novels among the Indonesian population.

When the Indonesian authorities launched the anti-Chinese campaign in the late 1950s and early 1960s, the serialization of *kungfu* novels was prohibited in daily newspapers. Nevertheless, the pocketbook form was still allowed. After the 1965 coup, *kungfu* novels were published more in pocketbook form than in magazines. Many *kungfu* translators began to establish their own printing presses and publishing houses. Those better known were Mekar Djaja, Panca Setya, Sastra Kumala and Gema.

It should be noted that during the 1950s and 1960s, a great proportion of *kungfu* novels in Indonesia were made up of translations of the works of Liang Yusheng 梁羽生 and Jin Yong 金庸. Liang and Jin, both based in Hong Kong, have been recognized as the representative writers of the new type of *kungfu* novels. They were later joined by Gu Long 古龙 from Taiwan and were known as the three most influential *kungfu* writers in the twentieth century. Jin Yong is particularly popular and there was even a group of writers who formed a "club" to study Jin Yong's novels.

The best works of Liang Yusheng, such as *Pingzong Xiaying Lu* 萍踪侠影录 (Peng Tjong Hiap Eng) and *Baifa Monu Zhuan* 白发魔女传 (Giok Lo Sat, 玉罗刹, atau Wanita Gagah Perkasa), are available in pocketbook form. The best known work of Jin Yong, such as *Shediao Yingxiong Zhuan* 射雕英雄传 (Sia Tiauw Eng Hiong atau Memanah Burung Rajawali), *Shendiao Xialu* 神雕侠侣 (Sin Tiauw Hiap Lu atau Burung Rajawali Sakti dan Pasangan Pendekar) and *Yitian Tulong Ji* 倚天屠龙记 (To Long To atau Golok Pembunuh Naga), were also published in pocketbook form. *Shediao* was first translated by Oei Kim Tiang (OKT) and later rewritten by many based on his translation. There are many versions, the latest being published by Gramedia, the major publisher in Indonesia as late as 1997. In the 1970s and 1980s, the largest proportion of *kungfu* novels were translations of Gu Long's works, of which the most popular were *Juedai Shuangjiao* 绝代双骄 (Pendekar Binal) and *Chu Liuxiang* 楚留香 (Pendekar Harum), both translated by Gan Kok Liang (Gan K.L.). These too are available in pocketbook form.

There were three eminent post-war *kungfu* novels translators in Indonesia: namely Oei Kim Tiang 黄金长 (1903–95), Gan K.L. 颜国樑 (1928–2003) and Tjan Ing Djiu 曾荧球 (Tjan I.D. 1949–2020). All of them received some Chinese education and therefore read Chinese. The oldest among them was Oei (1903–95) who was the most established. In fact, before he translated the works of Jin Yong and Liang Yusheng, he had translated the well-known works of Wang Dulu 王度庐, depicting the story of a swordsman Li Mubai 李慕白. Wang Dulu was a pre-war *kungfu* writer whose style is similar to the new type of *kungfu* writers. Gan was younger (1928–2003) and Tjan is the youngest (born in 1949). Oei and Gan have passed away and Tjan has stopped translating new novels since the mid-1980s.

Speaking of *kungfu* novel, we have to mention a prolific *kungfu* writer of Indonesia, Kho Ping Hoo 许平和 (Xu Pinghe, 1926–94). He had produced more than 100 titles of works but these were not direct translations of Chinese *kungfu* novels, rather, they are creative writings. Kho was Dutch-educated and did not read Chinese. However, being a Peranakan he was very familiar with Chinese stories as well as Chinese *kungfu* novels in Indonesian translations. The storylines of his novels cannot be found in any one Chinese *kungfu* novel. Apparently, he was able to digest various *kungfu* stories and *kungfu* movies and recreate his own stories. But the titles of his works are often similar to translated *kungfu* novels, such as *Pek Liong Po Kiam* (*Pedang Pusaka Naga Putih*, 1959), *Ang Tjoa Kiam* (*Pedang Ular Emas*, 1963) and *Kisah Sepasang Rajawali* (1973). In fact, most of the recent "Chinese" *kungfu* novels in Indonesia are not direct translations. Many of these writers are not well versed in Chinese and hence have resorted to producing *kungfu* novels on their own. Their works, therefore, are not within the scope of this chapter.

It should be noted that *kungfu* novels were often published under the names of the translators rather than those of the original authors. Frequently it was stated that the novel was "*dituturkan*" (narrated) by so and so. Like pre-war *kungfu* novels, many novels after the war were adaptations rather than literal translations. When they were published, the titles often differed from their original. The work of Gan K.L., *Tjhau Guan Eng Hiong* 草原英雄 (Pendekar Padang Rumput, Hero from the Grassland), is a good example. It was an Indonesian translation of Liang Yusheng's novel *Saiwai qixia zhuan* 塞外奇侠传 (The Story of an Extraordinary *Kungfu* Hero). Because of this, it is quite difficult and often time-consuming to identify the original titles of those novels.

Other Literary Works

Unlike *kungfu* novels in Indonesian translation, which are large in number, serious literary works in Indonesian translations are limited, and the translators are not confined to ethnic Chinese. There are also indigenous Indonesian writers who have undertaken such translations. Understandably, many of these translations are from Western languages.

To the best of my knowledge, Chinese classical poems in book form were introduced to Indonesian readers by Mundingsari. His booklet entitled *Himpunan Sadjak Tionghoa* (collection of Chinese poems), published in 1949, is based on French and German translations.[16] The poems of Li Bai 李白 and Du Fu 杜甫, two great Chinese poets, are included in this small volume. In 1963, another small pamphlet called *Tu Fu* (Du Fu) was published, in commemoration of the 1,250th birthday of this great Chinese poet. Twenty-one poems by Du Fu in Indonesian translation were collected in this volume.

Many of them were translated by leading Indonesian writers such as Amir Hamzah, Ramadhan and Pramoedya Ananta Toer.[17] However, the translations were in fact done earlier and put together in book form by the committee for that occasion. In 1976, a book consisting of a collection of classical Chinese poems was published. It was compiled by a leading Indonesian poet Sapardi Djoko Damono. Again, this translation did not follow the original closely, and it has thus been criticized for its "inaccuracies".

It was twenty-five years later, after the fall of Suharto, that a Chinese Indonesian, Wilson Tjandinegara (alias Chen Donglong 陈冬龙 or Chen Tung Long), published his *Antologi Sajak Klasik Dinasti Tang* (An anthology of classical Tang poetry). Tjandinegara himself wrote both Indonesian and Chinese poems, and has been very active in translating works from Chinese into Indonesian. Although this book on Tang dynasty poems was directly translated from Chinese, it was not based on the original text of the poems. Chen used the modern Chinese version of the poems written by Xu Fang 徐放 as the sources of his translation. Tang dynasty poems were written in classical Chinese and are often too difficult to be translated. The collection has 100 poems by Tang dynasty poets such as Li Bai, Du Fu, Wang Wei 王维, Li Shangyin, 李商隐 and Meng Haoran 孟浩然 etc. The book collects mainly short poems and many well-written longer poems are left out.

In fact, prior to the publication of Tang dynasty poems in Indonesian translation, Tjandinegara already published a book of translation of Chinese modern poems in Indonesian: *101 Puisi Mandarin: Antologi Puisi Dwi Bahasa* (101 Mandarin poetry: an anthology of bilingual poems). The book includes the works of modern Chinese poets from mainland China, Taiwan and Hong Kong. Again, these are very short poems. One can argue that the quality of his translation is uneven, but one has to agree that he is one of the most productive translators of Chinese language works into the Indonesian language at the moment.[18]

The most ambitious and comprehensive collection of Chinese classical poems in Indonesian was done by a young architect, Zhou Fuyuan, who is an Indonesian-born Chinese with some Chinese school education. A self-taught man with a good command of the Chinese language, he also writes essays and poems in Chinese. Zhou spent five years translating 555 classical Chinese poems and eventually published a 367-page book entitled *Purnama di Bukit Langit: Antologi Puisi Tiongkok Klasik* (The moon on the Tian mountain: an anthology of Chinese classical poetry) (Jakarta: Gramedia, 2007). Unlike the previous collections of classical Chinese poems in Indonesian, Zhou's translations were based on the original, from the oldest poetry of *Shi Jing* 诗经 (The Book of Songs) to that produced in the Qing dynasty. Also, the collection was not confined to *shi* 诗 but also included other forms of Chinese classical verses and songs (*ci* 词 and *qu* 曲).

If classical and modern Chinese poems are not many in Indonesian translations, Chinese classical novels are a plenty. As mentioned earlier, *Sanguo yanyi* had appeared in Indonesian in the late nineteenth and early twentieth centuries, but since World War II, it has been re-translated. In the 1980s, Lee Chun Seng re-translated *Sam Kok* and published it in twelve volumes under the same title. Another version is called *Kisah Tiga Negara*, which was done by A.S. Udin. In addition to this, *Shuihu* was also re-translated into Indonesian, one done by Lee Chun Seng under the title of *Shuihu Zhuan* (108 Pendekar Liang San) based on the Chinese original and the other entitled *Batas Air* by Setiawan Abadi based on the English translation by J.H. Jackson. The early translation of *Shuihu Zhuan* was incomplete and the language was in the style of Chinese Malay. However, the new Indonesian translations of these Chinese classics are in "standard" Bahasa Indonesia. A few titles even used Pinyin rather than Hokkien in transliterating Chinese terms and names. Some titles also used Indonesian and the term *perampok* (robbers) which was used to refer to the rebels in Liang San who are now called *pendekar* (heroes).

It is worth noting that the translation of the great classical novel, *Dream of the Red Chamber* (*Honglou Meng* 红楼梦) was only published after World War II (1989). The book, which is entitled *Impian di Bilik Merah*, is not really a translation.[19] It is based on a re-writing of the story of 120 chapters by Marcus A.S. This Indonesian version consists of a few volumes. Volume 1 has fifteen chapters and many drawings are taken from Chinese comics. No name of the translator is given. It is possible that the book was based on the English abridged version as it uses neither Hokkien nor Pinyin but the Wade-Giles spelling. After all, *Honglou Meng* is not easy to translate.

Modern literary works such as novels, short stories and drama have also been translated into Indonesian after World War II but the quantity is still small. The earliest work of modern Chinese literature translated into Bahasa Indonesia in book form is perhaps Chen Quan's 陈铨 drama entitled *Mawar Hutan* (*Ye Meigui* 野玫瑰, Wild Rose), published by Balai Pustaka in 1950. The translator is Teng Ying Siang 邓应祥—not much is known about him but this drama was quite popular in the 1950s. It was put on stage in 1958 by Sin Ming Hui, a major Peranakan socio-cultural organization in Jakarta. In the same year, Cao Yu's 曹禺 drama, *Taufan* (雷雨, Thunderstorm), was also put on stage by Sin Ming Hui. It was directed by Steve Lim (Indonesian name: Teguh Karya), a playwright who later became a leading movie director in the early 1950s. Mao Dun's 茅盾 novel, *Midnight* (*Zi Ye* 子夜), was also translated into Indonesian under the title *Tengah Malam*. The novel, which deals with the story of Chinese businessmen and industrialists in Shanghai, was serialized in a leftwing magazine called *Republik*. As far as I know, the novel was not published in book form.

The works of Lu Xun 鲁迅, a great Chinese modern writer, were only introduced to Indonesian readers in the mid-1950s. *Ah Q zhengzhuan* 阿Q正传 (The True Story of Ah Q) was first translated into Indonesian jointly by Go Gien Tjwan and Soekotjo in 1956. This version, *Riwajat Kita Ah Q*, was translated from English because neither Go, a sociologist and political activist, nor Soekotjo, an indigenous Indonesian, read Chinese. In 1961, a self-taught local-born Chinese, Tannin (陈燕生, Chen Yansheng), translated *Ah Q* again (*Riwayat Asli Ah Q*), this time straight from the original. But the translation was less lucid. In 1964, Shannu, another Chinese Indonesian translated *Ah Q* again from the original. Comparing Shannu's translation with that of Tannin, one is in no doubt that Shannu has consulted the work of Tannin, as shown in the similar terms used and footnotes added in the two translations. However, Shannu's translation appears to be more lucid. In the preface of the translation, Shannu acknowledges the help given by Rukiah Kertapati, a well-known Indonesian woman writer, in improving the Indonesian translation.

As a matter of fact, Shannu has done more than his predecessors. In addition to *Riwayat Asli Ah Q*, he has also translated most of the important short stories by Lu Xun. These translations have been put together with Ah Q in a book entitled *Pilihan Tjerpen Lu Sin*. The book has not been in circulation since the 1965 coup partly owing to the fact that it was published by a leftwing publisher.

It should be noted that the publications of modern Chinese writings in Indonesian translation took place during the period when relations between Indonesia and Beijing were cordial. In fact, many were published by the Penerbit Pustakan Asing (Beijing Foreign Language Press). Apart from popular Chinese folktales, the publisher also published many serious works, mainly by communist writers. These publications were also distributed in Indonesia. For instance, *Wang Kui dan Li Siang Siang* 王贵与李香香 (The love story of Wanggui and Li Xiangxiang) by Li Tji (李季 Li Ji), *Sadjak-sadjak Li Ju-tjai* (*Li Youcai banhua* 李有才板话, Story of the traditional story teller Li Youcai), and *Dewi Uban* (*Baimao Nu* 白毛女, The white-haired girl) by He Tjing-tse (He Jingzhi 贺敬之) and Ting Yi (Ding Yi 丁易). Most of these works were directly translated from their original by "returned overseas Chinese" from Indonesia but their names were not mentioned anywhere. However, *Dewi Uban* was translated from the English translation by Pramoedya Ananta Toer, the most eminent Indonesian novelist. Not surprisingly, his name is clearly stated in the book as the translator.

Prior to the 1965 coup, ethnic Chinese in Indonesia were also translating and publishing modern Chinese works. The selected works of Lu Xun by Tannin and Shannu mentioned earlier were published by Indonesian Chinese publishers (Jajasan Kebudajaan Zamrud and Jajasan Kebudajaan Sadar). Lekra, a PKI (Partai Komunis Indonesia) affiliated organization, also published *Njanjian Remadja* (*Qingchun zhi ge* 青春之歌, Song of Youth), a novel by Yang Mo 杨沫 which deals with the radical student movement in China. However, many Chinese works published during this period were highly partisan. With the change of Indonesian government in 1965 and the deterioration of Indonesia-China relations, these publications were prohibited.

During the first fifteen years of the Suharto era, there were no new translations of modern Chinese literary works. But since late 1989 the Yayasan Obor Indonesia, a new foundation which is interested in translating good foreign literary works into Indonesian, began to publish well-known mainland Chinese literary works. At least three books were published: Lu Xun's short stories, Zhang Xianliang 张贤亮 and other Chinese contemporary writers' short stories, and Zhang Henshui's 张恨水 novel on Liang Sanbo and Zhu Yingtai 梁三伯与祝英台. The first two books were re-translated from the English version by indigenous Indonesians and edited by well-known Indonesian writers such as Sapardi Djoko Damono. Leading author Mochtar Lubis and scholar A. Dahana wrote the prefaces for the books. Only the last book was translated straight from the original Chinese by Oei Kim Tiang 黄金长 (OKT).[20]

However, there are very few of these titles; much more popular are the *kungfu* novels. Many popular novels by Taiwan and Hong Kong writers have also been translated. One of them is the work of Qiong Yao 琼瑶 (Chiung Yao). In the early 1980s, some of Qiong Yao's earlier novels such as *Bara Burung Api* (*Ranshao ba huoniao* 燃烧吧, 火鸟) were translated into Indonesian. The novels were so popular that Gramedia, a major publisher in Jakarta, later followed suit and published a series of Qiong Yao's novels such as *Putri Sinyue* (*Xinyue gege* 新月格格, Princess New Moon) and *Enam Mimpi* (*Liuge meng* 六个梦, Six Dreams). According to the information provided in the book, the translation was done by a team of translators. The publication coincided with the broadcast of Taiwan's TV series based on Qiong Yao's novels. Not surprisingly, the covers of these novels are taken from the TV serials. The novels were so popular and Gramedia formed "The Chiung Yao Fan Club" inviting readers to join the club to get more information on the writer and her works.[21]

The fall of Suharto brought about the re-emergence of the translations of Chinese works. Not many new serious novels were translated but some Chinese Indonesian writers began to translate their own works (either short stories or poems) into Indonesian. The Indonesian Chinese Writers' Association (Yinhua Zuojia Xiehui 印华作家协会) in Jakarta and the Komunitas Sastra Indonesia in Tangerang collaborated and translated Yinhua poems into Indonesian. The book was launched and many indigenous Indonesian writers were present at the function. A seminar and poetry reading in both languages were conducted, marking the new era in relations between Indonesian Chinese and the indigenous literari. Earlier we mentioned Chen Tung Long (Wilson Tjandinegara) who has done a few of the translations. Apart from Tang dynasty poems, his most notable work was the translation of short stories and poems by Indonesian Chinese writers. For the first time in Indonesian literary history, a bilingual book in Indonesian and Chinese entitled *Resonansi Indonesia* (*Yindunixiya de hongming* 印度尼西亚的轰鸣, Indonesia's Resonance) was published in 2000. The book consists of the works of 100 poets, half indigenous Indonesian and half Yinhua poets.

III. Post-war Translations in Malaysia/Singapore

Unlike in Indonesia, *kungfu* novels have not been translated into Malay in independent Malaya (Malaysia after 1963). Modern Chinese literature in Malay translations also received far less attention, at least initially. In fact, it was the Indonesian Chinese who started the translation of Chinese works into Malay. Lie Tjwan Sioe 李全寿 (Li Chuanshou), a graduate from the University of Indonesia, was the first Chinese who translated Shen Fu's 沈复 work on the Qing era into Malay: *Hidup Bagaikan Mimpi* (Life as a dream) 浮生六记 (1961), a Chinese novel which tells the story of a dedicated wife who encourages her husband to take a concubine. Later, Lie also translated a few short stories by Lu Xun including "Ah Soh Hsiang Lin" (*Xianglin sao* 祥林嫂, Aunty Xiang Lin).[22]

Lie Tjwan Sioe was a Malay language lecturer at Nanyang University at a time when there was a group of students who were eager to learn the language and to introduce Chinese literature to the Malay speaking community. Periodicals in Malay, namely, *Mimbar Universiti* (University Tribune) and *Budaya* (Culture), were partially used for that purpose. The Shanghai Book Store in Singapore also published the translations of Chinese folktales and Lu Xun's *Riwayat Asli Ah Q*. The latter was a revised version of Tannin's translation. In the 1950s, most of the Chinese in Malaya and Singapore were not well versed in Malay and Malay writers were not yet interested in Chinese literature. As a result, very few Chinese works were translated into Malay. However, after the independence of Malaya in 1957, Chinese-educated Malayan Chinese started learning Malay seriously and by the 1960s, some had acquired a reasonable command of the Malay language. The translation of works was also gradually done in Kuala Lumpur rather than Singapore. To my knowledge, the earliest translation in book form was Chan Tat Cheong's *Hidup dengan Mati: Antoloji Cherpen Tiongkok* (Life and Death: An Anthology of Chinese Short Stories) which is a collection of short stories by Lu Xun and Ba Jin 巴金 published by Pustaka Antara in 1966.

The establishment of diplomatic ties between China and Malaysia in 1975 also helped the promotion of modern Chinese literature in Malaysia. More translations were published after that year. The most outstanding figure was probably Goh Thean Chye (Wu Tiancai 吴天才), a Nanyang University graduate who later became head of the Chinese Studies Department at the University of Malaya. In 1975 Wu published *Puisi Baru Tiongkok* (*Zhongguo xinshi xuan* 中国新诗选) which comprises numerous Chinese poems from mainland China. Being a poet himself, Goh has concentrated on the translation of poems rather than other kinds of literary works. In 1981 he published five books of translations, including the poems of Guo Moruo 郭沫若 and Ai Qing 艾青, two leading poets in mainland China's literary world.[23] Other Chinese Malaysian translators followed suit. E.T. Tang (Chen Yingde 陈应德) published the Malay translation of Bing Xin's 冰心 *Air Musim Bunga* (Spring Water, *Chun shui* 春水) while Li Yucai translated her *Bintang-Bintang* (Numerous Stars, *Fan xing* 繁星). Bing Xin was well known among the Chinese for her short "philosophical" poems similar to those of Rabindranath Tagore.

Apart from publications in book form, there are also translations published in *Dewan Sastra* (*Literary Monthly*, published by Dewan Bahasa) and Malay newspapers. For instance, Lie Tjwan Sioe translated two more short stories by Lu Xun which were published by Dewan Bahasa dan Pustaka. In 1984, he republished his earlier translations of Lu Xun's short stories together with the ones that he published in *Dewan Sastra* under a new title, *Lampu yang Tak Kunjung Padam.*[24] In 1987, *Utusan Malaysia*, the Malay newspaper, also serialized a short novel by a Taiwanese writer, Li Ang 李昂, entitled *Membunuh Suami*

(*Shafu* 杀夫 or To Kill a Husband). The translator was Chew Hock Tye 周福泰, an ex-school master who is effectively trilingual. Also in 1987, *Dewan Sastra* serialized a well-known Chinese drama entitled *Ribut* (*Leiyu* 雷雨 or Thunderstorm), Cao Yu's masterpiece which had been put on stage in Singapore in 1962 by a Singapore Malay cultural association.[25] Apart from poems and novels, more philosophical works such as two Confucian classics, *Daxue* 大学 and *Zhongyong* 中庸, and the Daoist classic, *Daode jing* 道德经, were translated into Malay.[26] The translator was Yap Sin Tian (Ye Xintian 叶新田). In fact, a Malay scholar at the Universiti Kebangsaan Malaysia, Obaidellah Haji Mohamad, also translated *Lunyu* 论语 and *Mengzi* 孟子, both published by Dewan Bahasa dan Pustaka in 1994.[27]

It is worth noting that some Chinese literature produced by Mahua (Malaysian Chinese)[28] writers were also translated into Malay. The first Mahua literary work which was translated into Malay (in 1960) was "Baiqu lai de xiaoxi" (白区来的消息, The News from the White Territory), a short story by Wei Yun 韦晕. The translator was Li Chuan Siu whom I mentioned earlier.[29] In 1975, Goh Thean Chye, a Nanyang graduate, published the Malay translations of Malayan Chinese poems entitled *Puisi Mahua Moden* (*Mahua xinshi xuan* 马华新诗选, An Anthology of Malaysian Chinese poems). In 1981, he also translated his own poems into Malay entitled *Imbauan Subuh* (The Call of Dawn). Three years earlier, Yassin Tani (i.e. Yap Sin Tian) had published a collection of Mahua poems. In 1982, Moo Kiow Chai 巫运才 also published an anthology of Mahua short stories. Earlier Teng Shin Min 邓盛民 had translated the short stories of Mahua writer Yuen Li Fung 云里风 (Tan Chon Tik).[30] Chan Yong Sin 曾荣盛 translated the poems of Sarawak poet Wu An 吴岸 under the title *Gelombang Rejang* (Waves of Rejang) which was published in 1986 by Pustaka Selatan.

In fact, the group of people who were active in translating Chinese works into Malay was made up of those who were associated with the Persatuan Penterjemahan dan Penulisan Kreatif (Perspektif, Translation and Creative Writings Association). Perspektif was established in 1986. Many translators such as Chan Yong Sin and Yang Quee Yee 杨贵谊 are members of this association. The association, in collaboration with Dewan Bahasa, published three collections of Mahua short stories:

Angkatan Ini (This Generation, 1988), *Gadis Dalam Gambar* (Girl in the Photo, 1994) and *Dalam Hujan Renyai* (Drizzling Rain, 1995).[31] Dewan Bahasa dan Pustaka also published *Perkembangan Kesusasteraan Mahua Moden 1919-1965*, a history of modern Mahua literature which was mainly based on Fang Xiu's 方修 well-known work in Chinese.

In the 1990s, Dewan Bahasa dan Pustaka also published a number of Chinese short stories and classical works in Malay, for instance, *Rakyat Sahni: Antologi 20 Buah Cerpen Penulis Wanita Republik Rakyat China* (*Xani Dadie* 撒尼大爹, A collection of works by Chinese women writers), *Pilihan Cerita Aneh dari Balai Pustaka* (*Liao Zai* 聊斋, better known as Chinese ghost stories), and *Keluarga* (*Jia* 家), a well-known novel by Ba Jin 巴金 which deals with the cruelty of feudalism in pre-war China. The latest publication was *Hikayat Pinggir Air* (*Shuihu Zhuan* 水浒传), or *Water Margin* also known in the West as *All Men are Brothers* (translated by Pearl Buck).[32]

In Singapore, Chan Meow Hwa 陈妙华's *Antologi Cerpen Xinhua* (An anthology of Singapore Chinese short story) was followed by Goh Choo Keng 吴诸庆's *12 Cerpen Xinhua* (Twelve Singapore Chinese short stories). Chan was a journalist while Goh, also a journalist, was a graduate of Nanyang University.

Conclusion

The translation of Chinese works into Malay/Indonesia began with the rise of ethnic Chinese cultural nationalism in the two colonial states in the late nineteenth century. These translation works were first meant to satisfy the need of the Chinese themselves who had already lost their command of the Chinese language. The works were mainly done by those Peranakan Chinese who were still able to read Chinese, but some were done with the cooperation of the migrant Chinese. Gradually, the local Chinese-educated ethnic Chinese played a more important role.

It is worth noting that the emergence of Malay/Indonesian translations of Chinese works appeared to have played a leading role in using Romanized Malay in colonial Indonesia (Dutch East Indies) and British

Malaya. They both emerged before the colonial powers decided to "standardize" the languages. This is particularly the case in British Malaya where the Malays in general preferred to use Jawi (Arabic scripts) to publish newspapers, magazines and books.

Chinese literary works in Indonesian and Malay translations are still very modest in terms of quality and quantity, with the possible exception of *kungfu* novels. The majority of the translations have been in the category of popular literature.

In Indonesia, the translation of Chinese popular novels is more advanced than in Malaysia. This was due to the presence of a large number of Peranakan Chinese who read these translations in the past. Even indigenous Indonesians were also interested in this type of popular literature, especially *kungfu* novels. Since many Chinese Indonesians have lost the command of the Chinese language, they have to rely on the translations of Chinese works. In the future, it is likely that more translations in both serious and popular literatures will be published, but good old translations will be rewritten to suit the development of the Indonesian language. It is worth noting that the impact of Chinese translations, especially *kungfu* novels, on indigenous literature has been very significant. It gave rise to the emergence of indigenous *silat* novels.

In Malaysia, the number of Baba is small and the readership is much more limited than Indonesia. Moreover, Chinese Malaysians appear to be more interested in reading works in English and Chinese rather than in Malay. As a result, Chinese popular novels in translations ceased to exist in the early 1950s. It should be noted that after Malaysia's independence those Chinese who translated Chinese works—especially literary works—were Chinese-educated ("*totok*") rather than Peranakan Chinese.

However, as the number of Malaysian Chinese who are Malay-educated increases, more Mahua writings and Chinese works will be translated into Malay in the future. With the rise in the standards of the Malay language among Malaysian Chinese, more quality works in translations will also emerge.

Notes

*This is based on my earlier conference paper entitled "Chinese literature in Indonesian/Malay translations" prepared in 1988 but published in 1989. A few years ago, Professor Henri Chambert-Loir invited me to join his project on "History of Translation in Indonesia and Malaysia". As my contribution to this project, I conducted additional research and rewrote the above paper and gave it the present title. I am indebted to Dr Liaw Yock Fang for his comments and Dr Yang Quee Yee for providing me with useful information on relevant new publications in Malaysia. This English paper was later translated into Indonesian and included in Professor Chambert-Loir's edited book entitled *Sadur: Sejarah Terjemahan di Indonesia dan Malaysia* (Jakarta: KPG, 2009). The original English version was first published in *Asian Culture* 34 (June 2010), and this chapter is based on that version.

1. There are a few studies on the Chinese literature in Malay/Indonesian translations. Below are substantive works: Claudine Salmon, *Literature in Malay by the Chinese of Indonesia: A Provisional Annotated Bibliography*, Etudes Insulindies-archipel 3 (Paris: Editions de la Maison des sciences de l'Homme, 1982); Claudine Salmon, "Writings in Romanized Malay by the Chinese of Malaya: A Preliminary Inquiry", *Kertas-kertas Pengajian Tionghoa: Papers on Chinese Studies* 1 (December 1977): 69–95; Tan Chee Beng, "Baba Chinese Publication in Romanized Malay", *Journal of African and Asian Studies* 22 (1981): 158–93; Leo Suryadinata, "Chinese Literature in Indonesia and Malay Translations: A Preliminary Study", in *Chinese Literature in Southeast Asia*, edited by Wong Yoon Wah and Horst Pastoors (Singapore: Goethe-Institut and Singapore Association of Writers, 1989); Yang Guiyi (杨贵谊, Yang Quee Yee), "Xinma tusheng huaren fanyi wenxue de xingshuai 新马土生华人翻译文学的兴衰", in *Dongnanya huaren wenxue yu wenhua* 东南亚华人文学与文化, edited by Yang Songnian 杨松年 and Wang Kangding 王慷鼎 (Singapore: Singapore Society of Asian Studies, 1995), pp. 32–55.

2. Leo Suryadinata, *The Pre-World War II Peranakan Chinese Press of Java: A Preliminary Survey* (Athens, Ohio: Ohio University, Center for International Studies, 1971).

3. Salmon, *Literature in Malay by the Chinese of Indonesia*, p. 21; also Suryadinata, "Chinese Literature in Indonesia and Malay Translations", p. 255.

4. See Salmon, "Writings in Romanized Malay by the Chinese of Malaya", pp. 87–88. The Mercantile Press also published *Sam Kok*, I suspect that the Mercantile Press was owned by ethnic Chinese.

5. Salmon, *Literature in Malay by the Chinese of Indonesia*, p. 21. According to her, the original title of the book in Malay is: *Boekoe tjerita Tjioe Koan Tek anak Tjioe Boen Giok, terkarang oleh soeatoe orang Tjina* (Batavia:

H.M. van Dorp, 1882). It was the translation of the last chapters of *Haigong xiaohongpao quanzhuan* 海公小红袍全传.

6. Tan Chee Beng, "Baba Chinese Publications in Romanized Malay", p. 181.

7. For a discussion on the Peranakan and Baba, see Leo Suryadinata, "Peranakan Chinese Identities in Singapore and Malaysia: A Re-examination", in *Ethnic Chinese in Singapore and Malaysia: A Dialogue between Tradition and Modernity*, edited by Leo Suryadinata (Singapore: Times Academic Press, 2002), pp. 69–84.

8. Suryadinata, *The Pre-World War II Peranakan Chinese Press of Java*.

9. Kwee Tek Hoay, "Atsal Mulahnya Pergerakan Tionghoa yang Modern di Indonesia" (1933), republished in *Kesastraan Melayu Tionghoa dan kebangsaan Indonesia: Empat Karya Kwee Tek Hoay*, Jilid 4 (Jakarta: Kepustakaan Populer Gramedia, 2001), pp. 395–534.

10. Salmon, *Literature in Malay by the Chinese of Indonesia*, p. 492.

11. Salmon, "Writings in Romanized Malay by the Chinese of Malaya", pp. 74–75.

12. Yang Guiyi, "Xinma tusheng huaren fanyi wenxue de xingshuai 新马土生华人翻译文学的兴衰", p. 48.

13. Salmon, *Literature in Malay by the Chinese of Indonesia*, pp. 492 and 499.

14. Leo Suryadinata, "Peranakan Chinese Identities in Singapore and Malaysia: A Re-examination", in *Ethnic Chinese in Singapore and Malaysia: A Dialogue between Tradition and Modernity*, edited by Leo Suryadinata (Singapore: Times Academic Press, 2002), especially pp. 75–76.

15. Liao Jianyu 廖建裕, "Yinni wuxia xiaoshuo gailun 印尼武侠小说概论", in *Yinni huaren wenhua yu shehui* 印尼华人文化与社会 (Singapore: Singapore Society of Asian Studies, 1993), pp. 161–62.

16. See Mundingsari, *Himpunan Sadjak Tionghoa* (Jakarta: Balai Pustaka, 1949), p. 9.

17. *Tu Fu*, published in Jakarta by Komite Perdamaian Indonesia, no date (c.1963).

18. For instance, the *Mini Cepren Yinhua, Bulu Mata Menunjang Dunia* dsb.

19. *Impian di Bilik Merah* (Hung Lou Meng), karya Tsao Hsueh Chin, diceritakan kembali oleh Marcus A.S., Editor: Winarti (Jakarta: Bhuana Ilmu Populer, 1989).

20. *Catatan Harian Seorang Gila dan Cerita Pendek Lainnya*, diterjemahkan oleh Nur Rachmi & Rusti Surya dani, diredaksi kembali oleh Sapardi Djoko Damono, kata pengantar: Mochtar Lubis (Jakarta: Yayasan Obor Indonesia, 1989); *San Pek Eng Tay: Romantika Emansipasi Seorang Perempuan*, diterjemahkan oleh OKT (Jakarta: Yayasan Obor Indonesia, 1990); *Kisah Lelaki Tua dan Seekor Anjing* (Kumpulan Cerita Pendek Cina Kontemporer), pengantar: A. Dahana (Jakarta: Yayasan Obor Indonesia, 1991).

21. Chiung Yao, *Enam Mimpi* (Jakarta: Gramedia, 1997), "Join the Chiung Yao Fan Club", n.p.

22. The collection of Lu Xun's short stories was only published under the title of *Ah So Hsiang Lin dan Cerpen-Cerpen Lain* in 1963 by the now defunct Dewan Bahasa dan Kebudayaan Singapura.

23. Guo Moruo, *Ibuku Sang Bumi* 地球，我的母亲 (Kuala Lumpur: Universiti Malaya, 1981); Ai Qing, *Pemberitahuan Subuh* 黎明的通知 (Kuala Lumpur: Universiti Malaya, 1981).

24. Lu Hsun, *Lampu yang tak kunjung Padam* (Kuala Lumpur: Dewan Bahasa dan Pustaka, 1984). *Lampu yang tak kunjung padam* was one of the titles of Lu Xun's short stories *Chang ming deng* 长明灯.

25. I have come across the Indonesian script entitled *Taufan*, but I do not know whether it was officially published. In 1962 when the Malay Drama Society performed this drama, I suspect it was based on the same translation. The version published in *Dewan Sastera* was translated by Markaz Drama.

26. *Kitab Klasik Confucianisme: Pelajaran Agung Prinsip Kesederhanaan*, Diterjemahkan oleh Yap Sin Tian (Kuala Lumpur: Yap Sin Tian, 1994); *Tao Te Ching: Kitab Falsafah dan Moral Taoisme*, terjemahan dari bahasa Cina oleh Yap Sin Tian (Kuala Lumpur: Yap Sin Tian, 1994).

27. *Lun Yu: Pembicaraan Confucius* (Kula Lumpur: Dewan Bahasa dan Pustaka, 1994); *Meng Zi* (Kuala Lumpur: Dewan Bahasa dan Pustaka, 1994).

28. Chinese literature in Malaya/Malaysia is known as *Mahua wenxue*. *Ma* is the abbreviation of Malaya/Malaysia while *hua* is the abbreviation of *Huaren* (Chinese) or *Huawen* (the Chinese language).

29. The title was changed to "Kalau Nasib Malang Menimpa", published in *Budaya* (December 1960): 34–44.

30. Yuen Li Fung 云里风, *Anakku, Harapanku* (Wangzi chenglong 望子成龙) (Petaling Jaya: Syarikat Penerbit Universal, c.1980); *Pertemuan yang dikesalkan* (Xiang feng yuan 相逢怨) (Kuala Lumpur: Pelanduk, 1986).

31. *Angkatan ini* is the title of one of the short stories *Xin yi dai* 新一代 by Xia Ning; *Gadis dalam gambar* was a title of a short story *xiang zhong ren* 相中人; *Dalam hujan renyai* is also a title of a short story *Fenfen xiyu* 纷纷细雨. All of these books were edited by Yang Quee Yee (Yang Guiyi).

32. This classic was translated by three Chinese who are local university graduates. The Malay translation consists of four volumes, first published in 2001, reprinted in 2002.

7

INNOVATION AND TRANSFORMATION: PERANAKAN CHINESE LITERATURES/ PUBLICATIONS IN IMS

Introduction

Since the last decades, there has been a resurgence of interest in Peranakan Chinese culture in Singapore, Malaysia and Indonesia as witnessed by the opening of a Peranakan museum and the making of a popular TV series "Little Nyonya" (*xiao niang re* 小娘惹),[1] both in Singapore; the re-publication of pre-war Peranakan literature,[2] the exhibition of Peranakan furniture, and the publication of a Peranakan pictorial book, all in Jakarta, the establishment of the Benteng Heritage Museum in Banten, West Java;[3] and seminars on Peranakan Chinese and the renovation of Peranakan houses in Malacca, Malaysia. Although the resurgence is still rather weak, yet it has been noticeable.

This chapter examines the Peranakan Chinese culture with special reference to their literature in the above three countries, their developments, their similarities and differences, and their future development. By Peranakan Chinese literature, I mean the literature in Malay/Indonesian or Dutch/English produced by the Peranakan Chinese. It should be noted that this chapter does not mean to be comprehensive; rather, it aims to present the subject matter in a comparative perspective. Through a comparative study, we will be able to see different factors and conditions which result in the development of different literatures. I am fully aware that the topic is broad and complex, therefore I would like to treat this chapter as a preliminary survey rather than an in-depth study.

Publications in Peranakan Malay: Pre-Independence

The Peranakan Chinese elite in colonial IMS were either Dutch-educated or English-educated, but Peranakan Malay was used as the medium of communication with the Peranakan masses. It is not surprising that in IMS, Peranakan publications are divided into Malay and Dutch/English versions and those in Malay are the largest in number. Some publications use two languages (i.e. Malay and Dutch, or Malay and English), but the Malay portion is often larger than the foreign language section.

Let us look at the publications in colonial Indonesia (known as Dutch East Indies) and British Malaya and Singapore.

Colonial Indonesia

Towards the end of the nineteenth century, with the rise of Chinese cultural nationalism in Southeast Asia, especially in Indonesia, the Peranakan began to translate Chinese popular stories into the language that they are familiar with: Malay. Chinese classics such as *Shuihu Zhuan* 水浒传, *Xi Youji* 西游记 and *Sanguo Yanyi* 三国演义 were also partially or fully translated.[4] During the turn of the twentieth century, with the rise of Chinese political nationalism, Peranakan Chinese newspapers were also published in Java and the outer islands.[5] Peranakan Chinese newspapers, both weeklies and dailies, were large in number. In Java alone where the largest number of the Peranakan Chinese lived, there were at least fifteen Malay newspapers, of which a few are major daily newspapers: *Sin Po* and *Perniagaan/Siang Po* in Jakarta, *Warna Warta* in Central Java, *Pewarta Soerabaia* and *Sin Jit Po/Sin Tit Po* in Surabaya. These daily newspapers continued to publish up to the Japanese invasion. They were read not only by the Peranakan Chinese but also by "indigenous"

Indonesians. These publications were written in Romanized Malay (Indonesian) and were easy to follow.

With regard to publications of books in Malay, it consists of both the translations of Chinese stories and creative writings, marking the introduction of modern Indonesian language literature. Peranakan Chinese literature developed in Indonesia and played an important role in the Peranakan Chinese communities and has some influence on the indigenous Indonesians, especially the martial arts novels. Leading Peranakan writers before World War II include Gouw Peng Liang, Thio Tjin Boen, Kwee Tek Hoay, Tio Ie Soei, Liem Khing Hoo and Tan Hong Boen etc. One can argue that pre-World War II witnesses the golden era of Peranakan Chinese literature.[6] This literature continued to develop after Indonesia attained independence.

The language used by Peranakan Chinese journalists and writers at the beginning was known as Malay (later, it was called Low Malay). It was not called Chinese Malay yet until the 1920s when Indonesian nationalism proper emerged. There began to have a division between Melayu-Tionghoa and the Indonesian language proper. The vocabulary and grammar began to show their differences. This division continued until the 1950s.

Colonial Malaya/Singapore

Similar to colonial Indonesia, many liberal translations of Chinese popular stories were published in British Malaya and Singapore. In fact, Singapore tended to be the centre of Malay language publications. Those stories which were translated in colonial Indonesia were also translated in Malaya and Singapore. Most well-known translators were Chan Kim Boon of Penang and Wan Boon Seng of Singapore. However, unlike in colonial Indonesia, it seems that there were no significant Peranakan Chinese creative writings in pre-war Malaya and Singapore, with the exception of the *pantun* or *dondang sayang*, which strictly speaking, is the old form of Malay literature.

There were a few Peranakan periodicals and daily newspapers published in Peranakan Chinese: *Bintang Timor*, *Malaysia Advocate* and *Khabar Slalu*, but all were very short lived, lasting from five months to a year.[7] Unlike in colonial Indonesia, Peranakan publications, especially newspapers, were read by the "indigenous" Indonesians. In Malaya and Singapore, Peranakan writings (translations) in Malay were not read by the Malay readers as the Malays then read only publications in Jawi (Arabic script) while the Peranakans wrote in Rumi (Romanized Malay). Therefore, intensive interactions between Peranakan literature/newspapers did not take place in colonial Malaya and Singapore.

Unlike in colonial Indonesia, no major Dutch journals were published by Peranakan Chinese. There were quite a few English magazines which were run by Peranakan Chinese in Singapore and Malaya and were quite successful. One of the most well-known magazine was the *Straits Chinese Magazine*.

Publications in Malay/Indonesian: Post-Independence

Independent Indonesia

However, nation-building which started after Indonesian independence, especially in the late 1950s, caused Peranakan Chinese to identify more with Indonesia, hence the Indonesian language proper. Many more Peranakan Chinese received their proper education in Indonesian schools and they spoke and wrote like "indigenous" Indonesians. The further "Indonesianization" of Peranakan literature took place during the Suharto era when Peranakan writers produced "assimilationist works" which are almost identical with that produced by the indigenous writers.[8] The only exception is the *kongfu* (martial art) novels in Indonesian which are still very Chinese in contents.

After the fall of Suharto, the government has adopted a pluralist policy, which gives rise to Chinese ethnicity in Indonesia. The Chinese cultural pillars—organizations, dailies/radio/TV programmes and Chinese language schools—were restored. Writings in Chinese language re-emerged but the majority of the Peranakan writings remain in Indonesian. The younger generation who grew up during the New Order is especially very Indonesian. One can therefore argue that Peranakan Chinese literature tends to merge with the mainstream Indonesian literature. Major popular Peranakan writers such as Marga T. and Mira W. are considered as "indigenous" Indonesian writers, and their writings are not much different from other "indigenous" writers in both style and contents. The language used is standard Bahasa Indonesia.

It does not mean that the Peranakan identity has been lost. On the contrary, there has been a revival of interest in Peranakan culture and literature. Pre-war Peranakan literary works in Malay have been republished. More recently, books on Peranakan Chinese have also been published. Many Peranakan Chinese-based associations also reappeared after the fall of Suharto, showing the resurgence of Peranakan Chinese identity. Nevertheless, the reflection in the literature is not clear, except on the Indonesian version of Chinese *kungfu* novels.

Independent Malaya/Malaysia

While Peranakan Chinese literature continued to develop even after Indonesia's independence and eventually "merged" with Indonesian literature, Peranakan Chinese literature appeared to be left behind in Malaya and Singapore. Even the translation of Chinese work stopped for a while and only resumed long after Malaya attained independence; the quantity was also small. But in Indonesia, there were many more new translations of Chinese works, especially the new generation of *kungfu* novels by Jin Yong 金庸, Liang Yusheng 梁羽生 and Gu Long 古龙.

In the 1990s, Dewan Bahasa published quite a few Chinese classics and modern literature in Malay. The translators, unlike pre-war ones, are "*singkeh*" Chinese who are Chinese-educated.[9] Nevertheless, the Peranakan themselves began to write in Malay or Bahasa Kebangsaan. They no longer translated Chinese works into Malay but did creative writings. The most well-known Peranakan writers are Kelantan-born Lim Swee Tin and Pui Tiong Gee (pen name: Awang Abdullah),[10] and Sarawak-born Jong Chia Lai.[11]

It is interesting to note that unlike in Indonesia where those assimilated Peranakan Chinese writings are accepted as Indonesian literature, there has been resistance in Malaysia. It was reported that many Peranakan Chinese writers were even advised to write only about their own communities, not those of the Malay.[12] This is related to the concept of the Malaysian literature as many still habour prejudices against the Chinese.

Independent Singapore

In fact, the role of pre-war Singapore Peranakan literature is difficult to be separated from Malaya as the Straits Settlements established in 1826 included Singapore. Singapore at one time was also the centre of Malay publications. Peranakan Chinese in Singapore are also active in *dongdang* saying, a form of classic Malay literature rather than modern literature. I am not aware of Singapore leading Peranakan writers before the war who produced their works in Peranakan Malay. However, after the war, especially after Singapore's independence, there were quite a few Peranakan Chinese writers, but they mainly write in English, not Peranakan Malay, such as Goh Poh Seng, Goh Sin Tub, Robert Yeo, Catherine Lim, Arthur Yap, Lee Tzu Ping, Leong Lee Geok, Stella Kon, etc. Some, for instance Goh Poh Seng and Catherine Lim, were originated from Malaysia.

In fact, in Malaysia, there were a few well-known Peranakan writers who also write in English. For instance, Ee Thian Hong, Shirley Lim, to name but a few. However, these Peranakan writers eventually migrated to the West rather than staying in their own country, presumably because they did not have opportunity to develop in their country of origin.

Peranakan literature in Baba Malay re-emerged for a short period of time in the form of plays in Singapore. These Peranakan plays were performed in Peranakan Malay, not in English, but they did not last for a long time. In the past ten years or so, I have not heard of any Peranakan play being staged.

Similarities and Differences among Peranakan Chinese Literature

Why are there different types of Peranakan Chinese literature in these three countries?

Three factors may explain the developments of the Peranakan Chinese literature of these three countries: firstly, the size of the Peranakan Chinese community vis-à-vis the Chinese community, the size of the Chinese community vis-à-vis the indigenous population; secondly, the state policy towards the Chinese minority; thirdly, the continuity or discontinuity of foreign language (Dutch/English) education in the country concerned. In my view, these three factors influence, if not determine, the form and contents of Peranakan Chinese literature.

Firstly, Singapore has the largest ethnic Chinese population (76 per cent), followed by Malaysia (26 per cent) and Indonesia (2 per cent). It is clear that the Chinese in Indonesia formed an absolute minority and hence the most "integrated", if not assimilated, into the "indigenous" society; this is especially the case in Java where 50 per cent of the Indonesian population lives.

Secondly, the number of the Peranakan vis-à-vis *singkeh* (culturally Chinese or Chinese-speaking Chinese) in Malaysia and Singapore is small. Towards the end of the nineteenth century, Peranakan Chinese only formed around 15 per cent of the total Chinese population in the Straits Settlement. This proportion continued to decline as more new Chinese migrants entered British Malaya (including Singapore). Therefore, the Chinese-educated formed the largest number and had been dominant culturally before World War II. However, after the World War II, especially after Singapore attained independence, the two countries took different paths linguistically. In Malaysia, Malay has become the dominant language while in Singapore English has become the administrative/working language in the government, and is also the medium of instruction for all government schools and universities. In the nineteenth-century Indonesia, especially in Java, the Peranakan Chinese formed more than 70 per cent of the total Indonesian Chinese population but the number declined somewhat in 1930 though it remained the absolute majority.

In other words, in Singapore and Malaya, there was a lack of critical mass for the development of Peranakan Malay publications, especially daily newspapers while in colonial Indonesia, especially in Java, there was a presence of this critical mass which could support Peranakan Chinese publications, including daily newspapers.

Thirdly, the government policy also differs from country to country. Suharto's Indonesia adopted an assimilation policy for about thirty-two years, transforming the Chinese community into Peranakan and made the Peranakans more Indonesian, while in Malaysia, the national language policy has been implemented together with the permission for the existence of vernacular schools. Singapore has adopted English, and more recently, Mandarin has been encouraged. As a result, Peranakan Chinese writers moved closer to English rather than Malay, but there has also been a trend for some Peranakan Chinese children to learn Mandarin in schools. A certain degree of re-Sinicization process has taken place. But this process is not as rapid as that of the Chinese in Malaysia.

In light of the above argument, it is understandable that Peranakan Chinese literature in Indonesia has moved closer to the Indonesian literature; in Malaysia, the new generation of Peranakan Chinese have also moved closer to the Malay literature, while some of them tended to go overseas, or even migrated to Singapore; and most Peranakan writers in Singapore have written in English rather than in Malay.

Conclusion

Ethnic Chinese culture outside China has changed over time. A good example is Peranakan Chinese literature. Peranakan Chinese began to write in Malay instead of Chinese as they have lost their command of the Chinese language. Many later also mastered Dutch or English and produced their literature in the language that they are familiar with. Peranakan Chinese literature has also encountered transformation depending on country.

Owing to their different historical backgrounds, the culture/literature of each community also varies. Before independence, Peranakan Chinese literature in Malaya and Singapore (especially in the Straits Settlements) was restricted mainly to translations of Chinese stories and *pantuns*; while in Indonesia (Dutch East Indies), Peranakan Chinese literature went beyond "translation literature" and expanded to creative works.

After independence, the Peranakan Chinese elite began to write in the colonial languages: Dutch in the case of Indonesia and English in the case of Malaysia. In Indonesia, Peranakan Dutch literature never developed while in Malaysia and particularly in Singapore, Peranakan English literature has flourished. At the same time, the promotion of the Malay language in Malaysia and Singapore also resulted in the emergence of Peranakan writings in Malay, which was more developed in Malaysia than in Singapore.

In the case of Malaysia, apart from some Peranakans who published creative works in Malay, the translation works from Chinese to Malay were done by non-Peranakans who received Chinese education; while some Peranakan Chinese continued to write in English. In the case of Indonesia, Peranakan Chinese literature has gradually merged into the so-called Indonesian national literature.

Notes

1. The TV series was produced by the Singapore Broadcasting Corporation, and it consists of thirty-four episodes. It was claimed to be the most popular SBC TV series in the last few years.
2. The collection of Peranakan literary works, entitled *Kesastraan Melayu Tionghoa dan Kebangsaan Indonesia*, has been published into nine large volumes until today.
3. The museum was built by Udaya Halim, a Peranakan culture enthusiast, in 2011. The museum mainly displays the material culture of the Peranakans from Tangerang, West Java.
4. For a rather comprehensive catalogue of Peranakan Chinese writings in Malay/Indonesian, see Claudine Salmon, *Literature in Malay by the Chinese of Indonesia: A Provisional Annotated Bibliography*, Etudes Insulindies-archipel 3 (Paris: Éditions de la Maison des sciences de l'Homme, 1981).
5. See Leo Suryadinata, *The Pre-World War II Peranakan Chinese Press of Java: A Preliminary Survey*, Papers in International Studies, Southeast Asia Series, No. 18 (Athens, Ohio: Ohio University, Center for International Studies, 1971).
6. Salmon, *Literature in Malay by the Chinese of Indonesia*; Leo Suryadinata, ed., *Sastra Peranakan Tionghoa Indonesia* (Jakarta: Grasindo, 1996).
7. Claudine Salmon, "Writings in Romanized Malay by the Chinese of Malaya: A Preliminary Survey", in *Literary Migrations: Traditional Chinese Fiction in Asia (17th–20th Centuries)*, edited by Claudine Salmon (Beijing: International Culture Publishing Corporation, 1987), pp. 441–96; also Tan Chee Beng, "Baba Chinese Publication in Romanized Malay", *Journal of Asian and African Studies* 22 (1981): 158–93; Tan Chee Beng, *Chinese Peranakan Heritage in Malaysia and Singapore* (Kuala Lumpur: Fajar Bakti, 1993).
8. Suryadinata, *Sastra Peranakan Tionghoa Indonesia*.
9. Yang Guiyi (杨贵谊, Yang Quee Yee), "Xinma tusheng huaren wenxue de xingshuai 新马土生华人文学的兴衰", in *Dongnanya huaren fanyi wenxue yu*

   wenhua 东南亚华人翻译文学与文化, edited by Yeo Songnian 杨松年 and
   Wang Kangding 王慷鼎 (Singapore: Singapore Society of Asian Studies, 1995),
   pp. 32–55.

10. Zhuang Huaxing (庄华兴), "Lim Swee Tin （林天英）诗歌初论", in *Nyanyian
    Sepi* 寂寞求音: *Lim Swee Tin* 诗选 *(1973–1998)*, by Zhuang Huaxing (Kuala
    Lumpur: University Malaya Chinese Studies Department Graduates Association
    中文系毕业生协会, 2000), pp. 119–25.

11. Wei Yueping (魏月萍), "Huayi zuojia de malaiwen chuangzuo: kuayue bianjie
    de huama wenxue 华裔作家的马来文创作: 跨越边界的华马文学", *Sin Chew
    Jit Poh* 星洲日报, 24 December 2004.

12. Ibid.

8

POLITICAL AND NATIONAL IDENTITIES OF PERANAKAN CHINESE LEADERS IN IMS: BEFORE AND AFTER INDEPENDENCE

As this book addresses the issue of Peranakan identities, it is therefore essential for us to examine the concept of political and national identities of a few major Peranakan leaders from the colonial period to after independence. As the situation of IMS differs from country to country, it is therefore imperative for us to have examples from the three countries and a brief comparison between these leaders and their political and national identities. The comparison would definitely throw new light on the characteristics of the Peranakan Chinese in each country and their likely different future.

For the purpose of discussion, two or three Peranakan leaders from each country during the colonial period and two or three leaders from each country after independence have been selected. The selection category is based on the position of the leadership, the influence they had on the Peranakan community, and the availability of information on their thoughts with regards to their political and national identities.

However, it is difficult to differentiate Singapore Peranakan leaders from those of Malaysia (or Malaya). As a matter of fact, both countries had the same leaders before the separation. It is only possible to differentiate Peranakan leaders of the two countries after Singapore left Malaysia and attained an independence status.

Before proceeding further, the Peranakan Chinese situation in IMS needs to be clarified. In Indonesia, the Peranakan Chinese remain quite influential politically as their number has become even larger after Indonesia attained independence, while in Malaysia and Singapore, the traditional Peranakans are declining in number. The leadership position of the Peranakans in Malaysia has gradually been taken over by the non-Peranakan Chinese, as reflected in the MCA leadership. While in Singapore, the leadership position of the Peranakan Chinese in the People's Action Party (PAP) has been strong, one can also see that Singapore Peranakans are adjusting to the international and national development.

Having mentioned the background, let us look at the Peranakan leaders that are selected in this chapter. For the colonial period, Tjoe Bou San, Kan Hok Hoei and Liem Koen Hian are selected for Indonesia; Lim Boon Keng and Song Ong Siang are selected for both Singapore and Malaya/Malaysia. For the independence period, Siauw Giok Tjhan, Yap Thiam Hien and Abdul Karim Oei Tjeng Hien are selected for Indonesia; Tan Cheng Lock and Lee Kuan Yew are selected for Malaysia and Singapore respectively.

Before Independence

Tjoe Bou San (朱茂山, 1891–1925)

Tjoe Bou San was a leading journalist and a community leader. Born in 1891 in Jakarta, he received some Dutch education. Largely through self-education, he was able to read and write Malay, English, and probably Chinese. In 1909 he became the editor-in-chief of *Hoa Tok Po*, a Jakarta-based weekly in Peranakan Malay, which had close links with a Chinese revolutionary association called Soe Po Sia (Reading Club). A few years later he left *Hoa Tok Po* for Surabaya, where he became the editor-in-chief of *Tjhoen Tjhioe* until June 1917. He then went to China to work as a *Sin Po* correspondent.

Sin Po was then led by Kwee Hing Tjiat (1916–18), a Dutch-educated Peranakan nationalist who started a movement to guide the Chinese community in political matters. In 1917 the Dutch were planning to create the Volksraad (People's Council) and wanted to include the Peranakan Chinese and indigenous representatives in the new political institution. In the same year, a conference of Chinese residents was held in Semarang to discuss the issue. *Sin Po*, under the leadership of Kwee Hing Tjiat and supported by other Peranakan organizations, rejected the proposal of Kan Hok Hoei (better known as H.H. Kan), a pro-Dutch Peranakan landlord, to participate in local politics on the ground that the Chinese were citizens of China. As foreigners, they should not get involved in foreign politics.

However, the Peranakan Chinese in reality were Dutch subjects and as Dutch subjects they were allowed to get involved in the politics of the Dutch East Indies. Despite *Sin Po*'s objection, pro-Dutch Peranakan Chinese eventually accepted the proposal and became members of the Volksraad. In fact, the Peranakan Chinese prior to 1955 were having dual nationality status. As long as the Peranakan Chinese lived in the Dutch East Indies, they were under the jurisdiction of the Dutch law. But when they were in China, if they got into trouble, the Chinese law will be applied.

In 1918 Tjoe returned to Jakarta and was appointed as the editor-in-chief of *Sin Po* and, in 1919, the director as well. Tjoe continued Kwee Hing Tjiat's tradition and developed it further. It was under his leadership that *Sin Po* became one of the most influential political forces in the Chinese communities before World War II.

During World War I, the Dutch colonial government attempted to introduce the concept of *Indie Weebar* (the defence of the Dutch Indies). Under this scheme, Dutch subjects would be asked to be the militia to defense the Dutch colony. *Sin Po*, under Tjoe's leadership, launched a campaign to abolish the Dutch "Nationality Law" (Onderdanschap), and within a short period of time, the newspaper succeeded in collecting about 30,000 Peranakan signatures that wanted to repudiate Dutch nationality. A representative was sent to China to present these signatures but Beijing did not accept *Sin Po*'s request. The concept of *Indie Weebar* was also scrapped and hence the protest movement subsided.

Because of his Chinese nationalist point of view, Tjoe was very critical of P.H. Fromberg, a Dutch lawyer, who advocated the identification of the local Chinese with an "Indies nation" by accepting Dutch nationality. Tjoe was of the view that the Chinese in the Dutch Indies were China's citizens and part of the Chinese nation. They did not want to be part of other nations.

Tjoe soon came into conflict with the Peranakan Chinese leaders who did not agree with him that the solution to the issue of the Indies Chinese was Chinese nationalism. His main opponent in the press was Gouw Peng Liang, the editor-in-chief of *Perniagaan*, who actively advocated cooperation with the Dutch authorities and the popularization of Dutch education among the Peranakan Chinese.

Before he led *Sin Po*, Tjoe was known as a novelist who published his works under the pseudonym Hauw San Liang. His rather well-known works include *Satoe Djodo Jang Terhalang* (The Obstructed Match, 1917), *Binasa Lantaran Harta* (Destroyed by Wealth, 1918), and *Badjingan Besar* (Big Crook, 1918). His novel entitled *The Loan Eng* was published in 1922 after he led *Sin Po*.[1] Nevertheless, Tjoe was better known as a community leader and a journalist.

Tjoe contracted tuberculosis, which stayed with him for quite a while and this led to his premature death in 1925 at the age of thirty-four. Towards the end of his life, it was reported that he was influenced by Chinese philosophers such as Lao Zi and Zhang Zi, and became less militant. Nevertheless, *Sin Po* continued to hold a Chinese nationalist point of view even after the demise of Tjoe Bou San.

Kan Hok Hoei (H.H. Kan, 简福辉, 1881–1951)

Kan Hok Hoei was a politician, landlord, and a leader of a conservative Peranakan organization Chung Hwa Hui (CHH).[2] CHH was a Dutch-educated Peranakan Chinese political party whose members were wealthy businessmen and professionals. It was supported by the largest Peranakan firm in Java, i.e. Oei Tiong Ham Concern.

Born in 1881 in Jakarta, Kan Hok Hoei received Dutch secondary education (HBS). Initially he was active in Siang Hwee (Chinese Chamber of Commerce) and later in the Municipal Council of Batavia (now Jakarta) as well. His wealth and his knowledge of Dutch soon made him the most outspoken Peranakan Chinese in Dutch circles. He was also well-known among members of the local councils and Dutch-appointed Chinese officers.

When the Volksraad ("People's Council") was to be formed by the Dutch colonial government and many organizations of the Indies Chinese decided not to take part in that new council (1917), Kan accepted the appointment of the governor as a "representative" of the Indies Chinese. Kan believed that Chinese interests would be well protected under Dutch colonial rule.

In 1918 a review commission was appointed to probe into the Indies' political structure. Kan and two other Dutch members submitted a report that was in favour of preserving the status quo. Kan believed that a large number of indigenous members in the Volksraad would jeopardize Chinese interests. In 1927 Kan voted against the proposal for an indigenous majority in the Volksraad, an action which stigmatized him in the eyes of Indonesian nationalists.

When the CHH was formed in 1928, Kan was elected as its president. Though the response of Peranakan Chinese newspapers was not favourable to Kan, he was elected every year until the dissolution of the CHH during the Japanese occupation.

In 1932 Kan was sent by a local Chinese business firm to tour China. His links with the Consul-General of China became closer after his return to Java. His daughter married a son of the Chinese Consul General. In 1934 the Federation of Siang Hwees of the Dutch East Indies was founded under the instruction of the Consul-General of China, who became the honorary president while Kan was elected as the president. The Dutch Governor-General was unhappy with Kan's association with the organization which was dominated by Chinese migrants, especially Kan's relationship with the Consul-General of China. Kan was eventually forced to resign from the position.

In 1935 he was knighted by the Dutch Government for his "outstanding service" and in the following year he visited the Netherlands to promote closer relations between the Indies Chinese and the Netherlands. After the outbreak of the anti-Japanese war in China, Kan supported China with donation. At the same time Kan continued to support Dutch rule. In 1942 when the Japanese occupied Java, Kan was imprisoned for his anti-Japanese activities. He was released after the Japanese capitulation and died in 1951.

Liem Koen Hian (林群贤, 1896–1952)

Liem Koen Hian was born in Banjarmasin, Kalimantan in 1896 into a businessman family.[3] He received a Dutch primary school education and by self-study managed to pass the qualifying examination for the law school in Batavia (now Jakarta).

Like many Peranakan Chinese journalists, Liem was first a Chinese nationalist. He was the editor-in-chief of the following China-oriented periodicals/newspapers: *Tjhoen Tjhioe* (1915–16), *Soo Lim Po* (1917), *Sinar Sumatra* (1918–21), and *Pewarta Soerabaia* (1921–25). He abandoned his Chinese nationalist view after the mid-1920s and declared himself an Indonesian nationalist. The idea of Indonesian nationalism for Peranakan Chinese was developed in the following newspapers of which he was the editor-in-chief: *Soeara Publiek* (Surabaya, 1925–29), *Sin Jit Po/Sin Tit Po* (Surabaya, 1929–32; 1939), and *Kong Hoa Po* (Jakarta, 1937–38).

In the 1920s, two trends were emerging. The number of Western-educated Peranakan Chinese grew and there was also a rise of Indonesian nationalism proper. In 1928 the CHH was formed by Dutch-educated Chinese businessmen and professionals. Liem was nominated as one of its executive members but was not elected. The CHH was supported by Oei Tiong Ham Concern, a multinational business firm. The firm was led by Kan Hok Hoei (better known as H.H. Kan), a right-wing politician who was pro-Dutch colonial government. Liem dissociated himself from the CHH as he became more sympathetic to Indonesian nationalists. This became obvious when Liem assumed the editorship of *Sin Tit Po* in 1929.

Liem believed that the Peranakan Chinese were linked to the Indonesian population and were in opposition to both Chinese nationalism (as represented by the Sin Po group) and the pro-Dutch colonialism (as represented by the CHH).

Liem argued that "the Peranakan Chinese cannot consider Indonesia a foreign country or a temporary residence. Their status, their interest ...

and their feelings are growing closer to the Indonesian Nation of which they form an increasingly integral part as time passes."[4]

Liem also dissociated himself from Chinese nationalism as "this was a weapon which could be used to drive away the enemy".

> In China, Chinese nationalism can be used to drive away the country's enemies. To the Peranakan Chinese, this weapon is useless. Who is the enemy that the Peranakan Chinese are going to drive away? They have armed themselves with [Chinese] nationalism now and will bring harm to the people of Indonesia in the future when China is strong, just as the imperialists are doing to China now.[5]

Liem criticized the CHH as being pro-Dutch and "wants the Peranakan [Chinese] to see the Peranakan's interest through the Dutch glasses".[6] He further argued that "There are not many Peranakan Chinese whose interests are closely linked with those of the Dutch and who are more anxious than the Dutch men to keep Dutch rule forever ... There are only a small number of people like H.H. Kan who regards the end of the Dutch as the end of the world."[7]

Due to his new conviction, in September 1932 Liem established the Indonesian Chinese Party (Partai Tionghoa Indonesia, PTI) which was an Indonesia-oriented Peranakan Chinese organization. The objective of the party was to support Indonesia's independence. He served as its chairman from 1932–33.

Liem was criticized for changing his ideology, i.e. from a Chinese nationalist to an Indonesian nationalist. However, he defended himself:

> Previously I called myself a Chinese nationalist ... [now] I called myself an Indonesian nationalist. It does not mean that I have changed my political convictions. I have merely changed their object. Because I lived in Indonesia, I believe that I can do more for Indonesia than for China. However, the content of my convictions has not changed, for the content of Chinese nationalism is identical to that of Indonesian nationalism. I genuinely believe that the change of object cannot be condemned.[8]

It becomes clear that Liem Koen Hian followed the political and social development in the Dutch East Indies and adjusted his political beliefs. But there was a consistency in his political beliefs that he was always anti-colonialism.

When the Semarang branch of the PTI was about to be formed, Liem was invited to give a lecture in October 1932. Liem argued that Chinese nationalists were anti-colonialist, and Chinese nationalists in Indonesia should work for Indonesia's independence because it coincided with anti-colonialist movement. China was too far away from Indonesia, and it was unrealistic to work for a land which was a mystery for most of the Peranakans.

During the question and answer session, many questions were raised. The following two questions, which were related to China, were asked by the participants.

> Question: Why does the PTI's constitution not mention anything about China?
> Liem's reply: Because we continue to live in Indonesia, not China.
> Question: Being *Indonesiers*, what should we do if China and Indonesia go to war?
> Liem's reply: The possibility of war between China and Indonesia is very remote, but we shall still discuss it. If they were at war, we would first have to probe the cause of the war. If it was caused by Chinese imperialistic ideas, I would definitely fight on the Indonesian side because China would have betrayed the ideas of Sun Yat Sen. I think the Chinese here would also side with the Indonesians and fight against China.[9]

Liem was eager to show his Indonesian identity. In 1939, when a left-wing Indonesian party (Gerindo) opened its membership to Peranakans, Liem left the PTI and became a member of Gerindo.

Liem was against Japanese imperialism and published a book in 1938 denouncing it. He had engaged in a debate with Dr Soetomo on Japan as Liem noted that Japan had developed into an imperialist power, but Soetomo praised Japan as a developed country which was a model for other Asian countries. Due to Liem's anti-Japanese stand, Liem was detained when Japan occupied Java but was released soon after. In 1945 he was appointed as a member of the Investigative Committee for the Preparation of Indonesian Independence (BPUPKI) initiated by the Japanese (but headed by Sukarno and Hatta). When the Indonesian constitution was drafted, he urged the committee to declare all Indonesia-born Chinese as Indonesian citizens.

After Indonesia gained its independence, Liem was appointed as a member of the Indonesian Central National Committee (1946). As time passed, he became more interested in the communist movement in China. He translated Gunther Stein's book, *The Challenge of Red China*, and published it in June 1949. In the preface of the book, he predicted the victory of the Communist over the Kuomintang.

In 1950 together with some indigenous Indonesians, he established a multiracial political party, Persatuan Tenaga Indonesia (the New PTI), advocating Indonesian nationalism. In 1951 he was arrested by the Sukiman government on suspicion of being a communist. He was tortured while in detention by his fellow Indonesians and became emotional. Upon his release he repudiated Indonesian citizenship which he had advocated in the last twenty or thirty years. He left politics and became a businessman running a drug store. A year later (1952) he died in Medan.

Lim Boon Keng (林文庆, 1869–1957)

Lim Boon Keng was undoubtedly a leading Peranakan Chinese social activist and intellectual in Singapore and Malaya. Born into a Peranakan family in Singapore, Lim Boon Keng's father Lim Thean Geow was born in Penang but moved to Singapore early. Lim Thean Geow was educated at the Raffles Institution and later worked for Hong Lim Firm. He married a Peranakan girl from Malacca who was related to Tan Cheng Lock's family.[10]

Lim Boon Keng was born in Singapore in 1869. At the age of ten, he entered the Raffles Institution. At the age of twelve his father passed away, but he was still able to continue his studies due to the help and support of Raffles Institution's headmaster R.W. Hullett. Lim completed his studies at Raffles Institution in 1887 and obtained a Queen's Scholarship to study at the Edinberg University in Scotland. He earned a first class honours degree in medicine from the same university in 1892.

He lived in the United Kingdom for six years (1887–93) and admired the success of Britain, but at the same time he also realized his own inadequacy as an ethnic Chinese. He was unable to speak Mandarin in front of students from China and he was embarrassed when his lecturer asked him to translate some Chinese exercises. He therefore made up his mind to study the Chinese language.

In the U.K. he also witnessed white racism. He often defended the Chinese when they were bullied by the whites. But he also discovered that the British loved their country. This made him be aware of China. Since the age of nineteen, Lim had become interested in the Chinese language and Chinese culture, especially Confucianism.

After returning to Singapore, Lim became active in its social and political life. He was appointed as a member of the Legislative Council since 1885. In the following year, he headed a committee which looked into the sources of poverty in Singapore. In 1897 he staged a campaign against wearing queues among the Chinese men, showing his opposition to the Qing dynasty. In 1899 he co-founded the Singapore Chinese Girls' School with Song Ong Siang in order to improve the status of Chinese girls.

Out of his many activities, the most significant was his long-time association with Confucianism and he was recognized as the leader of the Confucianism movement in Singapore and Malaya. His enthusiasm for Confucianism led him to become a "Confucianist". He even became very critical of Christianity although he was brought up in a Christian environment and his two wives were devout Christians.

There are two different views regarding Lim's religious beliefs. One view was that he was a Christian but also embraced Confucianism. The other, however, argued that Lim was not a Christian and was never converted into Christianity.[11] On the contrary, he was "anti-Christian" as shown in his published articles in the *Straits Chinese Magazine* between 1895 and 1896.[12] Lim was of the view that Christianity would not be able to make China strong but Confucianism would.[13] There was a debate on Christianity and Confucianism in Singapore where Lim was involved and he served as a serious critic of Christianity. Interestingly, many of his closest friends such as Song Ong Siang were ardent Christians.

Lim continued to propagate Confucianism not only among the Peranakan Chinese in Singapore and Malaya, but also among the Chinese in Java. He also helped the Tiong Hoa Hwee Koan of Batavia (Jakarta) to recruit Chinese teachers.

Lim made friends with British administrators, local and mainland Chinese leaders such as Tan Kah Kee and Sun Yat Sen. In 1921 Lim was invited by Tan Kah Kee to become the chancellor of Xiamen University in Amoy (Xiamen) until 1937. Not surprising, he became more Chinese in his culture and political orientation.

However, earlier his political orientation and loyalty were towards Britain. He and Song Ong Siang established the Straits Chinese British Association in 1890, considering the United Kingdom as the country of the Straits Chinese and paid their allegiance to Britain. His involvement in the Legislature Council also showed this sort of belonging. During World War I, Lim urged the Straits Chinese to help the U.K. to subscribe to the National War Loan as well as the Straits Settlements War Loan.[14] In 1918 because of his public service, Lim was conferred the order of O.B.E.

Lim's political view changed from period to period. Prior to the twentieth century, his political loyalty was with the British. However, between 1900 and 1921, his political belonging was unstable, but after 1921, he identified himself with China. Between 1942 and 1945, he was forced by the Japanese military government to direct his political loyalty to Japan. After the Japanese surrender, he refused to get involved in any activities and stayed in Singapore until the day he died.

His view on the Singapore and Malaya's education is worth noting. In 1889, he wrote an article on the Straits Chinese reform, in which he noted that: "To learn English is necessary, but when our children are already familiar with Malay and Chinese, to use English as the medium of instruction is inappropriate ...". Lim also noted that "Among us there are people who can read, write and speak English, can't we design a good way to educate our children to learn Chinese, Malay, English and the foundation of modern culture?"[15]

Basically, Lim is a professional and an intellectual, and he interacted with the British colonial elite and the Chinese community in Singapore, Malaya and China. His contact with the Malay community is unknown. Although he spoke Malay and occasionally made speeches in Malay to the Peranakan Chinese, there was no record of his speeches to the

Malay community. He did not write any Malay article that discusses Malay culture.

Therefore, from the life story of Lim, it is difficult to pinpoint his clear national identity.

Song Ong Siang (宋旺相, 1871–1941)

Song Ong Siang was a leading Peranakan lawyer, an elder in the church and a self-taught historian. Born in Singapore on 14 June 1871, he was a third-generation Peranakan. His father, Song Hoot Kiam, was a devout Christian who was a close mentor of Reverend James Legge. Song Hoot Kiam was baptized in England and later established the Chinese Christian Association in Singapore. Song Hoot Kiam's second wife, i.e. Song Ong Siang's mother, Phan Fung Lean, was also a Peranakan who was fluent in Malay. Song Ong Siang was influenced by his parents and had a good command of English and Malay.[16] Nevertheless, he was unable to read and write Chinese.

Song Ong Siang received his education at the Raffles Institution. He was a brilliant student who always topped his class. At the age of twelve, he received the Guthrie Scholarship and did so for a few years. He also sat for the Queen's Scholarship Examination and topped the list. But as he was underaged, the scholarship had to be given to others. Song continued to sit for the Queen's Scholarship Examination and eventually got it when he reached sixteen years of age.

Initially he wanted to study medicine like Lim Boon Keng, but he later changed his mind to study law at Cambridge University. He graduated with a second class in law in 1893 and in the same year he was called to the English Bar. In the same year he returned to Singapore and was immediately active in the local scene. He was elected as chairman of the Chinese Christian Association which was established by his father. Song was then twenty-two years of age. One scholar noted that Song took up the Christian challenges differently from his father. "As a Christian, the targets that he sets for himself were educational and cultural, and not, as might be expected, evangelical."[17]

In 1893, together with his fellow graduate from Cambridge James Aitken, Song established a law firm named Aitken and Ong Siang.

In 1894 he and his brother-in-law founded the *Bintang Timor*, a Romanized Malay daily, for the Straits Chinese who were only able to read Malay. Unfortunately, it only lasted less than a year owing to the lack of fund. In this aspect he was different from Lim Boon Keng who co-established the Chinese language daily, the *Tiannan Xinbao* (天南新报), with Khoo Sook Yuen, another local elite who was Chinese-educated.

It seems that he was not easily discouraged. In 1899, together with Lim Boon Keng, he established the *Straits Chinese Magazine* (1897–1907), an English-language magazine which was popular among the Peranakan elite. Song served as its chief editor. Later Dr Wu Liande, another well-known physician from Penang, joined the magazine as editorial staff. It was in this magazine that many Peranakan leaders published their articles.

On 17 August 1900, Song, Lim Boon Keng, Tan Jiat Kim and Seah Liang Seah established the Straits Chinese British Association (SCBA). Tan Jiat Kim was elected the first president while Song its secretary. The SCBA was an organization of Peranakan Chinese who have sworn their loyalty to the British crown. They were proud of being called the "King's Chinese" that differed from the new migrants.

In November 1901, Song also helped establish the first Chinese Company of the Singapore Volunteer Infantry and was appointed Sergeant of B Company. In the following year he was selected as one of the volunteers in the Straits Settlement contingent in the coronation of King Edward George VII.[18] During World War I, Song also mobilized the volunteers to guard Singapore. His contribution to the British crown eventually gained him recognition, including being knighted.

Song's efforts on promoting Chinese women education were also commendable. He and Lim Boon Keng co-founded the Singapore Chinese Girls' School in 1899, giving Chinese girls the opportunity to receive an education.

However, as a Christian leader, his influence on the non-Christian Chinese seemed rather limited. And indeed during his lifetime, most of the Peranakan Chinese were followers of Chinese traditional religions.

Song is now remembered for his monumental work, a book entitled *One Hundred Years' History of the Chinese in Singapore* (1923). This book which contains over 500 pages is an important source for studying Peranakan Chinese history in Singapore.

Song passed away in 1941 when countries in the Malay Archipelago were not yet independent. His identity was a colonial identity.

Towards Independence and After

Siauw Giok Tjhan (萧玉灿, 1914–81)

Siauw Giok Tjhan was born on 23 March 1914 in Surabaya into a wealthy businessman family.[19] He received an HBS (Dutch secondary school) education and hence could not speak Chinese. He became acquainted with Liem Koen Hian and joined the PTI when he was eighteen years old. He worked for a pre-war Peranakan daily, the *Mata Hari*, from 1934 to 1942. His leftist orientation appeared during this period.

Siauw went underground when the Japanese occupied Indonesia. During the Indonesian Revolution (1945–49), Siauw sided with the Indonesian nationalists. He and Tan Ling Djie joined the Partai Sosialis in 1946. Both were active in the Front Demokrasi Rakjat (FDR), a left-wing force during the Revolution. In 1948 Tan Ling Djie joined the Partai Komunis Indonesia (PKI, Indonesian Communist Party), but Siauw remained with the FDR. Siauw was appointed as a member of the BPKI (Indonesian Central National Committee) in 1946 and, in the following year he was made Minister without Portfolio for Peranakan Affairs[20] under Prime Minister Amir Sjarifuddin (July 1947–January 1948).

Siauw was probably a member of the illegal PKI before World War II.[21] After the 1948 Madiun Affair, he was suspected of involvement in the PKI rebellion and was imprisoned by the Indonesian authorities. He was soon released and became active again in Indonesian politics. He was first appointed, and later elected, as a member of the Indonesian Parliament representing the Chinese minority from 1950 to 1966. He was officially dismissed from this position because of his alleged involvement in the G-30-S 1965 Coup.

Siauw's career as a journalist after World War II is not well known. He edited *Liberty* (Malang, 1946) and *Pemuda* during the Indonesian Revolution. Between July 1951 and October 1953, he served as the director of *Harian Rakjat*, the official organ of the PKI.[22] He also edited *Republik*, the official newspaper of the Baperki in the 1950s.

In 1954 Siauw participated in the formation of Baperki, the most influential Peranakan socio-political organization during the "Guided Democracy" period (1959–65). Before its founding, there was a heated discussion on the name of this new organization. One group, represented by a leading Christian lawyer Yap Thiam Hien, wanted to call the new organization the Consultative Body for Indonesian Citizenship of Chinese Descent (Baperwat). The other, represented by Siauw, wanted the term "of Chinese descent" be dropped.

Siauw argued that this new body did not have to be limited to the Chinese. It should be open to any Indonesian citizens who agree with the organization's goals. Siauw added that the goal was to eliminate racial discrimination that was flaring up at the time. He felt that it would not be wise to brand the organization that fought against racial discrimination a Chinese organization. According to Siauw, the most important thing at that time was to "give meaning and substance to citizenship".

Yap felt that "the name was a very important matter. A name is a label to defend something. If this body is by the Chinese, why should we fear to use the term of Chinese descent?" But the two groups continued to debate. Finally, the Siauw group won. The name of the organization became the Badan Permusjawaratan Kewarganegaraan Indonesia (the Consultative Council for Indonesian Citizenship) or abbreviated as Baperki. Siauw was also elected as its chairman. He retained this position until 1965 when Baperki was banned.

Baperki under Siauw's leadership advocated Indonesian citizenship for Chinese Indonesians. It opposed racial discrimination and strived for equal citizenship. It also opposed name-changing into "Indonesian name" for Chinese Indonesians and wanted to retain Chinese ethnicity within the Indonesian state. However, he was influenced by Marxist and Leninist views of ethnicity. He was of the view that ethnic issues could not be resolved in a non-socialist society. Therefore, he advocated the realization of a socialist society because only in a socialist society when there was no more class division, ethnic issues would disappear. He gave China and the Soviet Union as the examples and noted that in these countries, ethnic issues have been resolved.[23] His view came into conflict with that of Yap Thiam Hien, a Christian human rights lawyer.

Nevertheless, Baperki under Siauw made significant contributions to Indonesian Chinese society as it succeeded in accommodating Chinese Indonesian students who were forced to leave Chinese-medium schools in Indonesia. In the 1957 regulation, children of Indonesian citizens were not allowed to attend Chinese-medium schools, and this affected hundreds of thousands of Chinese Indonesian children. These affected students were accommodated into the Baperki-run schools. Baperki also continued to educate Indonesian Chinese to be oriented towards Indonesia.

However, Baperki under Siauw was moving closer towards Sukarno and the PKI and became the target of the right-wing forces in Indonesia. The 30th September Movement in 1965 (G-30-S) resulted in the banning of the PKI, the fall of Sukarno and the rise of the military represented by Suharto. Siauw was detained without trial for thirteen years soon after the G-30-S affair. When released he went to the Netherlands using his Indonesian passport. However, his passport was suspended by the Suharto government and Siauw lost his Indonesian citizenship. His memoirs, *Lima Jaman: Perwujudan Integrasi Wajar* (Five Eras: Formation of Natural Integration) was published in May 1981 in Holland. Its Chinese and English editions were later published in Hong Kong and Australia. Siauw died on 20 November 1981 in Leiden, the Netherland.

Yap Thiam Hien (叶添兴, 1913–1989)

Yap Thiam Hien was a leading human rights lawyer and social activist who became the symbol of law and human rights for the people of Indonesia.

Born in Banda Aceh on 25 May 1913, he was the grandson of a Chinese *Kapitan* who was an appointed leader of a Chinese group by the Dutch. Yap was the oldest of three children. He attended ELS, an elementary school for Dutch children where he became aware of racial discrimination. He continued his studies at Mulo, a Dutch secondary school, also in Banda Aceh. In 1929, he graduated from Mulo and moved to Java.

Yap entered AMS A-II in Yogyakarta where he completed his high school education in 1933. Due to a lack of funding, he then entered the Dutch Teachers' College for the Chinese in Jakarta. After graduating in 1934, he began his teaching career in various schools and later worked in the Lloyd's Insurance Company in Jakarta. Apparently, Yap found office work to be unsatisfactory. He then registered in a law school that had just opened in Batavia (now Jakarta). But before he could graduate from the law school, the Japanese had landed on Java. Yap was forced to leave his classes and returned to office work. In 1946 after the Japanese surrender, Yap travelled to Holland to study in Leiden. A year later, he obtained his law degree MR (Meester in de Rechten). From 1949 until the end of his life, Yap made law his profession.

Yap did not limit himself to legal matters only, however. He became involved in religious and social causes as well. He was active in Tionghoa Kie Tok Kauw Hwee (Chinese Christian Organization) in West Java. In 1950, Yap helped found the Indonesian Foundation for church education. He was also involved in setting up Baperki (the Consultative Council for Indonesian Citizenship), a mass organization for Chinese descent, on 13 March 1954 in Jakarta.

Yap came into conflict with Siauw Giok Tjhan over the naming of Baperki (for the discussion on this issue, see the section on "Siauw Giok Tjhan"). As the meeting was dominated by Siauw's group, Yap was not elected as the office bearer, but he continued to donate his labour and ideas to the organization. In 1955, he was eventually chosen as the 4th Vice Chairman of the central committee of Baperki. From 1956 to 1960, he was the first Vice Chairman of the central committee of Baperki.

However, he did not share Siauw's view on the "Chinese problem" in Indonesia. They eventually clashed in December 1960 when Yap accused Siauw of having taken Baperki from its neutral stance into the midst of the communist movement. In addition, Yap was critical of a clause in the 1945 Constitution that states the president of Indonesia has to be a "native Indonesian". To Yap, this clause was discriminatory and was in opposition to all that Baperki was striving for. The fact that Baperki needed Sukarno's support and that the 1945 Constitution would strengthen the president's position may have caused Siauw to adopt the attitude he did. Yap refused to back down. To him, the principle of Baperki's struggle was more important than the strategy used. In the end, Yap lost and resigned from his position as Vice Chairman of Baperki but remained as a regular member. Nevertheless, he was no longer active in the organization.

In fact, both Yap and Siauw were in agreement that the Chinese Indonesians should be allowed to retain their ethnicity. But they disagreed on the method of resolving the "ethnic problem". As Siauw was influenced by Marxism and Stalinism, he believed that ethnic issues could only be resolved in a socialist society. Therefore, he supported Sukarno on having a socialist revolution. Siauw argued that there were no more ethnic problems in socialist Soviet Union and China.[24] Yap as a Christian was in opposition to communism. He believed that the basic problem was with the human hearts and only through "the purification of human hearts" could the problem of racial/ethnic discrimination be solved.

Yap was against the assimilationist group. He also opposed to name-changing for Chinese Indonesians. In his view, the minority group had the right to preserve their tradition and culture and he considered name-changing a form of discrimination against the minority group.

Yap sympathized with the oppressed. He wanted to defend them. He once said that, "I do not just defend the accused but also truth and justice." He and a few lawyer friends in 1966 established the Lembaga Bantuan Hukum (LBH, Legal Aid Institute) to provide legal assistance to the poor. The LBH later became Yayasan Lembaga Bantuan Hukum Indonesia, which continues to offer legal aid to any Indonesian who needs it.

During the Sukarno era, Yap wrote an article calling for the release of political internees like Moh. Natsir, Moh. Roem and Sutan Syahrir. He also defended a Chinese man named Liem Koe Nio who was accused of economic subversion because he was stock-piling goods. Liem had been identified as a member of KMT (Kuomintang), a Taiwanese political organization opposed by Sukarno at that time. But during the Suharto period, Yap was appointed by the military court to defend Dr Subandrio who was alleged to have been involved in the so-called 30th September 1965 Movement/PKI coup. Yap's defense impressed the prosecution. Many were surprised that Yap would choose to represent a political opponent.

Yap's activities were not limited to Indonesia. In 1980, he became one of the founders of the Regional Council on Human Rights in Asia. Yap was also a member of the International Commission of Jurists

(Geneva). On 11 January 1980, he received an honorary doctorate from Vrije Universiteit (Netherlands) for his work on law. He also held many positions in the international organizations. On 24 April 1989, he died while he was attending an international meeting of INGI (a self-help organization of the nations that provide aid to Indonesia through IGGI).

Abdul Karim Oei (黄清兴, 1905–88)

Abdul Karim Oei (Oey), or Abdul Karim Oei Tjeng Hien as he was better known, was a Chinese Muslim who was active both before and after World War II.[25] Before moving to Jakarta, he was a Muhammadiyah leader in Bengkulu. He founded the Persatuan Islam Tionghoa Indonesia (PITI, Indonesian Chinese Muslim Association) and was part of the *dakwah* movement within the Chinese community.

Oei Tjeng Hien was a second-generation Chinese born in Padang in 1905. His father and mother came from Fujian (Hokkien) Province in Southern China and had migrated to Indonesia in the mid-nineteenth century. At the age of one, Oei was given into the care of foster parents. His adoptive father died, and he was subsequently returned to his natural parents. Oei's father was a successful merchant and sent his son to HCS, a Dutch school for Chinese children.

Perhaps as a result of his Dutch education, Oei became an Adventist Christian but, by his own admission, he never actually practised it. Oei did not continue his studies after graduating from HCS. He moved from Padang to Bintuhan and went into business there. He said that his Chinese soul and the influence of the Minangkabau made him want to leave home and become a merchant. He sold jewellery and other produce. Soon he came to be known as a superior trader and was able to afford a Chevrolet sedan. His work often took him to Jakarta.

The young Oei was searching for something in the world of religion. At first, he became a Buddhist and Confucian. Then he converted to Christianity.[26] Oei said that Adventist Christianity did not bring him inner peace, but he felt "the light of God began to illuminate my (his) soul".[27] Oei converted to Islam in 1931 when he was twenty-six. After conversion, he continued to study under Fikir Daud. After becoming a Muslim, Oei found that his relations with his family became distant, but his relationship with native Indonesians became closer, especially with the Sumatrans at his birthplace.

Oei became a Muslim in Bintuhan where he founded a branch of the Muhammadiyah organization. He had two ideas then—to set up a branch of the Indonesian Islamic Union Party (PSII) or of Muhammadiyah. Following the majority of the community, he eventually established Muhammadiyah in Bintuhan and was elected as its leader.[28]

Oei travelled around West Sumatra and Bengkulu where he met local figures such as Hasan Din, the father of Fatmawati and future father-in-law of Sukarno. In 1937, Sukarno was exiled to Bengkulu, but he remained active there. One day, he convened a meeting of the Muhammadiyah organization for the purpose of choosing a new consul as H. Junus Djamaluddin, the present consul, was seriously ill. Hasan Din suggested Oei Tjeng Hien of Bintuhan be the head. Sukarno agreed. Oei received a telegram asking him to sell his possessions in Bintuhan and move to Bengkulu. Oei became closely associated with Sukarno in Bengkulu. Finally, Sukarno asked Oei to propose to Fatmawati, Hasan Din's daughter, on his behalf.[29]

During the Japanese occupation of Indonesia, Oei was told to disband his organization but when he refused, the Japanese did not force him. When Japan surrendered and the Masyumi Party was founded, Oei became the party chief in Bengkulu.[30] When the Dutch initiated military actions in 1948, Oei and some other Masyumi figures became guerillas.

Oei continued to live in Bengkulu after Indonesia's independence and still served as Muhammadiyah consul. In 1952, he moved to Jakarta and, in the capital city, became a member of the Muhammadiyah Organization Board (1952–73). From 1957 to 1960, Oei was chosen to sit on the Masyumi Party Council.[31] He was also a member of parliament representing the Masyumi Party from 1957 to 1960.

After the Masyumi Party was disbanded, Oei founded the Indonesian Chinese Muslim Association (PITI) and was elected as its chairman. He began to sermonize within the Chinese community.

During the New Order period (1966–98), Oei introduced some new blood into the leadership hierarchy of PITI, while continuing to act as its chairman. Lt. General Sudirman was put in charge, and seven native

Indonesians, including Buya Hamka, were selected as advisors. The first vice chairman and the secretary general of PITI (H. Yunan Helmy Nasution and Major Achmad Johansjah) were native Indonesians as well. In other words, although PITI was a Chinese Muslim organization, its membership and administration were multiracial.

However, because of the total assimilation policy introduced by Suharto, in 1972 PITI was dissolved, ten days later (on 15 December 1972), a new organization called Pembina Iman Tauhid Islam (PITI, Organization for the Promotion of Religious Beliefs) was formed. Oei Tjeng Hien remained as its chairman until 1973, after which he served as its honorary advisor.

When Oei moved to Jakarta, he became involved in several companies. In 1952, he and Hasan Din set up PT Mega to import cloves and other commodities.[32] "Mega" was short for "Megawati", the name of Sukarno's daughter.

Another source states that Liem Sioe Liong, a tycoon, once helped Hasan Din when Sukarno's father-in-law was being sought by the Dutch. Hasan Din introduced Liem to several leaders of the Republic's army. And "during the Orde Lama period, he [Liem Sioe Liong] made Hasan Din director of several of his companies in Jakarta, among them PT Mega and Bank Central Asia".[33] It is not clear whether PT Mega belonged to Liem from its inception or whether it was bought by him later.

Oei served as the director of BCA Bank from 1955 to 1973 and, at the same time, was the first commissioner of the bank.[34] He also opened a factory producing Asli 777 T-shirts in 1962 and was its director until 1980. From 1964 to 1973, Oei was head of the Muhammadiyah Economic Council. In other words, he carried out his economic activities concurrently with his religious ones. From 1972 to 1979, he served as the director of PT Sumber Bengawan Mas.

Although Oei converted to Islam in 1931, he did not make a pilgrimage to Mecca until 1969 together with a group from HUSAMI (the Association of Indonesian Muslim Businessmen). HUSAMI was headed by Sjafruddin Prawiranegara. Two years earlier, Oei had been chosen by President Suharto to head the operations committee of the Istiqlal Mosque until 1974. He was an advisor of the Bakom PKB central

(Committee on the Understanding of National Unity) and was active in assimilation activities. Oei's wife and children, two daughters and a son, were also Muslim. Both his daughters married native Indonesians.

Oei died on 13 October 1988 in Jakarta at the age of eighty-three. He is recognized as an important Muslim figure in Indonesia. As Hamka noted, "He was a Muslim and a son of Indonesia ... who was fostered, nurtured and became a true Indonesian nationalist."[35]

Tan Cheng Lock (陈祯禄, 1883–1960)

Tan Cheng Lock is recognized as a Malaysian Chinese leader who contributed to the independence of Malaya and was considered by Tunku Abdul Rahman as "an outstanding patriot".[36]

Tan Cheng Lok was born in 1883 into a fifth-generation Peranakan Chinese family in Malacca. His father, Tan Keong Ann, was a businessman. Tan Cheng Lock was sent to Raffles College in Singapore and graduated in 1902. He was eager to study law in England but failed to obtain the Queen's Scholarship. Without the scholarship his family could not afford to send him overseas. Tan decided to stay at his alma mater as a teacher, teaching English literature for six years before returning to his birthplace.

In 1909 he returned to Malacca to work as an assistant manager at the Bukit Kajang Rubber Estate, and at the same time managed his family business. Later he found his own companies and became a successful businessman. In 1912 he was appointed as a member of the Malacca Municipal Council. In 1923 he was appointed as an unofficial member of the Legislative Council representing the Chinese community for twelve years. It was in this council that he urged for the end of discrimination against the Chinese in the civil service, the police force and in the immigration policy.

In the Chinese community, Tan was equally active. He revived the SCBA in 1915. However, he only became its chairman from 1928 to 1935. Like many Straits Chinese elite Tan was loyal to the British crown. In 1937 he was elected as a representative of the Straits Settlements to attend the coronation of King George VI. He was also knighted because of his long service to British Malaya.

Tan escaped to India when the Japanese occupied Malaya and stayed in India for four years (1942–46), where he met British officials and submitted memorials for the future of Malaya after occupation. It was during this period that he submitted a memorial to the Secretary of State for the Colonies, London, in 1945 which he argued:

> the future Government of Malaya should be to rally to its support those true Malayans, who passionately love the country as their homeland and those who intend to settle there, and who are united by the legitimate aspiration to achieve by proper and constitutional means the ideal and basic objective of Self-Government for a united Malaya within the British Commonwealth and Empire, in which the individuals of all communities are accorded equal rights and responsibilities, politically and economically ....[37]

When he was in India, he also formed the Overseas Chinese Association in exile. When he returned to Malaya after the Japanese surrender, he rejoined local politics and made contacts with the Malay politicians. When the Federation of Malaya was announced and Chinese Malayan citizenship was no longer guaranteed, Tan began to strive for Malayan citizenship for the Chinese. On 27 February 1949, he established the Malayan Chinese Association (MCA) and started to strive for Chinese interests.

It should be noted that Tan Cheng Lock was interested in a multiracial Malaya and hence preferred multiracial party rather than ethnic party. Jaafar Onn, the chairman of UMNO, wanted to open the membership of UMNO to all Malayans and proposed to change its name from the United Malays National Organization to the United Malayans National Organization, but he was not supported by UMNO members. As a result, Jaafar Onn left UMNO in 1951 and established a new party—the Independence of Malaya Party (IMP). His position was succeeded by Tunku Abdul Rahman. Jaafar Onn solicited the support of both Malay and non-Malay leaders.[38] Tan Cheng Lock joined the inauguration of the party and appealed to the Chinese to support the party.

However, Tan's position was opposed by many MCA leaders, especially Lau Pak Khuan from Perak. UMNO leaders wanted to form an alliance with the MCA in the municipal election of 1953. As ethnic feelings were strong and the MCA leaders preferred to cooperate with

UMNO rather than IMP, towards the end, Tan Cheng Lock backed down and formed an alliance in the municipal election and won the seats. This shows that in a plural society like Malaya, ethnic/racial feelings were too strong and the multiracial party concept did not gain much support in the 1950s.

Tan Cheng Lock was able to cooperate with the Malay leaders, especially Tunku Abdul Rahman. His efforts for racial harmony and his contribution to Malayan independence eventually won him the highest title of the land. In 1957 he was conferred the title of Tun.

However, Tan Cheng Lock's leadership was challenged in the MCA. During the 1957 MCA election, Tan was defeated by a young leader Lim Chong Eu and lost his chairmanship. Tan later retired from politics. He died in 1960 at the age of seventy-seven due to heart attack.

Lee Kuan Yew (李光耀, 1923–2015)

Lee Kuan Yew was the leader who shaped Singapore.[39] He was born into a Peranakan family in Singapore. His father was Semarang-born Lee Chin Koon and his mother Chua Jim Neo was English-educated and spoke to each other and to him in English,[40] while his paternal grandmother spoke to him in broken English and Javanese Malay.[41] He only learned Chinese when he entered politics. He noted that in 1955 during the assembly elections, he was challenged by his opponent in Tanjong Pagar to debate in Mandarin and Hokkien, but he was unable to do so and felt very embarrassed. From that time on, he began to learn Mandarin seriously.

In fact, Lee was sent to a traditional Chinese school for a short while but was uncomfortable there. He then went to Telok Kurau, an English-medium school. He later went to the Raffles Institution but before finishing his education at the Raffles College, the Japanese occupied Singapore. During the Japanese occupation he took on various jobs in order to survive. After the Japanese surrender, he went to Cambridge to study law for four years and earned first class honours and was called to the Bar. While in Cambridge he married Kwa Geok Choo, who was also a brilliant law graduate from Singapore.

After returning to Singapore, he first worked at a local British law firm and soon he and his wife established their own law firm named Lee & Lee. However, Lee became involved in local politics and served as the defense lawyer of many leaders of the trade union and student organizations who were in trouble. Influenced by Fabian Socialism, Lee, Goh Keng Swee, Toh Chin Chye and other English-educated Singaporeans established the People's Action Party (PAP) in 1954. Many left-wing Chinese-educated unionists and activists also joined the party. Therefore, initially the PAP was a leftist leaning party with the aim of getting self-government and eventually independence for Singapore. It should also be noted that the PAP aimed at building a multiracial and multilingual society.

At this juncture, it is worth noting that Lee Kuan Yew joined the SCBA soon after his return from England. He initially intended to use the Association as his political vehicle,[42] but he soon abandoned it.[43] Lee probably realized that SCBA was too conservative and too close to the colonial authorities. It is also too narrow in its basis as it excluded the Chinese-educated who formed a majority in Singapore then.

In the 1950s, the non-Communists and the pro-Communists were working together to gain independence for Singapore. However, after achieving self-government in 1959, there was a bitter struggle in the party between the anti-Communist and the pro-Communist groups. The former was represented by Lee Kuan Yew while the latter was represented by Lim Chin Siong. The PAP eventually split and the left-wing group established its own party—the Barisan Sosialis. This was in 1961.

As the pro-Communist Barisan Sosialis remained strong in Singapore politics, the Lee Kuan Yew-led PAP might not be able to defeat the Barisan Sosialis. Both Lee Kuan Yew and Tunku Abdul Rahman were concerned about the growing strength of the pro-Communist forces in Singapore and beyond. The merger with Malaya might be the way to defeat the Barisan Sosialis. Not surprisingly, the PAP was supportive of merger while the Barisan Sosialis was anti-merger. On 16 September 1963 Lee announced Singapore as part of Malaysia and on 21 September a general election was held in Singapore. This was seen as a struggle between the pro-Malaysia and anti-Malaysia camps.[44] PAP gained 47.4

per cent of the votes (43 seats) while the Barisan Sosialis obtained 32.1 per cent (13 seats).[45]

Nevertheless, after the merger, Lee's concept of "Malaysia for Malaysians" and Tunku's concept of "Malaysia for the Malays" came into conflict, leading to the departure of Singapore from Malaysia. Singapore became an independent state on 9 August 1965.

Nevertheless, Lee recognized that Singapore is in the Malay seas, and therefore, Malay is retained as the national language but the Singapore Government accepted four official languages, namely English, Chinese, Malay and Tamil. However, soon after independence, Kheng Chin Hock of the Singapore Chinese Chamber of Commerce demanded that Mandarin be made the first language among the official languages. Lee saw this as a suggestion which would create racial tension and political instability. He was of the view that in a multiracial Singapore, English, not Mandarin, should be the working language or common language of the people.[46] But he recognized the importance of Mandarin for Chinese Singaporeans and hence advocated "bilingual education". Bilingualism in fact was already in the PAP constitution since its inception.

Lee noted that his English-educated colleagues within the PAP also shared his thinking that their children should not forget their Chinese roots but "English had to be the working language of the country."[47] He further argued:

> There was a need to preserve the Chinese language. [But] we know that Chinese could never be made the common language of Singapore, we were in a sea of the Malays. We would not be able to link up with the international community if we chose Chinese. To top it all, we would be seen by the British as a vanguard of the Chinese Communist Party.[48]

Based on this thinking, the Singapore educational system also moved towards this direction. Understandably, with the exception of the Malay madrasah, all Singapore's national schools used English as the medium of instruction. This also affected the university education. Nanyang University began to change its medium of instruction in 1975 and merged with the University of Singapore in 1980 to become the National University of Singapore.

However, at the elementary and secondary school levels, vernacular languages—they are often called mother tongues—have become the second language. Each Singaporean has to learn his/her mother tongue as defined by the state. This is because Lee discovered that English-educated Chinese often lost their culture and hence experienced "deculturalization". He said that he had realized it when he was in England. Therefore, he sent his three children to Chinese schools up to the secondary school level.[49]

It is also worth noting that initially Lee Kuan Yew's Singapore adopted the melting pot policy. He would like to make Singapore a nation without referring much to one's ethnic background. However, this is impossible. His son Lee Hsien Loong eventually abandoned the melting pot policy and argued that Singapore would remain a plural society.

However, with the rise of China, Lee Kuan Yew became aware of the importance of the Chinese language for Chinese Singaporeans. Towards the end of his life, he established the Lee Kuan Yew Fund for Bilingualism, placing emphasis on pre-school bilingual education.[50] Although it is not confined to the Chinese language, but as the majority of the population in Singapore are Chinese, it seems that the Chinese language might gain the most benefit.

In *Great Peranakans: Fifty Remarkable Lives*, the profile on Lee Kuan Yew ended with the following sentences:

> Lee never publicly declared himself a Peranakan, since his chief concern for the nation was to foster a collective sense of identity that would surmount ethnic divisions. Nonetheless, his wife said: "Both Kuan Yew and I come from Peranakan families, speaking no Chinese, not even dialect."[51]

This background is important. If we look at Lee's language policy and Singapore's cultural and national identity, his vision is indeed a Peranakan one.

Conclusion

Examining Peranakan leaders during the colonial era, apart from the colonial factor, the size and socio-cultural background of the Peranakan community in each country also serves as an important factor in shaping their political thinking and national identity. In Indonesia, the number of Peranakan Chinese was larger in Java but smaller in the Outer Islands, and the socio-cultural background of the Peranakan Chinese leaders was more diversified. Therefore, the political and national identity of the Peranakans appeared to be more complex than those in Malaya and Singapore.

In pre-World War II Indonesia, Kan Hok Hoei who was Dutch-educated and a landlord, was very pro-Dutch and identified himself with the Dutch colonial power. He led the CHH, a conservative Peranakan Chinese organization. His political stand was also conservative and represented the interest of the Peranakan upper class. Initially he was not linked to China, but later when his economic interest was tied to China, he moved closer to China but his political loyalty remained towards the Dutch colonial government. He was different from Peranakan leaders who were journalists and came from the middle class such as Tjoe Bou San and Liem Koen Hian.

From the beginning, Tjoe Bou San was influenced by overseas Chinese nationalism and identified himself with China. He considered the Peranakan Chinese as part of the Chinese nation. Tjoe and his Sin Po Group rejected the Dutch "nationality" (in fact it should be called "Subject-ship") and refused to get involved in colonial politics and administration. But he passed away in 1925 when Chinese nationalism was at its peak. Liem Koen Hian, a Peranakan leader and journalist, was initially imbued with overseas Chinese nationalism and anti-Dutch colonialism, but he later became Dutch East Indies oriented and attempted to be associated with the CHH. But he soon broke up with the CHH and became the champion of Indonesian nationalism. His Indonesian nationalist stand and left-wing ideology made him a target of the Chinese nationalists, pro-Dutch colonialist, Peranakan Chinese, and the colonial authorities. Yet towards the end of his life, his Indonesian nationalism was being challenged by the right-wing Indonesian nationalists after Indonesia achieved independence.

The situation in Malaya and Singapore differed. The number of Peranakans was small and their Chinese cultural identity appeared to be stronger. There was no intensive assimilation like in Java where the term Peranakan at one time was used to refer to the Muslim Chinese. Moreover, there was a strong Indonesian nationalist movement in colonial

Indonesia, but there was no such movement in Malaya and Singapore. The independence of Malaya and Singapore was gained without a revolution. Besides this, the Peranakan Chinese were cultivated by the British colonial power to support the colonial regime. Many argued that they became "compradors" and were proud of being "King's Chinese". But the Dutch were less successful in cultivating the Peranakans to side with the colonial power as anti-colonial movement was strong among the Peranakans.

In British Malaya and Singapore, especially in the Straits Settlements, a Peranakan Chinese Christian leader Song Ong Siang was beholden to the British residents for his English education. He was awarded the Queen's Scholarship to study in England. He and other Peranakan leaders established the SCBA and declared his loyalty to the British crown. Song who was a lawyer was proud of being a "King's Chinese". His contemporary Lim Boon Keng who was a physician was also loyal to the British crown. But Lim Boon Keng's interest in Confucianism eventually led him to identify with China. He even went to China to serve as the Vice-Chancellor of the Xiamen University. After 1937 he returned to Singapore and during the Japanese occupation, he was forced to collaborate with the Japanese which made him a controversial figure. He withdrew from social life after the Japanese surrender.

If during the colonial era the political and national identities of the Peranakan Chinese in British Malaya and Singapore were between the colonial power and China, in colonial Indonesia the Peranakan Chinese were faced with more challenges: Dutch colonialism, Chinese nationalism and Indonesian nationalism. As there was no revolutionary Malay nationalist movement in Malaya and Singapore, and China and the colonial power were not yet antagonistic, the Peranakan's dual loyalty in Malaya and Singapore was not much a problem, but this is not the case with the Peranakans in Indonesia as the anti-colonialist movement became a mainstream during and after the 1945 revolution.

By this time, the pro-Indonesian nationalist group had become prominent. However, the birth of the People's Republic of China had an impact on the Peranakan Chinese in Indonesia. Siauw Giok Tjhan who was a journalist and political activist, identified himself with the

Indonesian nationalists, and later became an admirer of socialist China. His Marxist ideology pushed him closer to the left-wing Sukarno as well as Chairman Mao. He strived for an Indonesian Chinese identity, with a component of Chinese culture. He wanted the Chinese in Indonesia to be united, and refused to separate the Peranakans from the *totoks*. His organization Baperki also rejected the assimilation of the Chinese Indonesians into the indigenous population and favoured the realization of a socialist Indonesia.

This is different from another Peranakan leader, Yap Thiam Hien. Yap was a teacher and later became a lawyer, and was a staunch Christian who was critical of socialism/communism. Although a leader of the Baperki before 1960, he appeared to side with the Peranakans rather than the *totoks*. He agreed with the idea that the Peranakan Chinese should not be forced to merge with the indigenous Indonesians, but was more concerned with the human rights issue. He succeeded in championing for the establishment of the Legal Aid Institute to help the poor, regardless of race. Yap had defended various clients regardless of their ethnic background, class and ideology. Although not against natural assimilation, he strongly opposed "forced assimilation" and "elimination of ethnic identity" as this was against his belief.

Another Peranakan leader, Abdul Karim Oei (Oei Tjeng Hien), who was a businessman, was not against assimilation but was an advocate of Chinese conversion to Islam. After conversion he became close to the indigenous population and was elected chairman of the Muhammadiyah (Bengkulu). He became close to Sukarno when Sukarno was in exile in Sumatra. He also collaborated with the indigenous political elite. Karim Oei later established the Persatuan Islam Tionghoa Indonesia (PITI, Indonesian Chinese Muslim Association), making distinction between the Chinese Muslims and non-Chinese Muslims, yet in the organization, the indigenous Indonesians could join and held high positions.

While in Indonesia the number of Peranakans was significant, it is not the case in independent Malaya/Malaysia and Singapore. The Peranakan Chinese were overwhelmed by the migrant Chinese majority. Moreover, the number of Chinese was large in comparison to the Malay population in Singapore. These factors, of course, would influence the thinking and identities of the post-war Peranakan leaders.

Peranakan leader Tan Cheng Lock who received an English education in Singapore, did not have the opportunity for tertiary education. However, being in Malaya and working for a foreign company and later founding his own companies, he was able to make a fortune for himself. However, he was aware that Malaya was moving towards independence. While declaring loyalty to the British crown, Tan was aware that he needed to protect his own Chinese group. Although he was a leader of the SCBA, he knew that he needed a new political party to represent the Malayan Chinese rather than just the Peranakans. A few years prior to independence, Tan established the MCA to promote the Malayan Chinese interests, especially gaining Malayan citizenship for all local-born Chinese. When the multiracial party of MIP was established, he joined the party function while remaining in MCA. But MIP was unpopular among the Malays. Tan eventually collaborated with Tunku's UMNO in the assembly election and won the seats for MCA. He was the one who led the Chinese towards independence. But his leadership was soon challenged and he was defeated by a younger group in the MCA.

A Cambridge-trained lawyer Lee Kuan Yew was another Peranakan leader who eventually led Singapore towards independence. He too initially wanted to use SCBA as a political vehicle but immediately realized its limitations, and instead formed the PAP in 1954. He was the one who advocated for a multiracial and multilingual Singapore. But when it came to his political and national identity, it became clear that he was in favour of using English as the working language/common language and Mandarin as the mother tongue of the Chinese. He was in opposition to the Chinese-educated who wanted to use Chinese as the main language of the island state. It was under Lee that a national education system of Singapore was established and bilingualism was promoted.

From the above brief description and analyses, it is clear that the political and national identities of the Peranakan leaders are rooted in the local culture but with different degrees of Chineseness. However, Western culture also played an important role. Nevertheless, it was the condition of the country that they lived in which shaped their different identities.

Notes

1. Claudine Salmon, *Literature in Malay by the Chinese of Indonesia: A Provisional Annotated Bibliography*, Etudes Insulindies-archipel 3 (Paris: Éditions de la Maison des sciences de l_'Homme, 1981), pp. 362–63.

2. Kan's biography is mainly based on Leo Suryadinata, *Prominent Chinese Indonesian: Biographical Sketches*, 4th ed. (Singapore: Institute of Southeast Asian Studies, 2015), pp. 86–87, and Mary Somers Heidhues, "Kan Hok Hoei", in *Southeast Asian Personalities of Chinese Descent: A Biographical Dictionary*, Vol. 1, edited by Leo Suryadinata (Singapore: Institute of Southeast Asian Studies, 2012), pp. 393–95.

3. For a brief biography of Liem Koen Hian, see Suryadinata, *Prominent Chinese Indonesian*, 4th ed., pp. 151–52.

4. Liem Koen Hian, "Ka-Indonesierschap", *Sin Tit Po*, 2 April 1930.

5. Liem Koen Hian, "Haloean Kita II", *Sin Tit Po*, 10 April 1930.

6. Liem Koen Hian, "Haloean Kita IV", *Sin Tit Po*, 12 April 1930.

7. Ibid.

8. Liem Koen Hian, "Sekali Lagi boeat Toean Soedarjo Tjokrosisworo", *Sin Tit Po*, 25 August 1936.

9. Liem Koen Hian, "Causerie Pikiran Indonesia dan Peranakan Tionghoa", *Djawa Tengah*, 11–12 October 1932.

10. This biography relied heavily on Song Ong Siang's book, *One Hundred Years' History of the Chinese in Singapore* (with an introduction by Edwin Lee) (Singapore: Oxford University Press, 1984), pp. 234–38; also Li Yuan Jin (李元瑾, Lee Guan Kin), *Dongxi wenhua de zhuangji yu Xinhua zhishifenzhi de sanzhong huiying* 东西文化的撞击与新华知识份子的三种回应 (Singapore: Department of Chinese Studies, NUS and Global Publishing Co, 2001). Lee's book was based on her PhD dissertation submitted to the Hong Kong University, an in-depth study on three Singapore Chinese leaders, namely Khoo Seok Guan, Lim Boon Keng and Song Ong Siang. I have also relied on the information provided in the book.

11. Ibid., p. 266. However, another source noted that he embraced Christianity. See *Great Peranakans: Fifty Remarkable Lives* (Singapore: Asian Civilisations Museum, 2015), https://www.nhb.gov.sg/peranakanmuseum/~/media/tpm/document/exhibitions/english%20gallery%20guide.pdf (accessed 25 April 2021).

12. For a brief description of the Straits Chinese Magazine, see https://eresources.nlb.gov.sg/infopedia/articles/SIP_2015-10-19_160335.html (accessed 21 April 2021).

13. Ibid., p. 267.

14. Song, *One Hundred Years' History of the Chinese in Singapore*, pp. 237–38.

15. "Straits Chinese Reform 3—The Education for Chinese", 1899, p. 103. This is the English translation of Li Yuan Jin's book which was written in Chinese.

16. For a brief and insightful biography of Song Ong Siang, see Edwin Lee, "Introduction", in *One Hundred Years' History of the Chinese in Singapore*, pp. v–xiv. See also Kevin Y.L. Tan, "The King's Chinese: The Life of Sir Song Ong Siang", *BiblioAsia*, 1 April 2020, https://biblioasia.nlb.gov.sg/vol-16/issue-1/apr-jun-2020/king (accessed 22 April 2021). This section benefitted from the above essays. Song Ong Siang also wrote about himself in his book (1984 edition), pp. 242–47.

17. Lee, "Introduction", in *One Hundred Years' History of the Chinese in Singapore*, 2004 edition, p. viii.

18. Tan, "The King's Chinese".

19. For a brief biography of Siauw Giok Tjhan, see Leo Suryadinata, *Prominent Chinese Indonesian: Biographical Sketches*, 4th ed. (Singapore: Institute of Southeast Asian Studies, 2015), pp. 247–48; see also Siauw Tiong Djin, *Siauw Giok Tjhan: Bicultural Leader in Emerging Indonesia* (Victoria: Monash University Publishing, 2018) for a full biography of Siauw.

20. This was often miswritten as the Minister for Minority Affairs (Menteri Urusan Minoritas). See Siauw Tiong Djin, *Perjuangan seorang Patriot membangun Nasion Indonesia dan masyarakat Bhineka Tunggal Ika* (Jakarta: Hasta Mitra, 1999), p. 109.

21. Siauw denied that he was a member of the illegal PKI. See Siauw Tiong Djin, *Siauw Giok Tjhan: Bicultural Leader in Emerging Indonesia*, p. 24. "However, being close to its prominent members like Tan [Ling Djie] and Amir Sjarifuddin, he was probably involved in some of the party meetings and activities." See ibid., p. 25.

22. Some argued that *Harian Rakjat* became the PKI organ only after the departure of Siauw, although many PKI leaders had already worked in *Harian Rakyat* under Siauw. The announcement in the newspaper when Siauw left noted that there was only a change of management, and not the ideology of the paper.

23. See his letter sent to *Star Weekly*, 1960. Siauw did not know that the ethnic problem was unsolved in these two countries. The Soviet Union eventually disintegrated into ethnic states.

24. Siauw was not aware that the USSR was dissolved due to ethnic issues and China has been troubled by ethnic problem.

25. Most of the information has been taken from Oei's autobiography entitled *Mengabdi Agama, Nusa dan Bangsa: Sahabat Karib Bung Karno* (Jakarta: Gunung Agung, 1982).

26. *Apa dan Siapa: Sejumlah Orang Indonesia 1985-86* (Jakarta: Grafitipers, 1986), p. 618.

27. Oey's autobiography, p. 14.

28. "H. Abdul Karim Oei: Pengabdi Agama, Bangsa dan tanah Air", *Kiblat*, No. 2/XXX (1982): 11–13.

29. Oey's autobiography, pp. 90–96. In Fatmawati's memoirs, she mentioned that Oey helped Sukarno approached her and "H. Abdul Karim [Oey] ... was Bung Karno's closest friend." See Fatmawati, *Catatan Kecil Bersama Bung Karno* (Part 1) (Jakarta: Sinar Harapan, 1983), pp. 45–48.
30. "H. Abdul Karim Oei: Pengabdi Agama, Bangsa dan tanah Air", *Kiblat*, No. 2/XXX (1982): 18.
31. Oei's autobiography, p. 245.
32. Junus Jahja, *Kisah-kisah Saudara Baru* (Jakarta: Yayasan Ukhuwah Islamiah, c.1988), p. 150.
33. Eddy Soetriyono, *Kisah Sukses Liem Sioe Liong* (Jakarta: Indomedia, 1989), pp. 10–11.
34. Oei's autobiography, p. 245.
35. "Dakwah dan Asimilasi" (Brochure) (Jakarta, 1979), pp. 11–12.
36. Some information on Tan Cheng Lock has been taken from "Tan Cheng Lock: Learned Politician", in Wang Chen Fa (王琛发), *Wei wanshi kai taiping: Chen Zhen Lu sixiang guoji yantaohui lunwenji* 为万世开太平: 陈祯禄思想国际研讨会论文集 (Kuala Lumpur: MCA School of Political Studies, 2007), pp. 39–51; see also Yeo Siew Siang, *Tan Cheng Lock: The Straits Legislator and Chinese Leader* (Petaling Jaya: Pelanduk Publications, 1990); and *Great Peranakans: Fifty Remarkable Lives*.
37. "Tun Tan Cheng Lock", https://img.mca.org.my/MCA/article/bd571db3-6bb3-4483-904e-0fcd46e6edb0.pdf (accessed 22 April 2021).
38. For a discussion on this event, see Khoo Kay Kim, "The Making of Malaya, 1946–1955: The Fruits of Ethnic Cooperation", in *Malaysian Chinese and Nation-Building: Before Merdeka and Fifty Years After*, edited by Voon Phin Keong (Kuala Lumpur: Centre for Chinese Studies, 2007), pp. 142–44.
39. This section is merely an interpretative short essay on Lee Kuan Yew with special reference to his thinking on political and national identity, using second sources.
40. Lee Kuan Yew, *My Lifelong Challenge: Singapore Bilingual Journey* (Singapore: Straits Times Press, 2012), pp. 24–25.
41. Ibid., p. 25.
42. See Kwa Chong Guan, "Political Dilemma and Transformation of the Straits-born Chinese Community: The Era of Decolonization", in *Peranakan Communities in the Era of Decolonization and Globalization*, edited by Leo Suryadinata (Singapore: Chinese Heritage Centre and NUS Baba House, 2015), p. 19.
43. Ibid.
44. Yeo Kim Wah and Albert Lau, "From Colonialism to Independence 1945–1965", in *A History of Singapore*, edited by Ernest C.T. Chew and Edwin Lee (Singapore: Oxford University Press, 1991), pp. 142–43.

45. Ibid. It is worth noting that several months before the election, the Internal Security Council launched the Operation Cold Store which led to the detention of Lim Chin Siong and twenty-three other Barisan Sosialis members.

46. Lee Kuan Yew, *My Lifelong Challenge: Singapore Bilingual Journey* (Singapore: Straits Times Press, 2012), pp. 60–61.

47. Ibid., p. 42.

48. Ibid.

49. Ibid., pp. 34–35.

50. Amelia Teng, "Lee Kuan Yew Fund for Bilingualism supports another nine proposals", *Straits Times*, 20 August 2015, https://www.straitstimes.com/singapore/education/lee-kuan-yew-fund-for-bilingualism-supports-another-nine-proposals (accessed 28 April 2021).

51. Alan Chong, eds., "Lee Kuan Yew 李光耀", in *Great Peranakans: Fifty Remarkable Lives* (Singapore: Asian Civilisations Museum, 2015), https://www.nhb.gov.sg/peranakanmuseum/~/media/tpm/document/exhibitions/english%20gallery%20guide.pdf (accessed 25 April 2021).

9

PROSPECTS OF THE PERANAKAN COMMUNITY: COMMENTS ON DR TAN TA SEN'S SPEECH*

The Four Periods

Dr Tan Ta Sen, President of the International Zheng He Society (Singapore), gave a speech to the Peranakan Chinese Association in Melaka in 2013, arguing that the "Peranakan [Chinese] community was born during the Cheng Ho [Zheng He] and Western colonial eras. Their main characteristics was at first being localized (indigenized-Malay or Indonesian), then Westernized during the colonial era, and re-Sinicized at the present national stage".

He divided the Chinese migrations to Melaka and Southeast Asia into "four periods", the first of which being the "Cheng Ho and [early] colonial period". Although he did not mention the years of this specific period, I believe he refers to 1405–1643. That is because 1405 was Zheng He's first voyage while 1643 was the end of the Ming dynasty. He also argued that this was the period when the Peranakan Chinese community came into being in Southeast Asia, and the characteristic of this period is the "localization" of the Chinese. However, the Zheng

He period in fact was very brief, i.e. 1405–33. After the demise of Zheng He, the Ming dynasty abandoned the expeditions and China began to be inward looking again. From the post-Zheng He period up to 1643, the Portuguese, Spanish and Dutch came to colonize maritime Southeast Asia.

The second period in Dr Tan's speech was from 1644 (the beginning of the Qing or Manchu dynasty) to 1840 (the eruption of the Opium War in China). During this period, i.e. between the seventeenth and nineteenth centuries, Southeast Asia countries were colonized by the West. Many Chinese who did not want to live under the Manchu rule left for Southeast Asia; some took refuge in Melaka and became the Peranakans. Dr Tan argued that the Peranakan Chinese culture was in fact a fusion of the "Chinese, Western and Malay cultures".

The third period, still in the nineteenth century, was after the Opium War (1840). China was then in turmoil and the Chinese came to Southeast Asia in large numbers for better economic opportunity. The number of Chinese new migrants outnumbered the Peranakans, and the Peranakans began to be "re-Sinicized".

The fourth period started since World War II and lasted until now. Dr Tan argued that the re-Sinicization process which characterized this period remained till the present day. But the process was interrupted by the nation-building projects which took place after the war. In Malaya/ Malaysia they were caught between Chinese nationalism and Malayan/ Malaysian nationalism. However, in the twenty-first century, because of the influx of a large number of new Chinese migrants, the Peranakans once again experienced re-Sinicization.

Dr Tan's periodization of the Chinese migrations to Southeast Asia is interesting, but a bit confusing; many might not share his system of periodization. For one thing, the Zheng He period is very brief; while the fourth period is too long. One can argue that the rise of China in the late twentieth century and the new wave of Chinese migrants known as *xin yimin* (新移民) should actually be seen as a new period. Unlike the previous Chinese migrations, this new wave of migrants mostly went to the developed countries, and according to some estimates only less than 20 per cent of them came to Southeast Asia, with the bulk of this group residing in Singapore. It is also arguable whether these

Chinese migrants have flooded Malaysia as the country imposes strict immigration policy on the citizens of mainland China.

"Localization", "Westernization" and "Re-Sinicization"

Nevertheless, Dr Tan's overall argument is thought-provoking as it points out that in general, the Peranakan Chinese community originated during the Zheng He period (1405–33) in Melaka, with the "localization" taking place during that period, but after the arrival of the West (post-1511) the Peranakan Chinese community encountered Westernization; and later in the nineteenth century the number of Chinese migrants outnumbered the Peranakans and there was a re-Sinicization process. Nevertheless, after World War II, all Southeast Asian countries attained independence, and the Peranakans were caught between nation-building and re-Sinicization. At the "national stage", Dr Tan argued that because of the presence of large numbers of new Chinese migrants, the Peranakan Chinese continue to experience re-Sinicization rather than "localization". Let us examine some of the arguments made by Dr Tan in his speech.

As the speech which he presented to the Peranakan Chinese Association in Melaka is not intended to be an academic paper, it is understandable that it need not be rigidly structured and equipped with footnotes. There were also no references to the works of other scholars. Moreover, many key terms, such as "localization", "Westernization" and "re-Sinicization", used in the speech were also not properly defined. Even the term "Peranakan" has not been elaborated.

Therefore, perhaps it is useful for us to examine the term "Peranakan [Chinese]" before we proceed further. Dr Tan was correct in saying that in Malaya and Singapore, the terms Baba and Nyonya/Nonya were more commonly used, while Peranakan was more often used in Indonesia, only to be adopted later in Malaysia and Singapore. Dr Tan maintains that the term refers to the foreigners (e.g. Chinese) who have experienced "localization", namely Malaya-nized, indigenized or Indonesia-nized. He did not explain what is Malaya-nized and Indonesia-nized. Does it mean that it is a process by which a Chinese was to become a Malay or Indonesian and abandoned all his original ethnic characteristics? Or was it simply for him to adopt some Malay/Indonesian features but still remains outside the boundary of the Malay/Indonesian ethnic group?

The original meaning of Peranakan refers to the offspring of a marriage between a foreigner male and a Malay/Indonesia female, or vice versa. However, if the female is a foreigner and the male a Malay/indigenous Indonesian, the Peranakan offspring from this pattern of marriage will often be absorbed into the Malay or indigenous Indonesian community; and he or she is more likely to become a member of the Malay/Indonesian community rather than that of the independent Peranakan community.

The Peranakan Chinese are supposed to be mixed blood, but these inter-racial marriages were likely to be something in the distant past when the male Chinese came to Southeast Asia without their spouses, and they had to marry local Malay/Indonesian women as there were no (or not enough) Chinese women around. After that period, there is no more intermarriage of this pattern. The more important defining trait of the Peranakan Chinese is actually their cultural characteristics. Many Peranakan Chinese had lost their command of the Chinese language and use the local language or creolized Malay as their medium of communication. Their daily life and customs had also been indigenized but they did not lose their Chinese characteristics. In the Malay archipelagos, the Peranakan Chinese formed an intermediate group between the Chinese migrant community and the indigenous population. However, the identity of these Peranakans were/are still Chinese. Professor Tan Chee Beng (CB Tan) called this process "localization" rather than "acculturation".[1]

Peranakan Chinese

It is also essential to remember that the so-called Peranakan community is not confined to Malacca, in fact one can also find them in the Straits Settlements such as Penang and Singapore. CB Tan even maintained that in Kelantan and Terengganu, there are "Peranakan-type Chinese", although they may not call themselves "Peranakan".[2]

There is also a large number of Peranakan Chinese in Indonesia, southern Philippines and southern Thailand. But here we will focus our discussion on three countries: Malaysia, Singapore and Indonesia.

Nevertheless, if we examine the characteristics of these three Peranakan communities carefully, we will see that their Malay-ness and Indonesian-ness are different in degree. The Penang Peranakan Chinese, for instance, are different from those in Malacca as the former used a mixture of Hokkien and Malay as their medium of communication rather than the so-called Baba Malay. The Peranakans in Java are the most Indonesia-nized compared to those "Peranakans" in Sumatra and Kalimantan where certain Chinese dialects are still used in their daily communication.

In addition, the meaning of "Peranakan" also changes from period to period. In colonial Indonesia during the eighteenth century and certain period of the nineteenth century, Peranakan Chinese were referred to as Chinese Muslims. But coming to the twentieth century, the term does not have the religious connotation anymore. It simply refers to the local-born Chinese who speak the local language and adopt local or both local and Western ways of life.

Peranakan Chinese since Zheng He?

Dr Tan mentioned in his speech that the Zheng He period witnessed the birth of the Peranakan Chinese community in Malacca, but elsewhere he mentioned that when Zheng He was in Malacca, the number of the Chinese was too small to form a community.[3] In fact, in many of CB Tan's writings which discuss the Chinese of the Zheng He period, it is noted that the Peranakan Chinese did not originate in the Zheng He era. He argues that there is a lack of historical evidence to back this claim and suggests that it may simply be a myth.[4]

It is worth noting that during the Zheng He period, Ma Huan and Gong Zhen had noted that in other parts of Southeast Asia, such as Java and Sumatra, there was already the existence of Chinese enclaves. Nevertheless, these Chinese were mainly Muslims rather than Confucians, Taoists or Buddhists. Some of them remained as Peranakan but the majority might have been assimilated into the local community and disappeared. That is because very few (if any) present day Peranakan Chinese families can trace their family trees to the early fifteenth century! The same could have happened in Malacca. I believe that Dr Tan would also agree with this argument as he mentioned that during the Zheng He and early colonial periods, the "localization" process had already taken place. I suspect that he actually meant a total "assimilation" process had taken place as many Peranakans eventually became "natives". It is difficult, if not impossible, to find any Peranakan Chinese in the twentieth century who is descendant of a Peranakan family from the Zheng He period.

During the height of Western colonialism there were a lot of new Chinese migrants (known as either *singkeh* or *totoks*) in Southeast Asia and the colonialists introduced the "divide and rule" policy, using race as the important social/ethnic marker to differentiate the population. Intermarriages between the Chinese male and Malay female were drastically reduced. By the nineteenth century the sexual/gender ratio of the Peranakan Chinese society was almost equal and the Peranakan Chinese married among themselves.[5] For the case of Malaya and Singapore, CB Tan has argued that the Peranakan Chinese either married among themselves or the Peranakan females married the new male Chinese migrants.[6]

Re-Sinicization of the Peranakan?

At the turn of the twentieth century there was a rise of overseas Chinese nationalism and many new Chinese migrants who were in Southeast Asia were also influenced by the movement. Many Chinese began to be China-oriented. In Indonesia and Malaya/Singapore, Chinese education flourished. In the Dutch East Indies, the Dutch responded to this by offering Dutch education to the Peranakan Chinese; whereas in the Straits Settlements, the British had already offered some English education to the Peranakans. One can see that the Peranakan Chinese community was thus divided by different educational background. Nevertheless, it became clear that those who had the privilege to receive a Western education were from the better off group, while those who went to Chinese schools were from the less affluent group. And the Chinese elite of the colonial period were often derived from the group of Western-educated Peranakans.

It is often believed that by attending Chinese-medium schools a Peranakan is undergoing the process of "re-Sinification". That is to say, the Peranakan Chinese have been transformed into migrant Chinese again in terms of their daily use of the Chinese language and adoption of migrant Chinese culture. However, this may not be the case. That is because many Peranakans, despite receiving a Chinese-education, continued to speak the local language at home and adopt a non-migrant Chinese lifestyle. Perhaps the situation in Malaya/Singapore on the one hand and Java/Indonesia on the other hand is rather different as the Peranakans in Malaya/Singapore continued to form a minority among the Chinese population, while in Indonesia, at least in Java, the Peranakans formed the majority of the Chinese population.

After independence, there has been the process of nation-building in Southeast Asia. For the Chinese population in Indonesia and Malaya (Malaysia)/Singapore, both the children of *singkeh* (*totoks* or foreign-born Chinese-speaking Chinese) and Peranakans have been influenced by the nation-building process. While the Indonesian nation model was based on indigenization, the nation-models in Malaya (Malaysia)/ Singapore were more pluralistic. Nevertheless, in Malaya/Malaysia, the model has a strong dosage of Malay-ness, because of this, citizenship rather than nationhood had been stressed.

In Indonesia, during the Sukarno's era, despite the indigenese-base of the nation, the idea of "total assimilation" of the Chinese into the indigenous society was not popular among the local born Chinese. In 1963 President Sukarno began to propose the new concept of the Indonesian nation (*Bangsa Indonesia*). He noted in the 8th National Congress of Baperki (the Consultative Council for Indonesian Citizenship) that Indonesians consist of various *sukus* (ethnic groups), which included suku Peranakan Tionghoa (Peranakan Chinese ethnic group).[7] Sukarno considered the "Peranakan Tionghoa" (Peranakan Chinese), not any Chinese Indonesian, as member of the Indonesian nation. This also shows that the "integration degree" of the Peranakan Chinese into the Indonesian society is significant. This concept allows the Peranakan Chinese to remain as they are without being absorbed into the indigenous population.

Unfortunately, when Suharto (1966–98) came to power, this Sukarno "policy" was abandoned, instead he introduced a "total assimilation policy" and urged the Chinese Indonesians to be "assimilated" into the

Indonesian "indigenous society" without delay. During his thirty-two years of ruling the country, Suharto abolished the three cultural pillars of the ethnic Chinese in Indonesia: Chinese media, Chinese schools and ethnic Chinese organizations. Under this kind of situation, it was impossible for the Chinese Indonesians to be "re-Sinicized". On the contrary, non-Peranakan Chinese had instead been transformed into Peranakans, or at least, becoming more akin to the Peranakan population.

The situation in Malaya/Malaysia is different. Some observers such as John Clammer noted that there was a "re-Sinicization" process in Malaysia in the sense that many Peranakan Chinese sent their children to Chinese-medium schools.[8] By doing so, these Peranakan Chinese started to learn Chinese again. It seems that the domestic situation contributed to this process. In Malaysia, especially after the departure of Singapore from the Federation, there was racial polarization. The Peranakan Chinese being the intermediate group was caught in between. They were pushed into the migrant Chinese side. Some began to pick up the Chinese language but the transformation was slow and many remained as Peranakan and Western educated. Nevertheless, these Peranakans as a group were not transformed into a Mandarin-speaking community.

The Singapore situation is the most interesting. Since the introduction of mother tongue language as a second language in the school curriculum, all Chinese Singaporeans, including the Peranakan Chinese, have to learn Mandarin as a second language. Although the standards are not high, many who were unable to cope went overseas for education. Some even migrated to Western countries for the sake of their children's education. Of course, the majority stayed in Singapore but they were not transformed into Mandarin-speaking Peranakans either. Some Peranakans have acquired some knowledge about the Chinese culture/language but they remain as Peranakan as they have a better command of the English language. One can also notice that the Singapore Peranakans differ from their Malaysian counterpart in terms of their knowledge of the Malay language. While the younger generation of Peranakan Chinese in Malaysia know and speak Malay, the younger generation of Singapore Peranakan Chinese can no longer speak the Malay language.

The Rise of China and the Peranakan

What about the recent development? With the rise of China in the late twentieth century and a new wave of Chinese migrants to the West and Southeast Asia, have the Peranakan Chinese in the three countries that we mentioned been re-Sinicized?

As stated earlier, more new Chinese immigrants went to the developed countries (North America, Europe, Japan, Australia and New Zealand) than to Southeast Asia. With the exception of Singapore, Indonesia and Malaysia have been quite reluctant to accept these new immigrants from China. Although there is a large number of Chinese tourists in these three countries, they are not to be regarded as migrants.

To my knowledge, in Malaysia and Indonesia, they are not yet flooded by Chinese new migrants. Nevertheless, there is no doubt that China's influence in the twenty-first century has started to be felt. The economic and political power of China, if not its military power, has been witnessed by Southeast Asians, including the Peranakan Chinese. There is certainly more economic opportunity in China or with the Chinese firms for those who are literate in Chinese. This could be an incentive for the Peranakans to be "re-Sinicized", i.e. to master the Chinese language and modern Chinese culture. Nevertheless, this has yet to be an obvious motivation among the Peranakans. On the contrary, there is a revival of the so-called Peranakan culture rather than "Chinese culture" among the Peranakans in these three countries. Peranakan-affiliated organizations have become active again and things "Peranakan" are being promoted. The revival is still weak as the Peranakans form a minority group in Singapore and Malaysia. In Indonesia, learning Mandarin is more prevalent among the children of the Peranakanized *totoks* than those who have been deeply Indonesia-nized and Westernized. As I see it, the Peranakan Chinese in these three countries are being globalized instead of being "re-Sinicized", i.e. to be *singkeh* or migrant Chinese again. If there is an element of "re-Sinicization", it is as part of globalization rather than "re-Sinicization" per se.

In fact, Dr Thung Ju Lan also feels that the Peranakan Chinese in Indonesia and Malaysia in the last thirty years are not "re-Sinicized". She suggests that the Peranakan is a malleable community that could be changed by outside forces in any way they want. With the establishment of Aspertina [Asosiasi Peranakan Tionghoa Indonesia], we see the resurgence of interest in Peranakan culture, similar to that which Lee Su Kim observed in Singapore and Malaysia with their Straits Chinese, i.e. the equivalent of the Baba-Nyonya Peranakan in Indonesia. As such, it proves that the Peranakan community is active and self-changing. Thus, we could argue that these processes of localization, Westernization (modernization), as well as of re-Sinicization operate at the same time within every Peranakan community, creating "glocalized" Chinese culture that encapsulates both global and local elements into a new blend of "modern, urban and/or cosmopolitan". Further studies are required to understand how these processes have worked in today's contemporary world.[9]

In fact, relevant to this issue is the Peranakanization of other Chinese (children of *singkeh* and *totoks*), especially in Indonesia if not in Malaysia and Singapore. During the Suharto era, the children of *totoks* had been Peranakanized, if not Indonesianized, but after the fall of Suharto, the three cultural pillars of Chinese culture have been largely restored. The so-called trilingual schools (Chinese, English and Indonesian) have been established, but they are actually Indonesian schools with two foreign languages, unlike the full-fledged Chinese schools in the pre-Suharto era, hence the command of the Chinese language of the students is limited. Is this a "re-Sinicization" process or "glocalized" process as mentioned by Thung Ju Lan? In the past, people may say that this is "re-Sinicization", but actually it may only strengthen their ethnic Chinese identity, but they cannot be transformed into migrant Chinese again.

Notes

*This chapter was first published in *Asian Culture* 40 (December 2016).

1. Tan Chee Beng, *Chinese Overseas: Comparative Cultural Issues* (Hong Kong: Hong Kong University Press, 2004), pp. 23–27.
2. Tan Chee Beng, *Chinese Minority in a Malay State: The Case of Terengganu in Malaysia* (Singapore: Eastern Universities Press, 2002); Teo Kok Seong, *The Peranakan Chinese of Kelantan: A Study of the Culture, Language and Communication of an Assimilated Group in Malaysia* (London: ASEAN Academic Press, 2003).

3. Tan Ta Sen, *Cheng Ho and Malaya* (Singapore and Malacca: International Zheng He Society and Cheng Ho Cultural Museum, 2014), pp. 120–21.
4. Tan Chee Beng, "Intermarriage and the Chinese Peranakan in Southeast Asia", in *Peranakan Chinese in a Globalizing Southeast Asia*, edited by Leo Suryadinata (Singapore: Chinese Heritage Centre and NUS Baba House, 2010), pp. 27–40 (especially pp. 27–28).
5. Leo Suryadinata, *Peranakan Chinese Politics in Java: 1917–1942* (Singapore: Marshall Cavendish, 2005), p. 2.
6. Tan, "Intermarriage and the Chinese Peranakan in Southeast Asia", in *Peranakan Chinese in a Globalizing Southeast Asia*, pp. 27–40.
7. Siauw Giok Tjhan, "Amanat P.J.M. Presiden Soekarno pada Kongres Nasional ke-VIII Baperki", in *Gotong Rojong Nasakom untuk Melaksanakan Ampera*, edited by Siauw Giok Tjhan (Djakarta: Baperki, 1963), p. 14.
8. John Clammer, *Straits Chinese Society: Studies in the Sociology of the Baba Communities of Malaysia and Singapore* (Singapore: Singapore University Press, 1980).
9. Thung Ju Lan, "Peranakan Chinese Community in Indonesia and Globalization", in *Peranakan Communities in the Era of Decolonization and Globalization*, edited by Leo Suryadinata (Singapore: Chinese Heritage Centre and NUS Baba House, 2015), pp. 135–36.

PART II

Focusing on Indonesia

10

PERANAKAN CHINESE AND THE INDONESIAN PRESS, LANGUAGE AND LITERATURE*

Introduction

Since the late nineteenth century, ethnic Chinese have been active in the Indonesian press, publications of books and creative writings in proto-Bahasa Indonesia (Malay). They have made significant contribution at least in the above three fields. This chapter examines briefly their role in these fields from the colonial period to the present. This is based on my earlier works and recent observation as well as the studies by other scholars. In the process of writing this chapter, I became more aware that more studies on the relevant topics should be conducted in order to fill the gaps. From available research findings however, one notice that the role of Indonesian Chinese was essential in the formation and development of the Indonesian press, language and modern literature, but this was often overlooked, if not neglected, by many Indonesianists in the past. There has always been a stereotype that ethnic Chinese are economic creatures and that they are only interested in making money, and nothing else.

Before discussing their role, it should be remembered that ethnic Chinese in Indonesia were and are not a homogeneous group. They can be divided at least into two types: the Peranakan or local-born Indonesian-speaking Chinese, and the *totok* (i.e. *singkeh*) or foreign-born and Chinese-speaking Chinese. In the first half of the twentieth century, the Chinese in Java were primarily Peranakan while those in the outer islands were primarily *totok*. With Indonesia's independence, *totok* Chinese have been rapidly Peranakanized, if not Indonesianized. Nevertheless, the process has been much more rapid in Java than in the outer islands, due to both the historical factor and settlement patterns. Speaking of Indonesian Chinese, I mean to include both the Peranakan and *totok*, but it seems that the Peranakans contributed more to the above three fields than their *totok* counterparts for obvious reasons: the Peranakans have stayed longer in Indonesia and have partially been assimilated to the local culture.

Apart from this socio-cultural background, it should also be noted that the role of ethnic Chinese has been facilitated by their socio-economic status in both colonial and independent Indonesia. Ethnic Chinese have been urban dwellers (especially in Java) and have been widely exposed to the development of capitalism. They formed a middle group in the colonial social strata and a middle class in independent Indonesia. Not surprisingly they became "pioneers" in the development of the Indonesian press, language and modern literature. In other words, ethnic Chinese were in the modern sector and naturally they played a "pioneering" role in the development of "print- capitalism".[1] They lagged behind the Dutch but were ahead of their indigenous counterparts (e.g., in owning printing press and running Malay language newspapers), at least during the colonial period.

The Republic of Indonesia today is more the product of Dutch colonialism rather than the extension of the old empires of Sriwijaya and Majapahit. It emerged in 1945 although the nationalist movement, which led to the establishment of the Indonesian nation-state, started several decades before that year. Strictly speaking, before 1945, there was no Indonesia but the Dutch East Indies. However, I have used "Indonesia" to refer to both the Indies and Indonesia.

Indonesia consists of more than 250 "indigenous" ethnic groups. Although ethnic Javanese were and are the largest group, their language was and is not used by non-Javanese. The lingua franca of various indigenous ethnic groups and ethnic Chinese was Malay. Not surprisingly, the newspapers, which were published for multiethnic/multiracial readership, were in Malay rather than in local ethnic languages. These newspapers should be considered as the forerunners of Indonesian newspapers.

The Indonesia Language Press

In-depth studies on the history of the Indonesian press before World War II are very few.[2] Generally, the history of the Indonesian press before independence can be divided into three broad periods.[3] The first period, between 1744 and 1854, was the era of the White Press. The press was solely published in the Dutch language, owned and run by the Dutch and its readership was confined to the Dutch-speaking community, with very few of them being non-Dutch. The press dealt with the Dutch community affairs and printed news relevant to this community. The Dutch language press was therefore irrelevant to the indigenous and Chinese populations.

Only in 1854, there was a change in the Indonesian press. With the victory of the liberals in the Netherlands, a more liberal policy was also introduced, resulting in the emergence of the non-Dutch press. The Indonesian press entered the second period. During this period, which covered the years between 1854 and 1908, the press was characterized by the emergence of the Malay language newspapers but owned and run firstly by Eurasians, and later by Peranakan Chinese and indigenous Indonesians. Nevertheless, the number of the Peranakan newspapers was very significant.

During the third period, between 1908 and 1945, the *pribumi* national press began to be more significant. However, the Peranakan press was still playing a major role. This was due to both economic and political reasons. The Peranakan Chinese press was financially better off and politically was more moderate compared to the indigenous nationalist press. Many indigenous newspapers were closed down due to economic difficulty; some were banned because of political reasons. For instance, in Surabaya, there was no indigenous newspaper for five years and the indigenous readers had to depend on the Peranakan press for information.

If we examine the situation of the press in Indonesia in 1928, we will notice the significance of the Peranakan press.

Nevertheless, it is also important to note that the Dutch press remained strong as reflected in terms of number and capital, but it continued to serve mainly the Dutch community. The majority of Indonesian readers did not read Dutch newspapers. As a result, the Malay press became the most important media for the non-Dutch.

The Peranakan press was not only read by ethnic Chinese but also by the indigenous readers. Indeed, initially all of these newspapers claimed that they were published for all Indonesian- ("Malay-") speakers regardless of race. One *pribumi* scholar, for example, has noted that the emergence of the Muslim organization Nahdlatul Ulama, was only fully reported in *Pewarta Soerabaia,* not elsewhere.[4] Another Indonesian observed that Indonesian radical nationalists used to publish articles in Peranakan newspapers simply because they had more readers.[5] Another writer noted that the indigenous Indonesian press maintained a precarious existence and that at times no Indonesian paper was published for a prolonged period in major towns.[6]

TABLE 10.1
Newspapers in the Dutch East Indies (1928)

City	Indonesian newspapers	Chinese (Peranakan) newspapers	Dutch newspapers
Surabaya	0	3	2
Semarang	1	2	2
Sala	1	0	0
Yogyakarta	1	0	2
Bandung	0	0	2
Batavia	2	3	4
Medan	1	1	1
Palembang	0	1	0
Padang	1	2	0
Makassar	1	0	0
Total	8	12	13

Source: Surjomihardjo (2001), p. 95.

During the pre-World War II period, major Peranakan newspapers were largely in Java. These major newspapers/publishers including *Sin Po, Perniagaan* (later it changed its name to *Siang Po*), and *Keng Po,* were all located in in Jakarta. *Djawa Tengah* of Semarang and *Pewarta Soerabaia* of Surabaya were also large and had a relatively long lifespan. In Medan, *Sinar Sumatra* was also quite large but could not be compared with its counterpart in Java. It is interesting to note that these newspapers did not share the same political ideology. Some were sympathetic to Dutch rule, some sided with Indonesian nationalism and others remained neutral in the conflict between the Dutch and Indonesians.

When the Japanese occupied Indonesia (1942–45), the Peranakan Chinese press was suppressed. Peranakan newspapers re-emerged only after Indonesia's independence. Pre-World War II newspapers such as *Sin Po* and *Keng Po* resumed publication and further developed. These two became the largest and most influential Peranakan Chinese newspapers in Indonesia, representing two different political ideologies. The former was "left-wing" while the latter was "right-wing". Due to their different political views, they were affected by Indonesian political developments.

Because of the pressure of Indonesian nationalism, the Peranakan press eventually became Indonesian newspapers. They even abandoned the original Chinese sounding names and adopted Indonesian names for their papers in the 1960s. *Sin Po* became *Pantja Warta,* and later *Warta Bhakti* while *Keng Po* became *Pos Indonesia*. However, the 1965 coup ended the Peranakan press. All Peranakan-run newspapers were closed down. The Peranakan press was transformed into the "national press" which is often seen as the *pribumi* press, as the leadership was taken over completely by *pribumi* Indonesians, with perhaps the exception of *Kompas* in its formative years.

Kompas may be a leading example of the Indonesian "national press" which was partially developed with the Peranakan's capital and participation. It was co-founded by Auwjang Peng Koen (later changed his name to P.K. Ojong), a Peranakan and Jakob Oetama, a Javanese, in June 1965 before the downfall of Sukarno.[7] Ojong was a senior editor in *Keng Po* and its Indonesian magazine *Star Weekly* (1951–62) until the magazine was banned in 1962. His association with *Keng Po*, especially his close association with Khoe Woen Sioe (1906–76), the director and editor-in-chief of *Keng Po*, was crucial for his success in the Indonesian press. He admitted that he learned about the press from Khoe. After *Star Weekly* was banned, Ojong established a new magazine (*Intisari*) in 1963. In 1964, he joined the Catholic party (1964–68), which was dominated by the *pribumi*. With the support of the Indonesian Catholics, he succeeded in getting a permit to start a new daily newspaper called *Kompas*. The newspaper developed rapidly during the "New Order" period. Its publisher, the Gramedia company, was later developed into a large publishing giant in Indonesia. [In fact, the close cooperation between peranakan and *pribumi* journalists can also be found in *Tempo*, which later became an influential Jakarta news weekly. The first chief editor of *Tempo* was Gunawan Mohammad (a Javanese) and his deputy, Christianto Wibisono (Oey Kian Kok, a peranakan)]. Ojong passed away in 1980 but his legacy still lives on. His name as the co-founder of *Kompas* is still listed on the front page of the newspaper.

The Indonesian Language

Before 1928, the language of the Indonesian press was called Bahasa Melajoe or Malay. However, the colonial government divided the Malay language into "Melayu Tinggi" ("High Malay"), which was based on Riau Malay, and Melayu Rendah ("Low Malay"), which was based on lingua franca. In the nineteenth century and the early part of twentieth century, these two types of Malay were similar, if not identical, in terms of syntax, vocabulary and grammar, but the latter was richer in vocabulary as it was influenced by other cultures/languages. It was also more widely used by the Dutch Eurasians, Peranakan Chinese and the indigenous press. Dutch Eurasians, Peranakan Chinese and the indigenous Indonesians called the language used in the press simply as "Melajoe" or "Melajoe Betawi" (Batavian Malay), the adjective "Rendah" ("Low") was attached only later after the rise of Indonesian nationalist movement. The so-called Melayu-Tionghoa (Chinese-Malay) also appeared later and was classified in the category of "Low Malay".

Lie Kim Hok, the father of the so-called Melajoe Tionghoa, did not call the language Melajoe Tionghoa nor Melajoe Rendah, but Malajoe

Batawi.[8] It was only after the rise of the Pan-Chinese movement and *pribumi* Indonesian nationalism that Melajoe Betawi was called Melajoe-Tionghoa. It was wrong to say that "Bahasa Melajoe Tionghoa" existed as early as the mid-nineteenth century.[9] For one thing, the term Tionghoa only came into being in the twentieth century.

With the new labelling, one creates the impression that the Malay language used by the Peranakans was a special kind and different from the Malay language used by *pribumi* Indonesians. Many pre-World War II *pribumi* writers (e.g. Sanoesi Pane and Sutan Takdir Alisjahbana) argued that this was not the case.[10] The Malay language used by the Peranakans, especially before the mid-1920s, was basically the Malay language used by the population in the Malay archipelago, especially in the Dutch East Indies.[11] Sutan Takdir Alisjahbana noted in 1934 that the difference between Indonesian and "Chinese Malay" was temporary and not much. The most important distinction, according to Alisjahbana, was the spelling but this would soon disappear.[12] I have compared the pre-World War II speeches of Sukarno and Liem Koen Hian and discovered that their languages were similar.

After World War II, more scholars argued that the so-called Chinese-Malay before the mid-1920s was not much different from the Malay language used by other Indonesians in Java.[13] Referring to the Malay language prior to the emergence of Indonesia, Pramoedya Ananta Toer, the leading Indonesian novelist, maintains that the non-Balai Pustaka Malay language should be called the working language (Bahasa Kerja)[14] or pre-Indonesian language (Bahasa Pra-Indonesia). He disagreed with the terms "Low Malay", "Market Malay" (Melaju Pasar)[15] and "Mixed Malay" (Melaju Campuran) to refer to the Malay language used by the majority of the population as this was politically motivated.[16] It was meant to downgrade the language and discredit the literature written in such language, because the Indonesian nationalist press and non-official Indonesian literature were written in such a language. This view was later confirmed by a Dutch scholar, Prof. Hendrik Maier, who argued that the Dutch colonial authorities had formulated a policy to marginalize the Chinese-Malay literature.[17] As part of the strategy, the Dutch colonial authority established a publishing house in 1908, which was later known as Balai Pustaka (1917) to sponsor the publication of "good" Indonesian literary works. All publications of Balai Pustaka were in "High Malay", which was later known as "standard Bahasa Indonesia".

In fact, the so-called Low Malay was so popular; and before the mid-1920s, the overwhelming majority of Indonesian publications were in this language rather than in "High Malay". Referring to "Low Malay" used by Lie Kim Hok, a leading Peranakan writer, Kwee Tek Hoay, commented in 1928 that, "The spelling [initiated by Lie Kim Hok] has spread and has been adopted in all over Indonesia. We believe that it will eventually defeat and destroy Riau Malay or the Malay language of C.A. van Ophuijsen, which is now protected by the government."[18] But this did not happen because of the success of the Dutch language policy.

Nevertheless, Chinese Indonesians played a very significant role in developing and popularizing this Language. Leading Peranakan Chinese writers before World War II such as Lie Kim Hok (1853–1912), Gouw Peng Liang (1869–1928) and Kwee Tek Hoay (1886–1951) were major figures who used and developed the language. Lie Kim Hok was the first person in colonial Indonesia and beyond to publish a grammar book on Batavian Malay (1884) in romanized characters, far ahead of the Dutch and *pribumi* scholars themselves. Although published over one hundred years ago, the book still retains modern features of the modern Indonesian grammar.[19] The Malay language of Lie Kim Hok was followed by many major Peranakan writers and perhaps some non-Chinese writers as well.[20] Gouw Peng Liang, a leading journalist and a Peranakan writer himself, admitted that he was heavily influenced by Lie.[21] Another pre-war major writer, Kwee Tek Hoay, was also within the same tradition.[22]

However, the colonial policy eventually crushed the Working Malay. Major Indonesian writers, many of whom were from Sumatra, adopted the standard Bahasa Melayu. Even Peranakan writers themselves began to accept the term "Melayu Rendah" to refer to their own language, as if their works were inferior to those of Balai Pustaka. It is worth noting that the publications in Bahasa Kerja were excluded from the Indonesian literature proper as they were not worth studying. This situation remained until the 1990s.

The impact of the colonial policy on the Indonesian language is far reaching. The division between the so-called Chinese-Malay and the standard Bahasa Melayu (later, standard Bahasa Indonesia) became wider. The post-World War II Chinese Indonesian writers such as Arief Budiman (Soe Hok Djin), Abdul Hadi WM (An L.K.), Marga T. (Tjoa) and Mira W. (Wong?) write in standard Indonesian and can no longer be differentiated from their *pribumi* counterparts.

Nevertheless, it is wrong to say that Melayu Betawi or Batavian Malay, which was developed prior to World War II, has disappeared completely. It has survived in the spoken language in urban Indonesia. Indonesian movies and TV programmes continued to use this kind of language. This fact has often been ignored by many observers as if Indonesians only speak standard Bahasa Indonesia.

Indonesian Language Literature

Language and literature cannot be separated. Peranakan literature started prior to the rise of Chinese nationalism but developed during the nationalist movements. As stated earlier, Peranakan literary works were written in Melajoe Betawi,[23] which was later known as Bahasa Melayu Tionghoa.[24] It emerged together with other literary works in the late nineteenth century. However, the creative works, which were independent of the Malay classical works, appeared at the beginning of the twentieth century. The writers were also journalists, and hence their works were taken from news stories. Over sixty to seventy years, Peranakan Chinese had produced a large number of "literary works", larger than the indigenous writers themselves.[25] According to Claudine Salmon, between the 1870s and early 1960s, there were 806 Peranakan authors who produced about 3,000 titles, which consist of 73 plays, 183 syair, 233 translations of Western works, 759 translations of Chinese works and 1,398 novels and short stories. She maintained that these numbers are larger than those of the indigenous writers (175) and publications (400).[26]

Salmon also argued that some of these Peranakan works were of high quality but she did not identify them. Nevertheless, one can argue that some of Kwee Tek Hoay's works, for instance, *Drama di Boven Digul* (1927–31, 718 pages), was a major work which could be put at the same level with any pre-war *pribumi* writings such as *Salah*

Asuhan (1928) by Abdul Muis and *Layar Terkembang* (1935) by Sutan Takdir Alisjahbana. Kwee's novel discusses politics, philosophy, race-relations, and social issues, including women emancipation. In fact, the appearance of Peranakan novels was also earlier than the so-called modern Indonesian novels, which dated in 1920 with the publication of Marah Rusli's *Azab dan Sengsara* (1920).[27] For instance, Gouw Peng Liang's novel entitled *Lo Fen Koei* and Thio Tjin Boen's novel entitled *Oey See* were both published in 1903.

With regard to the role of Peranakan literature in the history of Indonesian literature, there are a number of questions to be answered. Some writers argued that the quality was low while others held the opposite view. More research is needed. Besides, there is also a question of influence over Indonesian literature. Did Peranakan literature influence the *pribumi* literature, or there were parallel developments? Did they mutually influence each other?

Some scholars are of the view that the indigenous Indonesian literature was influenced by the Peranakan literature which emerged earlier. C.W. Watson (1971), for instance, argues that there is evidence that modern Indonesian literature was influenced by the literature written in Low Malay. He maintains that some of the plots in *Sitti Nurbaya* were influenced by *Tjerita Njonja Kong Hong Nio* (on the poison plot) and by *Nji Paina* (on sacrificing oneself in order to save one's family). John Kwee's PhD thesis (1977, pp. 232–35) gives more examples: for instance, *Pertjobaan Setia* by Soeman Hs. (1931) resembles *Saltima* by Tio Ie Soei (1925); the theme of *Salah Asoehan* by Abdul Muis (1928) is similar to that of *Nona Olanda Sebagai Istri Tionghoa* by Njoo Cheong Seng (1925); the theme of *Salah Pilih* by Nur Sutan Iskandar (1928) also resembles that of *Nona Lan-Im* by Tan Boen Kim (1919); *Gadis Modern* by Adlin Afandi (1941) resembles that of *Gadis Modern* by Chang Mung Tze (1939); the theme of *Taufan* by Bajolis (1936) resembles that of *Berdjoeang* by Liem Khing Hoo (1934) and *Manoesia Baroe* by Sanoesi Pane (1940) is similar to *Merah* by Liem Khing Hoo (1939).

Jakob Sumardjo, a *pribumi* writer, also argues that Indonesian translation work done by the Peranakans influenced the publications of Balai Pustaka.[28] For instance, Alexandre Dumas' work *The Three*

Musketeers was translated by Nur Sutan Iskandar in the 1920s under the title of *Tiga Panglima Perang*. In fact, he borrowed the title from Kwee Kim Hong's translation of the same work in 1914. Sumardjo also points out that the development of indigenous *kungfu* novels in the 1970s was undoubtedly connected with the popularity of Chinese martial arts novels in Bahasa Indonesia.

Nevertheless, there was evidence that these two literatures share a lot of similarities, some of which are far from coincidental. However, one needs to conduct further studies before drawing a conclusion. Peranakan Chinese literature is rich, but it was ignored by many scholars until Claudine Salmon produced her study on the subject. The reasons are complex but the fact that it was written in "Low Malay" was a major reason. Even after the publication of Salmon's works, there are few new research on this literature. One of the reasons was due to the difficulties in locating these works as most of them were out of print.

One major Indonesian publisher, Grasindo (affiliated to the Kompas Group) planned to reprint the pre-World War II Peranakan literary works but this did not materialize.[29] However, the project was later undertaken by Kepustakaan Populer Gramedia (also affiliated to the Kompas group) and it published the first volume in 2000. It plans to publish twenty-five volumes in total. Between 2000 and 2002, four big volumes have been published, including Kwee Tek Hoay's major novel.[30] Hopefully, with the republication of these works, Peranakan literature will have a place it deserves in modern Indonesian literature.

If the number of Peranakan Chinese writers was large before World War II, it has been reduced drastically after the war, with the exception of the *kungfu* novel writers (translators). The reasons for this are complex but certainly this was linked to the government policy, which channelled ethnic Chinese towards the economic arenas rather than other fields. Also, the assimilationist policy pushed the Peranakan Chinese to the indigenous cultural world. Peranakan Chinese writers tended to merge with the *pribumi* writers and form the Indonesian national literature. Peranakan writers such as Abdul Hadi WM, Arief Budiman, Ariel Heryanto, Marga T. and Mira W. are no longer known as "Peranakan" but Indonesian writers.

Profiles of Pre-World War II Writers

Let us look at the profiles of Peranakan Chinese writers. Many early writers had a background in journalism. Better-known writers include Gouw Peng Liang, Thio Tjin Boen, Kwee Tek Hoay and Liem Khing Hoo.

Gouw Peng Liang (1868–1928) and Thio Tjin Boen (1885–1940) were the first Peranakan writers to publish novelettes. They wrote about the life of the Peranakan Chinese of their time and because of their journalistic background, the novels were often based on news stories. Gouw's first work, *Low Fen Koei*, was published in 1903. It tells the story of an opium farmer, Lo Fen Koei, who wanted to take a Chinese girl as a concubine. He plotted against her family and a young man who attempted to stop him. He even committed murder in order to achieve his objective. However, with the help of a Chinese officer, his crime was exposed and he eventually took his own life by shooting himself. The suicide scene was new in Indonesian literature. The story was written before the rise of overseas Chinese nationalism and it portrays the Dutch-appointed Chinese officer as a good guy.

Thio's work, *Tjerita Oey Se*,[31] which was also published in 1903, tells the story of a young Chinese widow who converted to Islam after marrying a Javanese aristocrat. But her father disowned her and refused to allow her to see her son from her first marriage, resulting in tragedy. This work also reflected the racial and religious tensions in Indonesia. However, Thio's other novel, *Tjerita Njai Soemirah*,[32] which was published in 1917 and considered by a Dutch scholar as one of the best pre-World War II Peranakan novels, depicts the enduring love of an indigenous girl (Soemirah) and a Chinese boy (Tan Bi Liang) in the Preanger (Priangan, West Java) area. Despite the difficulties encountered by the couple, they eventually got married and lived happily ever after. Unlike Thio's earlier novel where the marriage was between a Chinese woman and a Javanese man, in this novel the love story was between a Chinese young man and a Javanese girl. While the former was a tragedy, the latter concluded with a happy ending. This was perhaps a reflection of Peranakan thinking during that period.

However, the most successful novelist was probably Kwee Tek Hoay (1886–1951).[33] Born in Bogor, West Java, he received little formal education, and was active in journalism and publishing. He was the most prolific writer before World War II. Apart from essays on religion and politics, he published a few major novels and plays. His *Drama di Boven Digoel* (serialized between 1928 and 1931)[34] which uses the 1926–27 communist rebellions as a background, but tells the love story of Moestari, the son of a regent who was Dutch educated, and Noerani, the daughter of Boekarim, a communist leader who was eventually sent to Boven Digoel (in Papua, formerly known as Irian Jaya). Apart from these two characters there were also Noerani's friend Soebaidah, a communist leader Rodeka who loved Noerani, Noerani's acquaintances, Peranakan Chinese Tjoe Tat Mo and his daughter Dolores. Through these characters, Kwee not only attempted to present the love story of Indonesian youth in the turbulent years, but more importantly, also his Buddhist philosophy. In fact, the real protagonists of the book are Noerani and Soebaidah. The former represents a courageous but rational modern Indonesian woman while the latter represents an equally courageous but rebellious and often emotional modern Indonesian young lady. Kwee advocated female emancipation in the novel. This was the longest Indonesian novel before World War II, and was considered Kwee's greatest work.[35]

Kwee's earlier novel, entitled *Boenga Roos dari Tjikembang*, was very popular and was performed on the stage and made into a movie. It depicts the story of the offspring of an inter-racial marriage between a Chinese man and an Indonesian woman and deals with the theme of incarnation, reflecting the author's belief systems.

Liem Khing Hoo (pen name Romaro, 1905–45) was also an outstanding writer. He received his primary school education at the Tiong Hoa Hwee Koan, but learned Chinese and Javanese classics from his father. His family background was often reflected in his writings. He worked as the editor of *Tjerita Roman* and *Liberty*. Indeed, most of his novels and short stories were published in these two magazines. One of his famous works, *Berdjoang* (1934), depicts the story of a group of young Chinese Indonesians who went to Borneo to establish a new colony. Claudine Salmon noted that this was a novel which denotes an utopian idea of the Peranakan Chinese. His other work, *Merah* (1937), tells the story of a Javanese trade unionist who was accused of being a communist and suffered as a result.

Generally the works of the Peranakan writers reflected the life of the local Chinese, but some also wrote about the indigenous population. Their works can be considered as part of the new Indonesian literature. However, for a long time, the Peranakan works have not been regarded by the indigenous writers as an integral part of pre-war Peranakan literature. The indigenous Indonesian writers felt that the works were not written in the so-called standard Bahasa Indonesia and that many of these literary works still reflected Chinese nationalist sentiments. However, there are many that are locally oriented and have helped promote the development of Indonesian local literature.

Profile of Post-World War II Writers

Indigenous Indonesians, including some Peranakan Chinese, were involved in Indonesia's independence movement. Indonesia was eventually declared independence in 1945 but only gained political power in December 1949. The Peranakan Chinese were considered as Indonesian citizens unless they rejected Indonesian citizenship. There was a growing Indonesian identity among the Peranakan Chinese and this was also reflected in their literary works.

Between 1950 and 1965, it seems that there were no major writers or major works by Peranakan writers. Most of the works produced were short stories in Peranakan newspapers or magazines such as *Pantjawarna*, *Star Weekly*, *Liberal* (later *Liberty*), and *Mingguan Sadar*.[36] It was only after the 1965 coup which ended Sukarno's rule and gave rise to General Suharto that more new writers emerged. Peranakan literature became more "assimilated". Apart from the *kungfu* novels and some short stories and novels with a Chinese background, the majority of their works were very similar to those of indigenous Indonesian writers. The materials were seldom taken from Indonesian Chinese society. Among these post-World War II Peranakan writers, the most well-known are Arief Budiman, Abdul Hadi WM, Marga T., and Mira W. They identified themselves with the Indonesian culture because they were the post-World War II generation of Peranakan Chinese who grew up in independent Indonesia and went to Indonesian schools. In addition, the Suharto's state policy was to assimilate the Indonesian Chinese population. As a result, these Peranakan writers tended to merge with the Indonesian indigenous writers. In fact, many readers were not aware that these writers were of Chinese origin. Culturally they are "Indonesian". Even in terms of religion, many are Christians or Muslims.

Success was achieved by these Peranakan writers in the field of essays, poems and popular novels. Arief Budiman (former name: Soe Hok Djin, 1941–) is a sociologist, political activist, and literary critic. In the 1980s he proposed "Contextual Literature", denying the existence of "Universal Literature". In fact, in the 1960s, he was one of the signatories of the so-called "Cultural Manifesto", promoting "Cultural Universalism" and criticizing Realism in the literature. But after he went overseas, especially to the United States, he began to change his view. Together with another younger Peranakan writer/scholar, Ariel Heryanto, they are of the view that literature is part of an ideology and a political system, and every literary work should be seen from the socio-historical perspective.[37] According to Arief, Indonesian literature belongs to the middle class, which is wrongly called "Universal Literature". Arief's view was considered to be leftist, which resulted in heated debates during the Suharto era.[38]

In the field of poetry, Abdul Hadi WM was outstanding. Born in Madura in 1946 into a Chinese Muslim family,[39] he studied Indonesian literature at the FSUI (1965– 67) and Western philosophy at the University of Gadjah Mada (1968–71). From 1969 to 1970 he was the editor of the *Mingguan Mahasiswa Indonesia* (Central Java edition). In 1971 he moved to Bandung and served as the editor of the same student newspaper, West Java edition (1971–73). After attending the Nusantara Literature Seminar in Kuala Lumpur in 1973, he participated in the International Writing Program (at Iowa University) as a guest-writer (October 1973 to April 1974). In June 1974 he was invited to take part in the International Poetry Festival in Rotterdam.

Abdul Hadi is a prolific writer. Apart from poetry, he has also written essays, articles, commentaries, and book reviews, ranging from student life, literature, philosophy, to culture. His poems, which have appeared in book form include *Riwayat* [Life story], *Terlambat di Jalan* [Late on the road], *Laut Belum Pasang* [The tide is not high yet], *Potret Panjang Seorang Pengunjung Pantai Sanur* [Portrait of a visitor at Sanur Beach], and *Anak Laut Anak Angin* [Son of sea and son of wind]. He received the Southeast Asia Write Award in 1985 for his poems. He was quoted as saying in an interview that he is "interested in the Far East, including China — my grandfather is Chinese". In 2006 he published his selected poems: *Madura, Luang Prabhang: Seratus Puisi Pilihan* [Madura, Luang Prabhang: One hundred selected poems (Jakarta, 2006)]. He is seen as a poet who has been able to mix East and West, although his Islamic identity is clear. One of his poems, which is entitled "West and East", reflects his thinking:

Barat dan Timur adalah guruku (West and East are my teachers)
Muslim, Hindu, Kristen, Budha (Muslim, Hindu, Christians, Buddhist)
Pengikut Zen atau Tao (Followers of Zen and Taoism)
Semua adalah guruku (All are my teachers)
Kupelajari dari orang saleh dan pemberani (I learned from devoted people and brave men)
Rahasia cinta, rahasia bara api menyala (the secret of love and the secret of burning fire)
Dan tikar sembahyang sebagai pelana menuju arasy-Nya (and prayer's mat as a saddle to the Words of God)
Ya, semua adalah guruku (Yes, all are my teachers)
Ibrahim, Musa, Daud, Lao Tze (Abraham, Moses, David, Lao Tze)
Budha, Zarathustra, Socrates, Isa Almasih (Buddha, Zarathustra, Socrates, Jesus)
Serta Muhammad Rasulullah (and Prophet Muhammad)
Tapi hanya di masjid aku berkhidmat (But only in the Mosque I pay respect)
Walau jejak-Nya (although HIS footsteps)
Ku-jumpa di mana-mana (I encounter everywhere)

Abdul Hadi was invited to the Universiti Sains Malaysia to teach while at the same time doing his postgraduate study leading to a PhD degree from the same university. He later returned to Jakarta to teach at the Universitas Paramadina and in 2008 he was promoted to a full professor. His inaugural speech is entitled "Paradoks Globalisasi: Memikirkan Kembali Arah Kebudayaan Kita" (Paradox of Globalization:

Rethinking of Our Cultural Direction), examining the challenges of globalization to Indonesian culture.

Marga T.

Marga T. is one of the most well-known and productive female novelists in Indonesia. Many of her novels have been made into films. As a popular writer, she has also formed her own fan club, the MT Fan Club. Most of her novels have been published by a leading publisher, Gramedia, which also publishes the largest Indonesian daily newspaper in Jakarta, *Kompas*.

Marga was born on 27 January 1943 in Jakarta. By her own admission, she has been interested in reading and writing since her school days. She received her primary and secondary education in Catholic schools; first in Santa Josef (finishing in 1955), and later in Santa Ursula (finishing in 1961). Like many Peranakan Chinese during the pre-Suharto era, Marga also went to the Universitas Res Publica (URECA), a Baperki-sponsored university which admitted many Chinese Indonesians, as good Indonesian state universities were difficult to enter. She studied medicine at URECA, but before she graduated, a communist coup allegedly took place on 30 September 1965. Baperki was perceived to be close to the Communist Party of Indonesia and was thus "implicated". URECA was burned down by the "mob" and the name of the university was changed to Universitas Trisakti (USAKTI). The university building was only rebuilt in 1969; from late 1965 to 1968, therefore, Marga did not go to any lectures. She only resumed her studies in 1969 and in 1974 graduated from USAKTI's medical school.

Marga noted in her writings that the burning down of URECA was a "blessing in disguise" as she began to concentrate on reading and writing. Although she had published her first short story in the local newspaper in 1964 (when she was twenty-one years old), she became a serious writer only after 1965. From 1965 to 1969, she published at least fifty short stories. Even after she resumed her medical studies, she continued to write. In July 1971 she began to publish her first serialized novel, *Karmila I*, in *Kompas*. Encouraged by its popularity, she wrote a sequel (*Karmila II*) in April 1971. The novel was published as a book in 1973 and in the following year she published another novel, *Badai Pasti Berlalu*. These two novels established her as a popular Indonesian novelist. *Karmila* was reprinted twenty times. Both novels were made into movies and since then, she has become a popular novel queen of sorts. Coincidentally, there is another woman novelist, Mira W., who has a rather similar background; both women are medical doctors by training and are equally well known.

Although Marga was a qualified physician, she failed to get a posting in Indonesia as a doctor. There is a regulation in Indonesia that a young doctor must be posted in one area or another in the Ministry of Health before he/she could practise. Marga did not explain in her brief biography why she was unable to get a posting. She was given some comforting words by Pak Muharyo, the editor of *Femina*, who said to her, "Indonesia does not need doctors, Indonesia needs writers!" Indeed, had she practised as a doctor and given up writing, she might not have become as successful as she is today.

Marga has to date written more than 150 short stories and 50 novels. Her novels deal with urban dwellers rather than rural folk, and with young adults rather than elderly people. Most of her novels are about love and life. Although written with an ethnic Chinese background, her novels generally do not reflect Chinese ethnicity. A possible exception is *Gema Sebuah Hati* [Echo of the heart] (1975) which tells the story of Peranakan Chinese students at URECA/USAKTI before and after the abortive coup of 1965. Its sequel, *Setangkai Edelweiss* (1978), tells the story of Peranakan Chinese students in Europe. With the exception of these two novels, her characters are modern educated Indonesians who live in cities, and can be of any ethnic background.

Marga may be well-known for her popular novels, she is nonetheless interested in socio-political events. In her latest novel entitled *Sekuntum Nozomi* which consists of five volumes, volume three deals with the anti-Chinese riots which took place towards the end of Suharto's rule, and describes how one of the protagonists witnessed not only the violence but also the anti-Chinese campaign engineered by some elements in Indonesian society. This was the first Indonesian novel to deal with the May 1998 event. From the perspective of a woman writer, Marga recounted the experiences of some of the Indonesians, especially urban Indonesian women, in the turbulent period. As such she was also describing Indonesian society before the fall of the Suharto regime, capturing the atmosphere of those days.

Like many Chinese Indonesians before the rise of Suharto, Marga also had a Chinese name: Tjoa Liang Tjoe, with Tjoa being her Chinese surname. After Suharto introduced the name changing rule, Marga also changed her name. During the time that she was writing short stories and novels, she used her pen name, Marga T. It has been suggested that T was the initial for her former Chinese surname, Tjoa, but she said it was not the case. She pointed out that Marga T., when abbreviated, would become MT, and when MT is pronounced in English, it sounds like "empty". Her confession to the almighty God is that "in front of HIM, she is nothing".

As stated earlier, Marga was unable to get a posting as a doctor in Indonesia. She therefore moved to Germany, presumably with her husband. However, her Indonesian qualification was not recognized by the World Health Organization, and she had to study medicine again at Wolfgang von Goethe Universitat—Frankfurt. In 1979 she passed the examinations required by the ECFMG (Educational Commission for Foreign Medical Graduates) to allow her to practise as a physician in the United States. She worked for a while in Texas but decided to return home to be a "village doctor" in Indonesia. According to her, at the Dallas Airport before the plane took off, an officer could not believe that she wanted to return to Indonesia and said to her, "What? You want to go back? Is this country not good enough for you?"

Marga is a prolific writer. It was difficult to study her writings in the past as they were not compiled systematically. It is only in recent years that she has begun to publish both her short stories and novels. There are two sources which provide interesting information about the author herself: one in the appendix of *Sekuntum Nozomi*, vol. 4, and the other in the appendix of the same novel, vol. 5. She has so far published 120 short stories and 54 novels; 8 of her novels have been made into films.

Mira W.

Mira W. is younger than Marga T., but is equally well-known. Mira W. is the pen name of Mira Wijaya who was born in Jakarta on 13 September 1950 (1949?) as Mira Wong. She graduated from Trisakti University medical school in 1979. The daughter of a film producer whose Chinese surname is Oey (or Wong?), she emerged as a popular writer in the 1970s. She is a teaching staff at the Prof Dr Moestopo University in Jakarta and also works as a university physician. However, she is better known as a popular novel writer.

She began to write short stories in 1975. Her first work was published in *Femina* magazine. In 1977 she wrote her first novel, *Dokter Nona Friska*, which was serialized in *Dewi* magazine. (However, *Kompas* says that her first novel was *Cinta tak Pernah Berhutang* [Love never owes] published in 1978.) It was later published in book form with a new title: *Kemilau Kemuning Senja* [The yellow sheen of twilight]. Her second novel, *Sepolos Cinta Dini* [As pure as Dini's love] was serialized in *Kompas*, and later also published as a book.

Her most popular novel was perhaps *Di Sini Cinta Pertama Kali Bersemi* [Love first blooms here] (1980). However, her better novel is *Relung-Relung Gelap Hati Sisi* [Dark side of the heart] (1983), a story about lesbians. Sisi, a beautiful girl who is a lesbian, was forced by her parent to leave her lover and compelled to marry a man who does not bring her happiness. Her lesbian lover returned from the United States and wanted to continue their love affair. When their relationship was discovered by her husband, she asked for a divorce. However, she did not go off with her lover. Instead, she join a medical team to be sent to the remote areas serving those who needed medical care. Perhaps, this is Mira's most powerful novel.

Her other works include *Masih Ada Kereta Yang Akan Lewat* [There is still a train which will pass] (1989?) and its sequel, *Biarkan Kereta Itu Lewat, Arini* [Let the train go, Arini] (1990). The book tells the story of an elderly woman who falls in love with a young man. Mira seldom wrote about her own Chinese society as she claimed that she was fully integrated and did not feel any difference with other Indonesians. Nevertheless, her fiftieth novel, *Bukan Cinta Sesaat* [Not a love of a moment] tells the love story of a Chinese girl Nina and a Batak boy Rio. Nina went to Jakarta to study medicine and met Rio with whom she fell in love.[40] Nina's father was against her daughter's relationship with a native boy but Nina did not listen. When there was an anti-Japanese riot in 1974 and she lost her Japan-made car, Nina decided to go to Belgium to finish her studies. Upon her return, she found that Rio was still in love with her although he was already married. Nina continued their love affair which resulted in a murder case.

According to Myra Sidharta who has studied Mira's works, the women in Mira's story are "usually strong, independent, and have integrity because that is what she thinks a woman should be. The time when women are portrayed as weak creatures whom need men to support is over."[41] She has published more than fifty novels, many of which have been made into movies.

Soe Tjen Marching

Unlike the Peranakan writers who were active during the Suharto New Order when the assimilation policy was imposed, Soe Tjen came to the literary scene after the fall of Suharto when pluralism had replaced the assimilation policy. There has since been a revival of Chinese Indonesian identity. Soe Tjen may be one of the representatives of this generation. It is also worth noting that she has also been "globalized" in her personal life.

Soe Tjen Marching was born on 23 April 1971 in Surabaya to a Chinese family. Little is known about her family background. According to her interview with Zara Majidpour, Soe Tjen's father was imprisoned and tortured during the New Order "because he was leftist and all of our property were [sic] confiscated".[42] She was born after her father was out of the prison. Soe Tjen is multi-talented. Interested in music since childhood, she won the national competition for Indonesian contemporary composers held by the German Embassy in 1998. In 2010 her work was selected as one of the best compositions in the international competition for avant-garde composers held in Singapore.

She received a PhD from Monash University after submitting a thesis on "The discrepancy between the public and the private selves of Indonesian women", that was published as a book in 2007. She has also written at least three books in Bahasa Indonesia: *Mati, Bertahun yang Lalu* (Died, several years ago) is her first novel (published by Gramedia in 2010) and received good reviews. In fact it was not only a novel but also a satire. The main character is a woman who died but as her energy was still strong, she continued to work. In the story, not many people knew that in fact she had died, as the title indicated. In this 150-page novel, Soe Tjen wanted to show that many people who are still alive in fact are already dead, her famous words in the book: "*aku sudah mati sebelum mati*" (I had already died even before I died).

Kisah di Balik Pintu (Stories behind doors, published by Ombak in 2011) is not a novel but the nine profiles of Indonesian women based on their diaries. In fact the materials of this book were used in her PhD dissertation. Soe Tjen describes their behaviour in public and in private which are very different. The book presents a different side of Indonesian women based on their own accounts. The third book, *Kubunuh Di Sini* (I kill it here, published in 2013 by Kepustakaan Populer Gramedia) is her own story—her long and courageous struggle against cancer and how she eventually won the battle. Through this story she talked about her own body, about life, about the different public health systems in the three countries where she had lived: Indonesia, Australia and the UK.

Soe Tjen is a feminist and the above three books are all about women, especially Indonesian women. In 2009 she started the *Majalah Bhinneka*, a magazine in Bahasa Indonesia, which promotes critical thinking. She is married to a scholar Angus Nicholis. She has been frequently invited to give lectures in Australia, UK and Europe.

Some Remarks on the Peranakan Literature

Peranakan Chinese literature in Indonesia has a long history and has had imprints of the era. It is apparent that the Peranakan Chinese served as one of the pioneers in modern Indonesian literature. The writers, some of whom did not receive much formal education, were able to produce impressive works. Writers such as Kwee Tek Hoay has now been recognized as a major Chinese Indonesian writer who produced novels which reflected his era.

However, after World War II Indonesia achieved independence partly due to the activism of independent movements. Indigenous Indonesian writers have produced major works, reflecting their struggle and the changes in society. Peranakan Chinese literary works were at first quite limited. There were no major writers—it was as if they were not touched by the "baptism" of the Indonesian revolution. Only during the New Order period did a few major writers emerge. The backgrounds of these writers are different from those in pre-World War II. Post-World War II writers are well-educated—more often than not they have university degrees and even come from a professional background. Nevertheless, in the creative writings they have not yet produced mega works comparable to indigenous Indonesian writers such as Pramoedya Ananta Toer and Mochtar Lubis. It is noteworthy, however, that most recently in a book published by a group of young Indonesian writers which lists the most influential Indonesian writers of the last century, three out of thirty-three writers selected are Peranakan Chinese, namely: Kwee Tek Hoay, Arief Budiman and Abdul Hadi WM.[43]

Conclusion

The role of Indonesian Chinese in the development of the Indonesian press, language and modern literature is important. There was no doubt that the Peranakan Chinese press played a pioneering role in the initial stage of the development of the Indonesian language press. It constituted part of the pre-independent Indonesian press and merged with the *pribumi* press after Indonesia's independence. This was also the case with Peranakan literature, often known as Sastra Melayu Tionghoa before World War II. With regard to the language, Indonesian Chinese "have by far the largest group to communicate in a variety of Malay, admittedly not the one condoned by the colonial government, which later developed into a specific variety of modern colloquial Indonesia".[44] "Their role is, of course, more significant if one considers that with Malay they provided their own group as well as others in both pre- and post-independence Indonesia with a literature, a press and various genres of performing arts more accessible to the general population than those provided by the colonial government" (ibid.). In the past their contributions were seldom recognized because of political and other reasons. However, with the end of the Cold War and globalization, foreign scholars, followed by some indigenous writers, began to look at the role of this minority and discovered their forgotten role. Nevertheless, the study of their role in Malay and Indonesian history, society and culture is still few, and it is time for scholars to do more detailed research in these fields.

Notes

* The above chapter is based on two of my published articles: "The Contribution of the Indonesian Chinese in the Development of the Indonesian Press, Language and Literature", in *Chinese Studies in the Malay World: A Comparative Approach*, edited by Ding Choo Ming and Ooi Kee Beng (Singapore: Eastern Universities Press, 2003), and "Modern Peranakan Indonesia Literature: Past and Present", in *Peranakan Communities in the Era of Decolonization and Globalization*, edited by Leo Suryadinata (Singapore: Chinese Heritage Centre and Baba House, 2015).

1. Benedict Anderson discussed this "print-capitalism" in his well-known book in relations to the rise of nationalism. See Benedict Anderson, *Imagined Communities: Reflections on Origin and Spread of Nationalism*, revised ed. (London and New York: Verso, 1991), p. 44.
2. These studies include: Pramoedya Ananta Toer (1961?); Suryadinata (1971); Surjomihardjo, ed. (1980); Ahmat B. Adam (1994; 1995).
3. The periodization of the Indonesian press differs from writer to writer. I have borrowed Toer's broad outline over here, but not the details.
4. Dr Alfian's oral explanation to the paper on the birth of the Nahdlatul Ulama submitted to the Second Seminar on National History, Yogyakarta, 27 August 1970.
5. D. Koesoemaningrat, "Sin Po dan Bangsa serta Pergerakan Bangsa Kita", *Sin Po Jubileum Nummer 1910-1935* (Batavia: Sin Po, 1935).
6. Sudarjo Tjokrosisworo, "Pertumbuhan Pers Nasional di Djawa Timur", in *Kenangan Sekilas Perdjuangan Suratkabar*, edited by Sudarjo Tjokrosisworo, pp. 214–32 (Djakarta: Serikat Perusahaan Surat Kabar, 1958).
7. Helen Ishwara, *P.K. Ojong: Hidup Sederhana, Berpikir Mulia* (Jakarta: Penerbit Buku Kompas, 2001); Frans M. Parera, "P.K. Ojong: Intelektual yang Menganut Sosialisme-Fabian", in *Mencari Identitas Nasional: Dari Tjoe Bou San sampai Yap Thiam Hien*, edited by Leo Suryadinata, pp. 137–72 (Jakarta: LP3ES, 1990).

8. Lie Kim Hok, *Malajoe Batawi* (Batawi: W. Bruining & Co., 1884).

9. Ahmat Adam, *Isu Bahasa dan Pembentukan Bangsa* (Kuala Lumpur: Dewan Bahasa dan Pustaka, 1994), p. 5.

10. Tio Ie Soei, *Lie Kim Hok (1853–1912)* (Bandung: Good Luck, 1958), pp. 112, 115.

11. Dede Oetomo, "The Chinese of Indonesia and the Development of the Indonesian Language", *Indonesia* (special issue: The Role of the Indonesian Chinese in Shaping Modern Indonesian Life) (1991): 53–66.

12. Cited in Tio, *Lie Kim Hok (1853–1912)*, p. 115.

13. Claudine Salmon, "Apakah Bahasa 'Melayu Tionghoa' bisa diterima?", in *Tionghoa dalam Keindonesiaan: Peran dan Kontribusi Bagi Pembangunan Bangsa*, vol. 1, edited by Leo Suryadinata and Didi Kwartanada (Jakarta: Yayasan Nabil, 2016), pp. 171–80.

14. Tio Ie Soei has also used this term "Bahasa Kerdja" to refer to the Batavian Malay. See Tio Ie Soei, "Pers, Melaju-Betawi dan Wartawan", *Istimewa* (Surabaja, 1 August 1951).

15. The term Melayu Pasar is often meant to be "pigdins Malay" or "Bazaar Malay", as if the language was used as the language of the market place which is unable to express complicated ideas. In fact, the so-called "Low Malay" used in the press is quite advanced by the standard of that era. Therefore, it should not be called "Melayu Pasar".

16. Tan Ta Sen, *Yinni wenhua lunwen ji* (Essays on Indonesian Culture) (Singapore: Jiaoyu chubanshe, 1977), p. 7.

17. Hendrik M.J. Maier, "Forms of Censorship in the Dutch Indies: The Marginalization of Chinese-Malay Literature", *Indonesia* (special issue: The Role of the Indonesian Chinese in Shaping Modern Indonesian Life) (1991): 67–81.

18. "Ejaan dan spellingnja soeda mendjalar dan terpakai hampir seloeroe Indonesia dan kita pertjaja pada akhirnja akan kalahkan dan musnahkan sama sekali Melajoe Riauw atau Melajoe Ophuijsen jang sekarang masih dilindoengkan oleh pemerentah", cited in Kwee Tek Hoay, "Almarhoem Toean Gouw Peng Liang", *Panorama*, 3 November 1928, p. 1684.

19. Liaw Yock Fang, "Lie Kimhok and the First Modern Malay/Indonesian Grammar Book", in *Southeast Asian Chinese: The Socio-cultural Dimension*, edited by Leo Suryadinata (Singapore: Times Academic Press, 1995).

20. More detailed studies should be conducted on this point.

21. Tio, *Lie Kim Hok (1853–1912)*.

22. Kwee, "Almarhoem Toean Gouw Peng Liang", pp. 11683–85.

23. Betawi is the Indonesian term for Batavia. In the modern term, it is often called Melayu-Jakarta.

24. Dr Dede Oetomo has written a fine paper on the role of the Chinese in the development of the Indonesian language, especially on the comparison

between the pre-Indonesian Malay and the Chinese Malay. See Oetomo, "The Chinese of Indonesia and the Development of the Indonesian Language".

25. Claudine Salmon, *Literature in Malay by the Chinese of Indonesia: A Provisional Annotated Bibliography*, Etudes Insulindies-archipel 3 (Paris: Éditions de la Maison des sciences de l'Homme, 1981).

26. She was referring to A. Teeuw's book. However, in the revised edition of Teeuw's book, it cited 284 writers and 770 books.

27. In fact, non-Balai Pustaka novels such as *Student Hidjo* (by Mas Marco) was published in 1918 and *Hikajat Kadiroen* (by Semaoen) was published in 1920. They also appeared after Peranakan novels.

28. Jakob Sumardjo, "Meninjau Kembali Sastra Melayu Tionghoa", in *Tiongoa dalam Keindonesiaan*, vol. 1, edited by Leo Suryadinata, Didi Kwartanada and Eddie Lembong (Jakarta: Yayasan Nabil, 2016), pp. 259–69.

29. It should be noted that the idea of reprinting pre-war Peranakan literature was in the early 1990s when I discussed this with Frans Parera of Grasindo. We planned to publish them in several batches. For the first batch, we selected twenty-four titles, including Kwee Tek Hoay's *Drama di Boven Digoel*. However, Grasindo only managed to publish my introductory book (Suryadinata 1996). The rest, which have been typeset and proofread, were abandoned.

30. The series originated from my project with Grasindo. However, it has been taken over by another publisher (Kepustakaan Populer Gramedia, KPG), which is also in the Kompas group. I was consulted in the initial stage but in the published works, there was no mention of my project with Grasindo. Nevertheless, the KPG project is larger because it includes non-literary works. The general title of this series is: *Kesastraan Melayu-Tionghoa dan Kebangsaan Indonesia*.

31. The full title of the novel: *Tjerita Oey Se, jaitoe satoe tjerita yang amat endahdan lotjoe, jang betoel soedah kedjadian di Djawa Tengah* (Solo: Shi Dian Ho, 1903).

32. The full title of the novel: *Tjerita Njai Soemirah atawa pertintaan yang kekal, satoe tjerita dari Preanger* (Batavia: Kho Tjeng Bie, 1917).

33. On Kwee Tek Hoay, see Leo Suryadinata, *Eminent Indonesian Chinese: Biographical Sketches* (Singapore: Gunung Agung, 1981), pp. 57–58; also Myra Sidharta, ed., *100 Tahun Kwee Tek Hoay: Dari Penjaja Tekstil sampai ke Pendekar Pena* (Jakarta: Sinar Harapan, 1989).

34. The novel was first published before World War II, and republished by a Jakarta publisher under the Peranakan literature series: *Kesastraan Melayu Tionghoa dan Kebangsaan Indonesia*, vol. 3 (*Drama di Boven Digul*, Karya Besar Kwee Tek Hoay) (Jakarta: KPG, 2001), p. 759.

35. For a detailed analysis of the novel, see Thomas Rieger, "Roman 'Drama Di Boven Digul' oleh Kwee Tek Hoay: Sebuah Ulasan Ringkas", in *100 Tahun*

Kwee Tek Hoay: Dari Penjaja Tekstil sampai ke Pendekar Pena, edited by Myra Sidharta (Jakarta: Sinar Harapan, 1989), pp. 122–53.

36. For the names of the writers and their works, see Leo Suryadinata, "Dari Sastra Peranakan ke Sastra Indonesia", in *Sastra Peranakan Tionghoa Indonesia*, edited by Leo Suryadinata (Jakarta: Grasindo, 1966), pp. 20–21.

37. See Ariel Heryanto, ed., *Perdebatan Sastra Konstekstual* (Jakarta: Rajawali, 1985).

38. For a discussion on Arief 's ideas, see Jamal D. Rahman, "Arief Budiman: Sumbangan bagi Kritik dan Pemikiran Sastra", in *33 Tokoh Sastra Indonesia Paling Berpengaruh*, edited by Jamal D. Rahman et al. (Jakarta: Kepustakaan Populer Gramedia, 2014), pp. 457–80.

39. Abdul Hadi's Chinese surname is "An".

40. This is based on Myra Sidharta's article on Mira Widjaja, published in Leo Suryadinata, ed., *Southeast Asian Personalities of Chinese Descent: A Biographical Dictionary* (Singapore: Institute of Southeast Asian Studies, 2012), pp. 1268–70.

41. Ibid., p. 1270.

42. http://zara-majidpour.blogspot.com/2012/07/my-music-and-my-writing-are both_05.html (accessed 10 June 2014); http://www.soetjenmarching.com/en/profile.html (accessed 10 June 2014).

43. Rahman et al., *33 Tokoh Sastra Indonesia Paling Berpengaruh*.

44. Oetomo, "The Chinese of Indonesia and the Development of the Indonesian Language", p. 65.

11

MUSLIM CHINESE IN INDONESIA: BETWEEN CHINESE-NESS AND INDONESIAN-NESS

The Chinese Indonesian Muslim community has been active again in recent years. The presence of Chinese Muslims in Indonesia is not new; there were Chinese Muslims prior to the coming of Cheng Ho (also spelled as Zheng He), a Muslim admiral during the Ming Dynasty, to Indonesia and the Chinese Muslim community was boosted in size with his visit (1405–33) but those Muslims who came then had been largely assimilated and merged into the local population. The present Chinese Muslims are relatively newer; some of them are new converts during the Suharto era and after. This chapter attempts to briefly examine the Muslim Chinese in Indonesia in terms of their origins and developments with special reference to the post-independence development. The chapter would also address the issue of Chinese-ness and Indonesian-ness among the Chinese Muslim communities.

Pre-Colonial Era

Prior to the arrival of Western colonialists, some Chinese Muslims had migrated to the Malay archipelagos. When Cheng Ho visited the areas which are now known as Indonesia, he discovered Chinese Muslim enclaves. Many argued that although Cheng Ho's mission was not to spread Islam, but it is believed that as a Muslim, he was involved in spreading the religion. In addition to Chinese temples, he built many mosques. More researches in the spread of Islam in the Malay archipelagos during the Cheng Ho period are needed, but it is interesting to note that they are many Islamic legacies attributed to Admiral Cheng Ho. From historical records such as *Lidai Bao'an* (Ryukyu Kingdoms Records) and also Raffles' *History of Java*, it was reported that some Chinese Muslims were engaged in spreading Islam in Sumatra and Java. The rise of Islamic kingdoms in Java has also been attributed to Chinese Muslims. Although some Muslim scholars doubted this as a historical fact, the historical legacies, including the architecture of mosques and Muslim tombs, and local legends pointed to the influence of China and the Chinese in Java. Many Chinese Muslims gradually integrated into local society and disappeared, and new Chinese migrants were mainly non-Muslims, giving rise to a different type of Chinese community. Nevertheless, there were still Chinese Muslim enclaves in Indonesia even after the coming of the Dutch.

Chinese Muslims during the Colonial Period

When the Dutch East Indies (VOC) was in power, it issued a regulation prohibiting the ethnic Chinese from converting to Islam and assimilating into the "indigenous" society. The Dutch authorities accused these Chinese of becoming Muslims for economic benefits as Chinese Muslims were allowed to pay lower taxes, similar to the indigenous population,[1] and the trading activities of the Chinese would now be less restricted. After the fall of the VOC, the Dutch colonial government in the nineteenth century re-issued the regulation, banning ethnic Chinese from converting to Islam.

As early as the beginning of the nineteenth century, the colonial authorities appointed two Chinese kapitans in Sumenep, the capital of Madura. One of them was tasked to administer the Chinese population, while the other was instructed to administer the Peranakans—the term used to refer to Chinese Muslims during that period.[2] The colonial government ordered the Chinese kapitans to tell the Chinese to give their loyalty to the Chinese kapitans. The Peranakan Chinese were also instructed to pay as much taxes as their non-Muslim counterparts. According to the records, there were 986 Chinese in Sumenep alone in 1865, but in the whole of Madura, there were 1,036 Chinese and 4,260 Peranakans (i.e., Chinese Muslims).[3] The Dutch records show that 80 per cent of the Chinese in Madura were Muslims. Nevertheless, according to the colonial regulation, Chinese Muslims were required to live in the Chinese ghettos, to wear Chinese attire and to keep pigtails.[4] Despite such regulations, those Chinese Muslims who resided in remote areas were living among the indigenous population and could no longer be separated.[5]

In fact, in Java, especially after the 1740 Angke (Red River) Massacre of the Chinese by the Dutch, many Chinese converted to Islam to avoid persecution. Not only did they become Muslims but they also used "indigenous" names. They were no longer under the jurisdiction of the Chinese kapitans.[6] After 1766, however, the colonial government re-appointed the Peranakan kapitan to administer Chinese Muslims.[7] During the nineteenth century, there was the Rangga rebellion in East Java in which some Chinese Muslims supported.[8] During the Diponegoro War (1825–30), Prince Diponegoro also received some support from Chinese Muslims. One of his close associates was Tjan Ali, a Chinese Muslim.[9]

The conversion of Chinese to Islam in Indonesia during the colonial period is quite complex and requires further research, but one thing is clear: the Dutch colonial authorities did not want the Chinese to convert to Islam. Apart from the economic factor mentioned earlier, the political factor is equally important, if not more. The colonial authorities feared that the ethnic Chinese would unite with the indigenous population against the colonial power. Apart from the colonial policy of divide and rule, the influx of new Chinese migrants and the rise of overseas Chinese nationalism during the beginning of the twentieth century also served as another reason for the decline in the number of Chinese Muslims. Thirdly, social stratification in colonial society also discouraged the Chinese from converting to Islam. In the colonial society, the Dutch (European) constituted the upper class, while the indigenous population formed the lower class. Islam was the religion of the indigenous population and hence was less attractive to the Chinese population.

The Dutch policy since the nineteenth century had tended to make Chinese Muslims in Indonesia a separate group from the indigenous Muslim communities. Nevertheless, not much is known about the Muslim community in the early twentieth century. Only in 1935, a group of Chinese Muslims in Medan (Sumatra) formed an organization called Persatuan Islam Tionghoa (PIT),[10] and its chapters were established in a number of cities, including Padang, Jakarta, Madura and Banjarmasin. By 1942, it claimed to have 43,000 members.[11] However, according to Oei Tjeng Hien (黄清兴, 1905–88), PIT was founded in Jakarta in 1953, and one of the founders was Oei himself.[12] Oei was an Advent, he was converted to Islam in 1931 and became active in Muhammadiyah, firstly in Bengkulu, and later in Jakarta. It was during his stay in Sumatra that he became close with Sukarno who later became the first president of Indonesia. It was also through his introduction that Sukarno got married with Fatmawati.

Chinese Muslims after Independence

According to Oei, the idea of establishing a Chinese Muslim organization came from Haji Ibrahim, then the general chairman of Muhammadiyah, who said to him that Muhammadiyah should pay a special attention to the ethnic Chinese in Indonesia.[13] One of the Chinese Muslim leaders, Yap A Siong (叶亚祥, 1894–1984) alias Haji Abdussomad (Abdul Somad) also pressured Oei to do so. Together with Yap A Siong (who converted to Islam in 1929), Oei established the Persatuan Islam Tionghoa in 1953.[14] Apparently this does not coincide with other sources, including the one provided by Yap A Siong.[15]

In 1963, Kho Goan Tjin, leader of Persatuan Tionghoa Muslim (PTM), came to visit Oei and suggested to him that PTM and PIT should be merged into one association. Oei agreed with the proposal and served as the chairman of the newly-born Chinese Muslim association, Persatuan Islam Tionghoa Indonesia, abbreviated as PITI.

It should be noted that prior to the New Order, the *dakwah* movement in general and PITI in particular was not very active. The situation changed only after the rise of Suharto and the beginning of the New Order. The rise of the *dakwah* movement should be understood in the post-1965 Indonesian context.

It should be pointed out that prior to the establishment of the New Order, there were already a few Chinese intellectuals who were either born Muslims or converts, but they were not members of PITI. These Muslims included two brothers, Tjan Tjoe Som (曾祖森, 1903–69) and Tjan Tjoe Siem (曾祖沁, 1909–78).[16] The former was Professor of Sinology at the University of Indonesia and the latter was Professor of Javanese Culture at the same university. They were descendants of Tjan Ali who was with Prince Diponegoro during the anti-Dutch war. There were a few Chinese who were converted to Islam and served as cabinet ministers such as Lie Kiat Teng (Mohammad Ali, 1912–90), representing Partai Syarikat Islam Indonesia and Tan Kim Liong (Haji Mohammad Hassan, 1925–91), representing Nahdlatul Ulama.[17]

Since the 1965 coup, religion has been cultivated by the Indonesian military to combat the communists and left-wing movements. Indonesians are expected to observe one of the organized religions and it is required to state one's religion in the identity card. Anyone who does not do so is often treated as an atheist or a communist, and this would make life very uncomfortable in the Indonesian setting. Understandably, many Chinese in Indonesia began to identify themselves with one of the existing religious groups, especially Buddhism, Christianity or Confucianism. However, before the 1970s, very few became Muslims. Apart from the socio-political condition which did not favour Islam and the existing prejudice against the religion, many Islamic practices appear to be incompatible with the Chinese belief system (for instance, pork-eating and ancestor worship).

Despite the unfavourable conditions, PITI's activities began to increase after Suharto came to power. PITI branches in various areas were established and there were reports that more Chinese were converting to Islam and joining the organization. With growing Islamic influence following the resurgence of Islam in the Middle East, there has been a movement among Chinese Indonesians to embrace the religion. Unlike earlier converts, these new Muslims were from the middle-class: they were businessmen, professionals, students and intellectuals.

There are many interpretations for this phenomenon. One is the growing influence of Islam in the Indonesian socio-political scene. It has now become respectable to be Muslims. While some Chinese became Muslims through marriage, others convert for practical reasons: it is easier to do business after conversion because the Muslim communities are less hostile towards Chinese Muslims. Some were attracted to Islam because of their close association with their Indonesian Muslim friends. Others see the conversion to Islam as the only way to solve the so-called "Chinese problem in Indonesia".

A prominent leader of this movement is Haji Junus Jahja alias Lauw Chuan Tho 刘全道, a new PITI member and a member of Majelis Ulama Indonesia (MUI). Junus is an interesting figure. Born in Jakarta into an old Peranakan family, he lost his command of Chinese dialect and Mandarin. He was a former Protestant who became a Muslim in 1979 and went on a *haji* in the following year. He received his university training in Rotterdam and obtained a degree in Economics in 1959. He was active while in the Netherlands as an advocate of assimilation ideas and urged the Chung Hwa Hui, an Indonesian Chinese students' organization in the Netherlands, to dissolve itself as having a separate Chinese association was against "Indonesian unity spirit". Not surprisingly, when he returned to Indonesia in 1960, he joined the assimilation movement (Gerakan Asimilasi) and propagated total assimilation of the Chinese into the indigenous population.[18] He also changed his Chinese name to an Indonesian one as early as 1962, five years ahead of his Peranakan counterparts. However, this assimilationist group never advocated the conversion of the Chinese to Islam, because many of them are either Christians or non-Muslims. Junus was the first member of this group who proposed conversion to Islam as the solution to the "Chinese problem".

He published books (mainly compilations of newspaper and magazine clippings) on the conversion of Chinese to Islam in Indonesia, especially during the period of 1979–88 when he was most active.[19] He organized seminars and gatherings in order to promote Islam among the Chinese. When asked about his identity, Junus answered that he is "a Muslim, an Indonesian, and a Chinese descent".[20] He emphasized his "Muslim-ness" rather than his national and ethnic identities. For him, the Islamic identity is most important. He fails to see that there is a possible conflict between religious identity on the one hand and national as well as ethnic identity on the other. He believes that Islam is a unifying factor in Indonesia and does not see the possibility of conflict occurring among Muslims.

Convinced that Islam is the solution to the so-called Chinese problem, Junus and his friends—both indigenous and Chinese—established the Yayasan Ukhuwah Islamiah (Islamic Brotherhood Foundation) in 1981 and began to propagate Islam among the Peranakan Chinese. He initiated a *dakwah* movement to convert middle-class Chinese to Islam. He published a book on *Saudara Baru* (New Muslim Converts) detailing his activities on this mission.[21] It is interesting to note that the *dakwah* movement in Indonesia differs from its counterparts in Malaysia in the sense that the latter claims to be an inward-looking movement. It does not intend to convert non-Muslims but to work among the Muslims to purify their faith. In Indonesia, or at least for the Junus group, it aims at converting non-Muslims to Islam.

The Junus group initially intended to convert 50,000 ethnic Chinese and encouraged 150,000 ethnic Chinese to intermarry with *pribumi* over a ten-year period.[22] He got the assistance of some indigenous Indonesians, both individuals and organizations, to realize the goal. The Junus group even introduced the god-father system so that ethnic Chinese youth can learn Islamic teaching and way of life by having Muslim indigenous god-fathers.[23] In the last few years, a few Chinese had indeed been converted. Some businessmen (for instance, A Boen or Jusuf Hamka), university lecturers (such as Muh. Budyatna and Ahmad Setiawan Abadi) and a movie star (George Rudy) were all converted either under his sponsorship or encouragement. In the 1980s, when asked how many Chinese in Indonesia were Muslims, Junus said that there was no statistics and was not easy to identify them, because many Muslim Chinese did not want to be identified as Chinese any more. However, he believed that between 0.5 and 1 per cent of the Chinese in Indonesia then were Muslims, i.e., about 25,000 to 50,000.[24] The objective was to have more Chinese Muslim converts. During one of the discussions with the Muslim groups, Junus stated that since 90 per cent of the *pribumi* population was Muslim, gradually 90 per cent of Chinese descent would also embrace the same religion.[25] It appears that the Islamic groups, especially the Muhammadiyah, are interested in the movement. They welcome the *dakwah* movement among the ethnic Chinese and stated that indigenous Muslims should also help the Junus group in converting the Chinese. In their view, this is the sacred mission of the Muslims.

It should be noted that in early May 1986, the University of Muhammadiyah in Yogyakarta and Yayasan Ukhuwah Islamiyah (the Junus group) together with two other organizations jointly sponsored a seminar in Yogyakarta on Islam and National Integration. Islamic scholars and practitioners were invited to present their papers on the subject. The seminar, attended by about 100 participants, proposed that the most effective vehicle for "national integration" was Islam. Nevertheless, it is important to note that Junus was not only promoting "religious assimilation" (i.e. to become Muslims) among the Chinese, but also "economic assimilation", i.e. to form partnership between Chinese businessmen and less successful indigenous businessmen. Not knowingly, in fact, Junus was shifting his argument from the religious to the economic field. He held the view that "to have an economically strong indigenous group is the key to assimilation" (*pribumi kuat kunci pembauran*).[26] In other words, to be Muslims alone would not solve the so-called Chinese problem.

There is no doubt that more Chinese Indonesians were being converted to Islam than before, but some observers maintained that converts to religions other than Islam were still more numerous than Muslim converts. It is general knowledge that Indonesian Muslims are not a homogeneous group. They are split into *santri* (strict Muslim) and *abangan* (nominal Muslim).[27] Among devout Muslims, one can also discern the followers of Muhammadiyah and Nahdlatul Ulama (NU). The Junus group appears to be closer to Muhammadiyah. However, it seems that they do not address themselves to schism in Muslim groups. The important thing for this group is that such differences are no longer measured in ethnic terms. It is also worth noting that the group does not really address itself to the economic aspect of the "Chinese problem", which cannot be simply solved by the conversion to Islam. Furthermore, the *dakwah* movement may be welcomed in the Muslim areas, but in areas where Islam is not a major religion (for instance, in Minahasa and Maluku), the conversion of the Chinese to Islam may create friction rather than harmony. Not surprisingly, the *dakwah* movement centres more on the provinces where Muslims are the majority.

The Emergence of Cheng Ho as the Symbol of Chinese Muslims

The *dakwah* movement during the New Order era had a strong assimilation flavour; it rejected the view that Islam and Chinese-ness could co-exist. There was strong pressure on the Chinese Muslims to assimilate completely to an indigenous Muslim population. It was reported that in 1966, Haji Yap A Siong flew to Medan to "invite" the Chinese Muslims to "integrate". In 1969 in North Sumatra, 3,000 Chinese were converted to Islam.[28] They had their own Islamic school in Medan called Perguruan Islam Sam Po (i.e. San Bao, another name for Cheng Ho) but it was later changed to Perguruan Islam Imam Bonjol, named after a Sumatran Islamic leader. Apparently, Sam Po was not "indigenous" enough. The school building was owned by a Hakka association which was said to have been associated with the banned Baperki. It was therefore confiscated by the regional military authority headed by Major General Mokoginta and was given to the Chinese Muslims in 1967 for an Islamic school.[29] By 1980, there were 900 Chinese and non-Chinese students, some of them were non-Muslims.

In 1972, the PITI central committee in Java also received some pressure from the assimilation group which continued to accuse the Chinese of being "exclusive". Karim Oei wrote in his memoirs that in order to convert *totok* Chinese who were not proficient in Indonesian, PITI under his leadership applied to import the Chinese translation of Al-Quran and to publish *dakwah* publications in Chinese, but his application was rejected by the Department of Religious Affairs as the government wanted to speed up the assimilation process of the Chinese.[30] That happened in 1972. In the same year the central committee of PITI received a letter from the Attorney General, ordering PITI to dissolve itself because the term "Tionghoa" contains "exclusivism". Fifteen days after the ban, a new organization called Pembina Iman Tauhid Islam (Promoter of Islamic Faith of Only One God) was established, but it was still abbreviated as PITI.[31] The organization was still active in the *dakwah* movement while the leadership organization did not change much.[32] Karim Oei stayed as the general chairman until 1973 and was made honorary chairperson after the year.

This episode is significant as from 1972 onward it appeared that PITI was transformed into an ordinary Islamic organization and was no longer for Chinese Muslims, although in reality, it continued to target on the Chinese community. Apparently, the Muslim group in the central government wanted to eliminate the ethnic Chinese elements in Islam and was temporarily successful. Nevertheless, there was a group within PITI who would like to retain some sort of Chinese identity. This was only successful after the fall of Suharto. The name of PITI after the fall of Suharto has undergone another subtle change. The official name is still "Pembina Iman Tauhid Islam" but after the name, it was inserted the old name of the organization: d/h Persatuan Islam Tionghoa Indonesia. The Chinese name of PITI is either Yinni Zhonghua [Chinese] Yishilan lianhe hui (印尼中华伊斯兰联合会) or Yinni huayi [Chinese descent] Yishilan xiehui (印尼华裔伊斯兰协会). It has therefore re-established its Chinese identity without abandoning the name used during the New Order.

The development of ethnic Chinese identity was made possible after the fall of Suharto when monoculture was replaced by multiculturalism. Assimilation policy was quietly abandoned and pluralism was adopted. The three pillars of Chinese culture (organizations, mass media and schools) have been to a large extent restored. Nonetheless, the thirty-two years of Suharto rule has had a major impact and the "assimilation" policy has been deeply rooted in the minds of both the indigenous and the Peranakan Chinese populations. Indeed, it is not easy to get rid of this mindset overnight.

The development of new Chinese Muslim identity in general and Masjid Cheng Hoo[33] in particular, has also been helped by the fall of Suharto. In the past, Cheng Ho and Chinese Muslim contributions to the spread of Islam were rejected. Anything which had "Chinese cultural elements" was not acceptable. Not surprisingly, Professor Slamet Muljana's book which asserted that Islam in Java came from China and some *wali songo* (Nine Muslim Saints) were of Chinese descent was immediately banned after its publication in 1968. Only after the removal of Suharto, with rapid globalization, democratization and revival of ethnicity, some "indigenous" Indonesian Muslims, particularly those from Nahdlatul Ulama (NU, Islamic Scholars' Association), began to re-look at the history of the spread of Islam to Indonesia. Discussion was initiated on the role of Chinese Muslims in history. Books on the subject matters were published, and old books by M.O. Parlindungan and Slamet Muljana were republished. Some Chinese Muslims, especially those who had some Chinese educational background, look up at Cheng Ho as a new symbol of Islam. It was not surprising that although the foundation was registered in 1995, the actual building of Masjid Cheng Ho was only initiated in 2001, three years after the end of the New Order.

Before discussing the establishment of Masjid Cheng Ho,[34] it is important to note that the central organization of PITI is in Jakarta, but it has branches all over Indonesia. One of the most active branches is the PITI East Java chapter under the leadership of Haji Bambang Sujanto alias Lioe Ming Yen (柳民源), a successful businessman in Surabaya, who is in various businesses, including hotel business.[35] He received some Chinese education and is still able to speak Mandarin, although his daily language is Javanese and Bahasa Indonesia. In the 1980s Bambang already served as the chairman of the PITI East Java. Under his leadership, it has been reported that in Surabaya there are many new Chinese converts. The PITI East Java chapter also publishes a bimonthly magazine entitled *Komunitas*.[36] The person in charge is also Bambang himself. It was also under his initiative that Masjid Cheng Ho was built.[37] The Chinese name of the mosque is Zheng He Qingzhensi (郑和清真寺). *Qingzhensi* is a Chinese term that refers to a mosque in China.

A question can be posed as to why the Cheng Ho Mosque was able to be established in Surabaya, and not in other parts of Indonesia. Perhaps it is linked to the condition in East Java in general, and in Surabaya in particular. East Java has been the strong hold of NU which preaches a more liberal and tolerant type of Islam. In addition, there is a group of Chinese businessmen who are also keen in promoting Islam among fellow Chinese Indonesians. It appears that they became conscious that Cheng Ho visited Gresik and Surabaya and felt proud of this.[38] Nevertheless, the most important person is perhaps Haji Bambang Sujanto who conceived the idea of building a Cheng Ho Mosque inspired by the Niu Jie (i.e., Cow Street) Mosque in Beijing.[39] He was the one who mobilized the PITI communities in East Java to realize this idea. He was also the person who sought the support of the local Chinese and non-Chinese communities, particularly the local military and police authorities.

The story of Masjid Cheng Ho is fascinating. All of the thirteen founders of the mosque were linked to PITI. Two leading founders who donated their land for the site of the mosque were Trisno Adi Tantiono (Chen Qixing 陈启兴), Chairman of the Central Committee of PITI and a businessman, and Bambang Sujanto whose name was mentioned earlier.[40] Bambang is currently the chairman of the Cheng Ho Mosque Foundation. The building of the mosque was modelled on the oldest mosque in Beijing's Niu Jie which was built in 996 AD;[41] therefore, it has a uniquely Chinese style. It consists of three colours and has the shape of a Chinese temple. The architects of the mosque were Chinese Indonesians from PITI.[42]

It is also worth noting that many of the PITI leaders in Surabaya belong to the Fuqing dialect group which has been very strong during the Suharto era. They are still able to speak Mandarin with a strong Javanese accent. They identify themselves with Muslims and pray regularly. When meeting their Muslim fellows, they greet each other by using Arabic verse. The male Chinese Muslims wear Indonesian *pici* (black velvet cap) when going to the mosque and attend official functions, but at home and office, it is not worn. This is not unique as many "indigenous Muslims" only wear *pici* during special occasions. They address themselves by their Indonesian names although many have Chinese names prior to name changing. Nevertheless, in certain publications their original Chinese names were included. In their official Cheng Ho Mosque name cards, their Chinese names are also inserted.

In their own Chinese community, they often speak some Mandarin mixed with Javanese and Indonesian. In recent years, when interactions between China and Indonesia intensified, many Chinese-speaking Muslims from China came to Surabaya. The guests and hosts conversed in Mandarin.

Recent Celebration of the Cheng Ho Mosque

The mosque has been opened for more than five years. There was a big celebration at the 5th anniversary of the mosque in 2007, during which the committee invited the Chinese consul and the American consul in Surabaya. Of course, major Indonesian Islamic organizations, namely Muhammadiyah and Nahdlatul Ulama (NU), were also present. A DVD which recorded the whole proceeding of the celebration was made. The welcome ceremony was a Chinese lion dance. Before the actual speeches were made, there were dances performed by Chinese Muslim Senopati Dance Troupe, showing local dances, Chinese dances and Mandarin songs performed by kindergarten children wearing Chinese costumes. The Mandarin song was *Shi shang zhiyou mama hao* ("In the World, Only Mama is the Best"). During this celebration, a book entitled *Tuntunan dan Terjemahan Juz'Amma bagi Saudara Baru* (Guide to verses from Al-Quran for New Converts in translations) was launched. The book was published in four languages: Indonesian, Chinese, English and Arabic. An indigenous Muslim leader purchased 500 copies of the book and distributed them freely to those who attended the celebration.

The mosque is opened to all ethnic groups. Indeed, many indigenous Indonesian Muslims visit the mosque frequently and especially for Friday prayers during which the Cheng Ho Mosque is particularly crowded. It appears that the local "indigenous" Muslims did not mind praying in the Cheng Ho Mosque.

Masjid Cheng Ho in late April 2008 organized the first international conference, inviting scholars from China, Singapore and various Indonesian universities. The theme of the conference was "Cheng Ho, Wali Songo and the Muslim Chinese in Indonesia: Past, present and future". The chairman of the conference committee was Professor A. Dahana, the former dean of the Faculty of Arts at the University of

Indonesia. The keynote speaker was Gus Dur, the former president of Indonesia who is well known for his sympathy to Chinese Indonesians. He repeated his story that he was of Chinese descent although he could no longer speak Chinese. He also noted that four of the Islamic holy men who spread Islam in Java were of Chinese descent.

It is interesting to note that the occasion was not purely an academic conference but was used as a public relations exercise. Local government officials, PITI leaders and two embassies (the PRC and the US) were invited to give speeches before the conference began. It was interesting to note that the master of ceremony used three languages: Indonesian, Mandarin and English, as there was a big delegation from the Yunnan province. Yunnan was the homeland of Cheng Ho. The conference lasted two days, but the first day was an academic conference while the second day concerned the presentation of semi-academic topics. All the papers were presented in Indonesian with simultaneous translation in Mandarin. Since the Cheng Ho Mosque Foundation was the organizer, it understandably tended to glorify Cheng Ho. No doubt, Cheng Ho made significant contributions to the cross-cultural contacts in the region and beyond, but some speakers did not differentiate between Cheng Ho as a historical figure and as a legend. Nevertheless, many scholars agree that more studies should be conducted in order to understand Admiral Cheng Ho and his contributions.

With the establishment of the Cheng Ho Mosque, it has become clear that the Chinese Indonesians wanted to assert the fact that Islam and Chinese-ness can go hand in hand. By claiming Cheng Ho and "establishing the fact" that four Chinese Muslims spread Islam in Indonesia, the Chinese Muslims would like to show that there was no conflict between Islam and Chinese-ness in Indonesia. Indirectly, they were maintaining that there is no conflict between Chinese-ness and Indonesian-ness among the Chinese Indonesian Muslims.

In fact, during the Suharto era in the past, when a group of Chinese Muslims began to launch the *dakwah* movement and urged Chinese Indonesians to convert to Islam, to become a Muslim meant to become a "Malay". To become a Malay (*masuk Melayu*) was said to be "converted to Islam" (*masuk Islam*). However, with globalization and the re-emergence of China, the old concept of being a Muslim which means to be converted into "Malay", is no longer entirely true. This has given a new dimension to Chinese assimilation in post-Suharto Indonesia.

Witnessing the rise of Chinese Muslims in Surabaya and the retention of their Chinese-ness, an indigenous scholar noted that the situation in Surabaya is perhaps unique as many indigenous Muslims appear to be able to accept the Muslim celebration and activities with "Chinese cultural characteristics", but it is not the case in Sumatra where she came from. She said that in West Sumatra, for instance, the Chinese Muslims are much more subdued. Probably, the local indigenous population still finds it hard to accept the Surabaya-type of Islam.

Conclusion

The above brief historical survey of the Chinese Muslims in Indonesia reveals the complexity of the spread of Islam in the archipelago. It also shows the importance of the state in defining the religion and ethnicity. Although Chinese Muslims in Indonesia were present before and after the visit of Cheng Ho, the Indonesian Chinese Muslims today are relatively new, as most of the older settlers have been integrated/assimilated into the so-called indigenous Indonesian communities. But not all Chinese Muslims were assimilated as the Dutch colonial authorities since the eighteenth century discouraged, if not prohibited, the Chinese to be converted to Islam. Even after they were converted, the Chinese were administered under the Chinese kapitans, making them different from the "indigenous" Muslims. Nevertheless, there were Chinese Muslims who were assimilated into the "indigenous society".

However, the influx of new Chinese migrants and the rise of overseas Chinese nationalism in Indonesia since the beginning of the twentieth century gave rise to Chinese ethnic and national identity, resulting in the conversion of the Chinese to Islam becoming less common. Only those who were less well to do tended to become Muslims and in the Chinese community when Chinese Muslims did not enjoy high status. It was only after the independence of Indonesia did the situation change somewhat. More Chinese who came from well-educated circles became Muslims but their number was limited. Many of these new converts completely abandoned their ethnic Chinese identity and assumed Indonesian Muslim identities, but a few are still recognizable. Those who still maintained ethnic Chinese identity tended to join PITI. Nevertheless, during the Suharto era, due to the implementation of the assimilation policy, even the name of PITI was changed in order to eliminate the Chinese identity "Tionghoa". It was only after the fall of Suharto that the old name was resumed, indicating that it was a Chinese Muslim association. The revival of the study of Cheng Ho and the rise of the PRC as an economic power appeared to have encouraged the retention of Chinese ethnicity. Nevertheless, the path that this group of Muslims has travelled is far from smooth, as the Indonesian society is complex and the economic and political situations have crucial impacts on the Chinese as a whole. With the establishment of Masjid Cheng Ho, the Chinese Muslims in Indonesia, at least those in East Java, would like to show that there is no conflict between Indonesian-ness and Chinese-ness. However, some "indigenous" Indonesian Muslims may not accept this "new identity".

Notes

*This chapter was first published in *Asian Culture* 32 (June 2008).
1. Karel A. Steenbrink, *Beberapa Aspek tentang Islam di Indonesia Abad ke-19* (Jakarta: Bulan Bintang, 1984), p. 87.
2. Ibid.
3. Ibid., p. 88.
4. Ibid.
5. Ibid.
6. Amen Budiman, *Masyarakat Islam Tionghoa di Indonesia* (Semarang: Tanjung Sari, 1979), p. 34.
7. Ibid.
8. Peter Carey, "Changing Javanese Perceptions of the Chinese Communities in Central Java, 1755–1825", *Indonesia*, no. 37 (April 1984): 22.
9. See Hari Suryatmoko, "Prof. Dr. Tjan Tjoe Siem", *Intisari*, April 1979. Reproduced in *Zaman Harapan Bagi Keturunan Tionghoa: Rekaman Dakwah Islamiyah, 1979–1984*, edited by Junus Jahja (Jakarta: Yayasan Ukhuwah Islamiyah, 1984), pp. 9–13. In this article, the name of Tjan's ancestor was not mentioned. I knew Professor Tjan Tjoe Siem and I have seen the family tree that he compiled but do not remember the details. I vaguely remember that one of them was Temenggung Tjan Ali.
10. According to another source, Yap A. Siong asserted that from 1936 he was involved in the Islamic movement, and together with other Chinese Muslims,

he formed PIT in Medan to prevent Chinese Muslims from becoming beggars, because "this degrades the religion that we believe in". The first president of PIT was Liem Kian Gie (Abdullah Rasyid), the vice-president was So Kien Hoa (Usman) and the secretary was Yap A. Siong (Abdussomad) himself. See "Profil Seorang Ulama Islam Tionghoa", *Pelita*, 2 January 1979 and 3 November 1980.

11. "Bukan Sebuah Pecinan + Masjid", *Tempo*, 23 August 1980, p. 52.

12. Abdul Karim Oei Tjeng Hien, *Mengabdi Agama, Nusa dan Bangsa: Sahabat Karib Bung Karno* (Jakarta: Gunung Agung, 1982), p. 198.

13. Ibid., p. 195.

14. Ibid., p. 198.

15. See note 10 here (*Pelita*, 2 January 1979).

16. One of Tjan's ancestors served in the Solo court and received an award from Mangkunegara III because of his merit in the Diponegoro War. See Leo Suryadinata, *Prominent Chinese Indonesian: Biographical Sketches* (Singapore: Institute of Southeast Asian Studies, 1995), pp. 199–200.

17. Ibid., pp. 3 and 36.

18. On Junus Jahja, see Leo Suryadinata, *Eminent Indonesian Chinese: Biographical Sketches* (Singapore: Gunung Agung, 1981), pp. 35–36.

19. Junus Jahja, *Garis Rasial Garis Usang* (Jakarta: Badan Komunikasi Penghayatan Kesatuan Bangsa, 1983); Junus Jahja, *Zaman Harapan Bagi Keturunan Tionghoa: Rekaman Dakwah Islamiyah 1979–1984* (Jakarta: Yayasan Ukhuwah Islamiyah, 1984); Junus Jahja, *Muslim Tionghoa: Kumpulan Karangan* (Jakarta: Yayasan Ukhuwah Islamiyah, 1985); Junus Jahja, *Kisah-kisah Saudara Baru* (Jakarta: Yayasan Ukhuwah Islamiyah, 1988).

20. Ahmad W. Pratiknya, ed., *Tak Semua Kakek Meilan Tak Semua Pak Ogah* (Yogyakarta: Laboratorium Da'wah, 1986), p. 41.

21. Jahja, *Kisah-kisah Saudara Baru*.

22. See Muh Budyatna, "Harapan Baru Bagi Keturunan Tionghoa", *Merdeka*, 15 January 1982.

23. The system is called the "Anak Angkat" system. See Jahja, *Muslim Tionghoa*, p. 64.

24. Pratiknya, *Tak Semua Kakek Meilan Tak Semua Pak Ogah*, pp. 43–44. However, according to a study based on the Indonesian Census 2000, 5.41 per cent of the Chinese Indonesians were Muslims. See Aris Ananta, Evi Nurvidya Arifin and Bakhtiar, "Chinese Indonesians in Indonesia and the Province of Riau Archipelago: A Demographic Analysis", in *The Ethnic Chinese in Contemporary Indonesia*, edited by Leo Suryadinata (Singapore: Institute of Southeast Asian Studies, 2008), pp. 17–47.

25. Ibid., pp. 45–46.

26. See Riyanto D. Wahono, *70 Tahun Junus Jahja: Pribumi Kuat Kunci Pembauran* (Jakarta: PT Bina Rena Pariwara, 1997), pp. 542–45 (First published in 1994.)

27. On the division of Islam in Java, see Clifford Geertz, *The Religion of Java* (New York: Free Press, 1960).

28. "Bukan Sebuah Pecinan + Masjid", p. 52.

29. Ibid.

30. Oei, *Mengabdi Agama, Nusa dan Bangsa*, pp. 199–200.

31. Ibid.

32. Ibid.

33. Please note that the official name of the mosque is Masjid Cheng Hoo (not Ho).

34. Please note that the official name of the mosque is Masjid Cheng Hoo (not Ho), it is a special spelling used by the Chinese in East Java.

35. Jahja, *Kisah-Kisah Saudara Baru*, p. 83.

36. I have read recent issues of *Komunitas*, which published articles and reports not only on Islamic activities, but also activities on other non-Islamic Chinese organizations such as Klenteng Boen Bio and Klenteng Hong San Ko Tee. There are also reports on Chinese festivals, Chinese history and Chinese culture. See for instance, *Komunitas*, no. 35 (October 2007) and no. 39 (April 2008).

37. "Masjid Cheng Hoo Mengapa di Surabaya?", *Komunitas*, no. 35 (October 2007): 3.

38. The mosque is in contrast with Sam Po Tong atau Klenteng Sam Po (Sambao Miao) in Semarang. The former is a mosque while the latter is a temple, although both are visited by Chinese and non-Chinese believers.

39. "Masjid Cheng Hoo Mengapa di Surabaya?", *Komunitas*, no. 35 (October 2007): 3–4.

40. *Sekilas Tentang Masjid Muhammad Cheng Hoo Indonesia* (Brochure), n.d., p. 5.

41. Ibid.

42. These are Ir. Azis Johan, HS Willy Pangestu, Donny Asalim SH, Ir. Tony Bagyo and Ir. Rachmad Kurnia. See "Masjid Cheng Hoo Mengapa di Surabaya?", *Komunitas*, no. 35 (October 2007): 3–4.

12

STATE AND "CHINESE RELIGIONS" IN INDONESIA: CONFUCIANISM, TRIDHARMA AND BUDDHISM DURING THE SUHARTO RULE AND AFTER*

State and "Chinese Minority Religions"

For political scientists and political sociologists, "state" is an important actor to be considered in dealing with communities and societies in developing societies. This is also the case when one deals with religions in developing countries. Of course, there are strong states and weak states, and their role differs. A strong state tends to determine the form and contents of minority religions. A question can be posed here: is there strong evidence to substantiate this argument? If so, to what extent a strong state determines the form and contents of minority religions? I would like to use Suharto's Indonesia and post-Suharto's Indonesia as an example to illustrate the role of a strong state and its impact on "Chinese minority religions".[1]

A few words about the Chinese in Indonesia are in order. Indonesia is a multi-ethnic and multi-religious society. It has a population of around 238 million, consisting of more than one hundred ethnic groups and six major religions, namely Islam, Protestantism, Catholicism, Hinduism (Hindu-Bali), Buddhism and Confucianism. About 87 per cent of the Indonesian population are Muslim. Ethnic Chinese is one of the Indonesian ethnic groups and constitutes only approximately two per cent of the total population.[2] However, Chinese Indonesians are also multi-religious; the majority are Buddhists, followed by Christians (Protestants and Catholics), Confucians,[3] and Muslims. Economically, the majority of Chinese Indonesians belong to the middle class. Culturally, they are also divided into Indonesian-speaking and Chinese-speaking subgroups, but the former forms the majority.

When Suharto came to power after crushing the so-called 30th September 1965 movement, he introduced a total assimilation policy towards the Chinese minority group, urging them to integrate with and assimilate into the "indigenous society" (*masyarakat Indonesia asli*) without any delay.[4] He believed that the Chinese minority was a security risk and had a tendency to be oriented toward mainland China. But most importantly he had strong prejudice against things Chinese. He believed in establishing an indigenous-based nation, seeing Chinese culture as "foreign" and hence had to be eradicated. In order to achieve this goal, his newly established regime decided to eliminate four pillars of Chinese culture, namely ethnic Chinese organizations, Chinese schools, Chinese mass media (especially newspapers) and Chinese religions.[5] On 1 October 1965, all Chinese language newspapers and Chinese organizations were dissolved. In the following year, all Chinese-medium schools (which were then for non-Indonesian children) were closed down. In the same year (1966), a name-changing regulation was promulgated, "encouraging" Chinese Indonesians to change their Chinese names to Indonesian-sounding names in order to show their "political loyalty" to Indonesia. There is no clear definition what an Indonesian-sounding name is, but Sanskrit, Arabic and even Western names are all considered as "Indonesian-sounding names". Nevertheless, he did not ban the fourth pillar, Chinese religions, as Chinese religions were still useful in combating communist and "left-wing" ideology. The state ideology was another reason for not banning Chinese religions. This point will be discussed later.

Some observers have argued that during the absence of the other three Chinese cultural pillars, many ethnic Chinese have used Chinese religions as a means to retain their ethnic identity. Why did the Suharto government fail to eradicate Chinese religions? Apart from its utility value as mentioned earlier, another major reason was that the Republic of Indonesia has been based on Pancasila, or the Five Principles, which accepted "religious freedom" as one of the principles. This principle is not meant to protect the Chinese minority; it is merely a reflection of the multi-religious nature of the indigenous Indonesian society: there are Muslims, Catholics, Protestants, Hindu Balinese, Buddhists, Confucians and others. The Chinese minority has indirectly benefitted from this state ideology of Pancasila which was formulated by Sukarno, the first president of Indonesia, in June 1945 soon before Indonesia declared its independence.[6] In fact, during the Sukarno era (1959–65), the Republic of Indonesia recognized six official religions in Indonesia, namely Islam, Catholicism, Protestantism, Hindu-Bali, Buddhism and Confucianism. This was reflected in the 1965 Law no. 1. Nevertheless, when Suharto came to power in 1966, it took a while for his government to de-recognize Confucianism. This will be explained later. However, since 1967 Suharto promulgated Presidential Instruction no. 14 prohibiting Chinese festivals to be celebrated and religious ceremony to be performed in public places, signifying the government's decision to control and eradicate Chinese culture in Indonesia.

In the Indonesian context, Chinese religions include Confucianism, known in Indonesian as Khong Kauw (孔教) before the New Order (1966–98) or Agama Khonghucu after Suharto came to power; Sam Kauw (三教) before the New Order or Tri-religions, also known as Tridharma in Indonesia after Suharto assumed power; and Buddhism/ Chinese Buddhism. However, these Chinese religions have been highly Indonesianized in order to survive and to be accepted as "Indonesian religions".

Agama Khonghucu[7]

Khong Kauw as an organized religion only emerged in the twentieth century, although it had a temple in Surabaya known as Boen Bio (文庙,

Wen Miao) in the nineteenth century. But it developed into a movement at the turn of the twentieth century together with the establishment of the leading Chinese association called Tiong Hoa Hwee Koan (中华会馆) in Jakarta (Batavia), which honoured Confucius. However, Khong Kauw Hwee, the Confucian Religious Society, came into being with the rise of Chinese reform movement led by Kang Youwei 康有为 and Liang Qichao 梁启超 in China.

It should be briefly noted that there are two schools of thought in China regarding Confucianism; one regards it as a philosophy while the other as a religion. The worship of Confucius only happened after his death and Confucianism was transformed into a "popular religion" in China.[8] Toward the end of the Qing dynasty there was also an attempt to make Confucianism (Kongjiao) the state religion of China. The people behind this were Kang Youwei and his colleagues and followers. Kang's reform movement in China failed and he fled to Japan and later Singapore, Malaya and Java before returning to China after the 1911 revolution. During his stay in island Southeast Asia, he promoted Confucianism. However, there was no establishment of Kongjiao hui or Khong Kauw Hwee either in Singapore, Malaya or Java. While back in China, Kang Youwei and his followers still tried to revive his Confucian Order, he intended to establish Kongjiao hui to promote Confucianism. The idea was mooted much earlier but it never materialized until 7 October 1912 when he instructed his follower Chen Huanzhang (陈焕章) to set up the society in Shanghai.[9] Not surprisingly, Kongjiao hui in Southeast Asia only came into being after the emergence of Shanghai's Kongjiao hui. It was reported that the first Khong Kauw Hwee in Indonesia was set up in 1918 in Solo (Surakarta).[10] Khong Kauw Hwee later developed slowly and became a Chinese-Indonesian religious organization known as Agama Khonghucu.

With the rise of Indonesian nationalism in the twentieth century and the localized nature of the Peranakan Chinese society, Khong Kauw or the Confucian religion has been gradually Indonesianized, not only in terms of language but also some of its contents. This was to suit the development of Indonesian nationalism and politics. When Suharto came to power in 1966, the new government required every Indonesian to have an organized religion which had to be included in the Indonesian identity cards. Those who did not believe in any religion would be considered as atheists/communist sympathizers and would encounter difficulty in daily life. It was during this period (1967) that Khong Kauw Hwee changed its name to Majelis Tinggi Agama Khonghucu Indonesia (The Supreme Council for the Confucian Religion in Indonesia, abbreviated as Matakin) and Khong Kauw was transformed into an organized religion called Agama Khonghucu (Khonghucu 孔夫子 is an Indonesian Hokkien term for Confucius, and *agama* is an Indonesian word for "religion"). Khong Kauw has become an Indonesian religion which fulfilled the first requirement of the Indonesian state ideology, Pancasila: belief in one supreme god.

Since then, Agama Khonghucu has had its complete teachings. Its god is called Thian (Tian, 天), its prophet is Confucius, its "bible" is *Kitab yang Empat* (also known as *Su Si, Shishu* 四书), its place for worship is *lithang* (*litang* 礼堂, hall), and its priesthood consists of Kauw Seng (教生), Bun Su (文士) and Haksu (学师). Its song book is entitled *Kitab Nyanyian* (Song Book). There are sermons and hymns sung in the Confucian church (*lithang*) which are conducted in Indonesian. In fact, this is modelled on Christianity and Islam.[11] The priests are generally men although there is a Confucian woman priest (Bunsu) called Titis who is an indigenous Indonesian.[12] This is an exception rather than a rule. Agama Khonghucu is uniquely Chinese Indonesian as it cannot be found elsewhere.

Despite its Indonesian characteristics, its religious terms are derived from Hokkien Chinese, and the majority of its followers are Peranakan Chinese, the more localized Chinese. From the "assimilationist perspective", it is still considered as "Chinese", and became the target of the assimilationists. However, at the beginning of the New Order period, Agama Khonghucu was still useful for the state as it provided a religion to a minority group and hence it was believed that its followers would not be influenced by left-wing and communist ideology, which was regarded as the major threat of the new Indonesian state. In the 1967 Confucian Congress, Suharto himself wrote a speech, congratulating the Confucians and wishing the Congress a success. However, by 1978, the state changed its view on the Confucian religion. It felt that Agama Khonghucu was still "un-Indonesian enough" as it was based on Chinese culture and hindered the assimilation of the ethnic Chinese into the indigenous society. The Suharto group began to take action against Agama Khonghucu. On 18 November 1978, the Minister of Home Affairs issued a ministerial letter to announce that Confucianism was derecognized as a religion.[13] The fact that the letter was not issued by the Minister of Religious Affairs but that of the Home Affairs was significant as this shows that it was a political rather than a religious issue. The New Order government also began to argue that Confucianism was a philosophy, not a religion, and hence from November 1978, the government only recognized five official religions: Islam, Catholicism, Protestantism, Bali-Hinduism and Buddhism. Not surprisingly, the 1979 Congress of Agama Khonghucu did not get a permit and thus was unable to be convened. The impact of this decision was significant: the Confucian religion was taken out of the school curriculum. All Confucians in the Indonesian identity card would be listed as "Buddhist".

Under this difficult situation, the Confucians found ways and means in order to survive. A primary school in Surakarta (Solo) which is associated with the Confucius religious organization called UKS SD Tripusaka, for instance, had to adopt Hinduism as the official religion of the school[14] and teach Confucian religion outside school hours. A small *lithang* rather than a Hindu temple was established in the school. Another school in Tangerang (West Java) which was sponsored by the Confucian religious organization is called Perguruan Setia Bhakti, but the official religion of the school was Buddhism.[15] However, there is no *wihara* (Buddhist temple) on campus but a small *lithang*. Similar to the Solo school, Confucius teaching was only given outside school hours. It is also worth noting that near by the Tangerang school, there is a large *lithang* for the Matakin to hold major events.

As stated earlier, Suharto did not ban the Confucian religion but withdrew its recognition as an "officially recognized religion". As a result the Agama Khonghucu encountered tremendous difficulties and was unable to develop. Despite the suppression of the state, many Confucians continued to practise their religion and married in accordance with the rules set by the Indonesian Confucian religion, but there was no open challenge to the state's decision. The situation only changed towards the end of the Suharto rule.

In 1995, there was an event which showed that Indonesian Confucians attempted to challenge the state power. A young Chinese Indonesian couple (known as Budi Wijaya and Lany Guito), who are followers of Agama Khonghucu, got married in Boen Bio (Confucian Temple, Surabaya) and according to the Indonesian law, followers of religion other than Islam are required to register their marriages at the Civil Registry Office, failing which their marriage would be considered as illegal. The Civil Registry Office refused to register the Budi-Lany marriage because the state no longer recognized Confucianism. However, the officer offered to register their marriage as Buddhist. Budy and Lany refused to change their religion and sued the chief of Civil Registry Office for refusing to register their Confucian marriage. The court case received wide attention and lasted for a few months, even Abdurrahman Wahid (Gus Dur, who later became the president of Indonesia), who was then a general leader of the Nahdlatul Ulama, the largest Muslim organization in Java, attended the court hearing. The Budi-Lany lawyers argued that Pancasila guarantees religious freedom for Indonesian citizens and Confucianism is a religion and therefore the Civil Registry Office did not have the right to reject the registration of the Confucian marriage. But the Indonesian lawyers argued that Confucianism is not a religion and that even if it was a religion, it was no longer recognized and that the Civil Registry Office had the right to reject the registration. The Surabaya Court finally decided that it was beyond its authority to decide whether or not Confucianism is a religion. Since the Ministry of Religious Affairs no longer recognized Confucianism, the Civil Registry Office, which is a state institution, should follow the existing regulations. The court decision was not well received by the Chinese and some indigenous individuals. But not much could be done. Budi-Lany decided to appeal and the procedure was lengthy and they had to wait until the fall of Suharto (see below).

Agama Tridharma

While some Chinese in Indonesia consider Confucianism as an independent religion, others consider it as part of the so-called Sam Kauw or the Three Religions: Confucianism, Taoism and Buddhism.

Sam Kauw has been developed in Indonesia prior to World War II. The Sam Kauw organization (Sam Kauw Hwee) was established around 1934 by a Peranakan Chinese writer and community leader Kwee Tek Hoay (1886–1951) who attempted to unite these three Chinese religions. The Indonesian Chinese temples known as *klenteng* in Indonesian, in fact, is a manifestation of this belief as the deities worshipped in these temples consist of the three religious elements.

After World War II, Kwee Tek Hoay developed the Sam Kauw Hwee into Gabungan Sam Kauw Hwee (Federation of Sam Kauw Organizations) and served as its president, with its headquarters in Jakarta. In 1951 Kwee passed away and he was succeeded by a Dutch-educated geographer Khoe Soe Khiam who later changed his name to Sasanasurya. Kwee's daughter Kwee Yat Nio (better known as Mrs Tjoa Hin Hoeij) served as Khoe Soe Khiam's deputy.[16] When Suharto came to power, Gabungan Sam Kauw Hwee was changed to the Indonesian name "Gabungan Tridharma Indonesia" (GTI). The name changing was a reflection of the government's assimilation policy. Sam Kauw is not "Indonesian", thus it had to be "Indonesianized". In fact, Tridharma comes from Sanskrit but it has been accepted as an Indonesian word.

In 1967, in Surabaya a new organization called Perhimpunan Tempat Ibadat Tri Dharma (PTITD) was founded by a Chinese-educated Indonesian businessman by the name of Ong Kie Tjay, who has a family temple called Pek Yun King, which is located in Lawang, East Java. The PTITD is also a federation of the three Chinese religions, but it is more specific than the GTI (Jakarta) as the latter is the federation of Chinese temple associations. During the early years of the New Order (1966–98), the Indonesian military commander of the Brawijaya Division in East Java, General Jassin, was eager to implement the assimilation policy and prohibited the use of the term which reflects Chinese culture. He suggested that the term *tempat ibadat* (worship place) should be used, and Sam Kauw should also be changed to Tri Dharma. Nevertheless, Tri Dharma was not recognized as an official religion in Indonesia. Followers of Tri Dharma should be registered as Buddhist in their identity cards and there were no protest from the Tridharma community.

Initially, there was cooperation between GTI and PTITD. It appears that the PTITD was able to develop. In the mid-1980s, Ong Kie Tjay expressed his desire to step down and an election was to be held. The GTI sent a proxy called Samiaji to contest the general chairmanship of PTITD. Ongko Pra Wiro (alias Wang Qinghui 王钦辉), son of Ong Kie Tjay, was also proposed as a candidate. Ongko defeated Samiaji easily and succeeded his father as the general chairman of the PTITD.[17] The two organizations remain separated until today. In fact, GTI is closer to Buddhism while PTITD is closer to Taoism.[18] The former is dominated by Western and Indonesian-educated while the latter is controlled by Chinese and Indonesian-educated. Gradually, the PTITD grew rapidly and appeared to have taken over the leadership of the Tridharma movement. Although PTITD was allowed to exist and the Chinese temples were allowed to operate, during the Suharto period, it encountered a lot of difficulties as the government only recognized Buddhism and their *klentengs* at one time were subject to "reform". This point will be discussed later in the following section.

Buddhism

As stated earlier, during the New Order, the Suharto government attempted to intensify the assimilation of Chinese Indonesians into the indigenous society by eradicating "Chinese cultural elements". Chinese temples (*klentengs*) were considered as the manifestation of Chinese culture and hence had to be cleansed out. Drs W.D. Sukisman, a Brigadier-General who was also a sinologist, noted that the Chinese temple has four functions for the Chinese,[19] namely: a place to take oath; a place to hold a wedding ceremony; a place to perform an adopting child ceremony; and a gathering place for the Chinese organizations to keep the Chinese culture/tradition alive.

However, he argued that by the 1990s, the government succeeded in eliminating the four functions, but failed to eradicate the *klenteng* as a place to worship Chinese gods and goddess. Due to the strong Chinese characters, many indigenous Indonesian leaders during the Suharto era attempted to transform the *klenteng* to *wihara* (or *vihara*, Buddhist temple). *Wihara* is considered to be "Indonesian" while *klenteng* is not.

The Buddhist organization Walubi was given the task to help transform these *klentengs* to *wiharas*. In early 1984, Walubi organized a workshop to discuss "the problem of *Klenteng*". Oka Diputhera, the director of the Buddhist/Hindu Department in the Ministry of Religious Affairs, stated that in the transition period, the government divided the Chinese temples into three types, as follows:

1. Full *wihara*—There are only Buddha or Bodhisattva statues in the *klenteng*.
2. *Wihara*—There are some Buddhist elements in the *klenteng*.
3. Chinese worship place—The *klenteng* without Buddhist elements. These can be transformed into *wihara*.

General Sunarso, the head of the State Intelligence Body, disagreed with Oka's view. He stated that all *klentengs* are traditional Chinese worship places. They have to be transformed into *wiharas*. As mentioned earlier, the "Indonesianization" of *klentengs* took place soon after Suharto took over power, especially in East Java where all the *klentengs* were called *tempat ibadat* (*ibadah*, a worship place). However, the military government did not stop there. It wanted the Buddhist organization to lead the transformation process, which many Buddhists were reluctant. Nevertheless, under pressure from the government, many *klentengs* were forced to change to *wiharas*. Their Chinese names were changed to Buddhist names; this is especially the case in Jakarta. For instance, the large and old *klenteng* Kim Tek Ie (Jin De yuan, 金德院), which was located in the Chinatown area, was renamed Vihara Dharma Bhakti. This was managed by a foundation consisting of Indonesian citizens. Between 1990 and 1995 the chairman of this foundation was an indigenous Indonesian Muslim, not a Chinese Indonesian Buddhist.[20] One *klenteng* building which is also located in Jakarta, Vihara Dhamma Cakka Jaya, was even renovated to make it less Chinese.[21] This is due to the fact that the foundation of the Buddhist temple was headed by an Indonesian admiral D.P. Koesno who renovated the temple many times. In Malang (East Java), a Maitreya Buddhist temple was also "Indonesianized". Non-Buddhist gods and goddess, including the "Eight Immortals" (Ba Xian, 八仙) and Guan Gong (关公) statues were removed. Nevertheless, it seems that there was no unified view within the government and the religious issue is complex and sensitive. Therefore, apart from a few temples which were "transformed" into the so-called "Buddhist temples", the Chinese contents of the majority of the *klentengs* were rather unchanged; in other words, the destruction of Chinese *klentengs* by the Indonesian authorities was rather limited.

As stated earlier, the government intervention in "cleansing" Chinese religions also affected Buddhism in Indonesia. Buddhism under Suharto was developed to suit the first principle of Pancasila, i.e. to "believe in one supreme god". As many argued that Buddhism did not have the concept of god, therefore some Indonesian Buddhists attempted to establish a new Buddhist religion. The most well-known was Bhikkhu Ashin Jinarakkhita (1923–2002) who was a Peranakan Chinese called Tee Boan An (戴满安). His sect argued that in Indonesian Buddhism there was a concept of Adi Buddha (Great Buddha) which is equivalent to the Supreme God. He then looked at the old Javanese text to prove his point. However, many pointed out that the text did not exactly have the word "adi" but in the Ashin's translation, he added the word and gave his own interpretation.[22] The Ashin organization, known as Sangha Agung Indonesia, had a large number of followers who eventually came into conflict with other Buddhist sects which were more traditional in their concept. Interestingly Ashin's sangha, which was initially supported by the government, eventually lost the support. His group was expelled from the Indonesian Buddhist General Organization (Perwakilan Umat Buddha Indonesia, Walubi) and the government supported the group led by Siti Hartati Murdaya (alias Zou Liying 邹丽英), a wealthy business woman who is also a Buddhist. As a result, there was a major conflict within the Buddhist community.

Post-Suharto Situation

Suharto's thirty-two-year rule has restricted Chinese religions in Indonesia and affected the number of followers. There has been a drastic decline in the number of Confucians. But it also forced Chinese religions in Indonesia to be "more Indonesian" in terms of form and contents.

Agama Khonghucu which was de-recognized in November 1978 attempted to reclaim its loss after the fall of Suharto. In 1998 when

Habibie succeeded Suharto to become president, the political system was liberalized, and ethnic Chinese were allowed to form ethnic political parties but the restrictions on Chinese customs and religions, especially Agama Khonghucu, were not relaxed. The Presidential Instruction no. 14/1967 issued during Suharto's time was still enforced. It was not until Abdurrahman Wahid (Gus Dur) became the president succeeding Habibie that the Presidential Instruction no. 14/1967 was abolished.[23] Gus Dur declared that his government recognized the Confucian religion and ethnic Chinese were free to hold their festivals and performed their religious practices. With regard to Agama Khonghucu, the Minister of Religious Affairs, Surjadi, issued an instruction on 31 March 2000 (no. 477/805/Sj) abolishing the 1978 Ministerial Letter which only recognized five religions and restated that the Agama Khonghucu was now the sixth officially recognized religion in Indonesia.[24] To emphasize the change, Gus Dur as the president of Indonesia attended the Lunar New Year celebration organized by Matakin. Nevertheless, this did not mean that Agama Khonghucu was accepted to be registered in the Indonesian identity card. Many regional bureaucrats were still reluctant to implement the policy as many instructions had not reached the regional level. Despite Gus Dur's efforts, it took several years before Confucianism was eventually accepted as a religion for inclusion in the Indonesian identity card. That was in 2006 during the presidency of Susilo Bambang Yudhoyono.[25]

Agama Khonghucu was eventually recognized but the Confucian marriages which took place before the re-recognition of Agama Khonghucu were still considered invalid. For instance, Budi and Lany who got married in 1995 had to be re-married in order to get the marriage certificate based on the Confucian religion. It was done during Gus Dur's time and with the help of Gus Dur, but it seems that the legal procedure still required Budi and Lany to do this in order to make it legal. Many felt that it was too troublesome.

The Confucian religion re-emerged after the fall of Suharto. This is especially the case after President Gus Dur announced the Lunar New Year (often called Chinese New Year) as an Indonesian optional holiday and President Megawati declared it as a national holiday. During the Lunar New Year celebration organized by the Matakin, various

Indonesian presidents, beginning from Gus Dur to Megawati and Susilo Bambang Yudhoyono, attended the celebration. This has often given a wrong impression as if the number of Confucians after the fall of Suharto has increased. The fact is just the opposite.

In the 1971 population census Confucians constituted 0.82 per cent of the Indonesian population (970,000), many thought that their percentage and absolute number would have still been similar after the fall of Suharto. However, there was no data given on the number of Confucians in the 2000 population census as they were listed under the category of "Others". In the "Others" category which was only 0.20 per cent of the population, more than half were either Indians or Arabs.[26] Even if half of the 0.20 per cent were Confucians, their total number was only 201,242. In the 2005 inter-population census survey, however, the number of Confucians was recorded as 205,757, which constituted 0.1 per cent of the Indonesian population.[27] My estimate for the number of Confucians in 2000 is close to the inter-census population report. Nevertheless, a more reliable percentage and figure may be reflected in the 2010 population census:[28] there were 117,091 Confucians, constituting 0.05 per cent of the Indonesian population. Both the percentage and absolute number of Confucians are much lower than those in 1971! The explanation may lie in the following reasons: there has been a drastic decline in the population growth rate of the Chinese Indonesians vis-à-vis that of indigenous Indonesians, but the most important reason is the impact of Suharto's suppression towards Confucianism in particular and his assimilation policy in general. It is also possible that some Confucians have become either Buddhist or Christian.

The position of Buddhism in Suharto's Indonesia was definitely better than that of Confucianism. The Buddhists used the opportunity to develop Buddhism. Many new Buddhist temples (*wiharas*) were established, particularly in some cities where the number of ethnic Chinese population is large. For examples, Vihara Mahavira Graha Pusat (Dacongshan Xichan Si, 大丛山西禅寺) and Dharmasagara (Fahaishi, 法海寺), both are in Jakarta. Nevertheless, there are also new *wiharas* in the outer islands, for instance, the Maitreya Temple on the Batam island (Maha Vihara Duta Maitreya Temple), which was established during Suharto's time but was only completed in 1999. This was supposed to be the largest Maitreya Buddhist temple in Indonesia, if not in Southeast Asia. It is interesting to note that this mega temple is connected to a Taiwan Buddhist organization, showing the internationalization of religion in this globalizing era. It should also be noted that the doctrine of this Maitreya Buddhism has also been adjusted to suit Indonesian state ideology. The Maitreya Buddhism admits the existence of the Ming Ming God (明明上帝) and its Indonesian translation for this god is simply *Tuhan yang Maha Esa* (the one supreme god), which coincides with the first principle of Pancasila. While Buddha Thien Ran (Tianran Gufo, 天然古佛) and Bodhisattva Yue Hue (Yuehui Pusa, 月慧菩萨) are called Bapak Guru Agung (Great Teacher) and Ibu Guru Suci (Holy Mother) respectively.[29]

Indonesian Buddhists are far from being united as shown in the previous section. During the Suharto era, they were divided and after his fall they remained divided. After the fall of Suharto, the Buddhist organization, Walubi, which was under the leadership of Hartati and supported by the government, was challenged by the anti-Hartati group. In November 1998 Hartati dissolved Walubi but in December 1998 her group immediately formed a new organization called Perwakilan Umat Buddha Indonesia (Representatives of Indonesian Buddhist Community, also shortened as Walubi). Hartati was re-elected as its leader. The anti-Hartati group established a different Buddhist association called Konferensi Agung Sangha Indonesia (KASI, Indonesian Supreme Sangha Conference), which consists of the Ashin group and other Buddhist organizations. The split within the Buddhist community is still unsolved.

Finally, let us discuss Tridharma. Organizationally, like Buddhism, there is no united organization of Tridharma. The GTI is reported to be in existence with its headquarters in Jakarta but not much information is available; while the PTITD's stronghold is still in East and Central Java. The PTITD headquarters which is located in East Java, consists of Tridharma regional organizations known as Tempat Ibadat Tri Dharma (TITD), of which the strongest at the moment is the TITD Central Java. The TITD Central Java claims to have united 80 per cent of the Chinese temples in that region and is also the most active regional Tridharma organization. Next is the TITD East Java and the weakest is TITD West Java.[30] However, as Tridharma has never been recognized as a religion and the followers of Tridharma have officially been included as Buddhists, the presence of Tridharma as a religion is never officially recognized by the Indonesian government. In other words, it never entered into the school curriculum. Nevertheless, Tridharma can still operate as long as it does not demand the recognition of the Indonesian state as another official religion.

Unlike Confucianism, Buddhism/Chinese Buddhism was able to maintain its hold in Indonesia, but surprisingly, the percentage of Buddhists did not grow either, despite Suharto favouring Buddhism over Confucianism. According to the 2000 population census, there were 1,694,682 Buddhists which constituted 0.84 per cent of Indonesia's total population.[31] But according to the 2005 inter-population census survey, the Buddhists only formed 0.6 per cent,[32] and by 2010, according to the population census, it increased to 0.72 per cent, i.e. 1,703,254.[33] When compared to the percentage in the 1971 population census in which the Buddhists constituted 0.92 per cent of the total Indonesian population, the percentage of Buddhists in Indonesia in 2010 had obviously declined, but not its absolute number (1,092,314). There are two explanations for this: the Chinese Indonesian population in general has declined significantly; some Chinese might have converted to other religions, especially Christianity (Protestantism and Catholicism). The distribution of Chinese Indonesians in the 2010 population census by their religions is shown in Table 12.1.

TABLE 12.1
Chinese Indonesians by Religions in the 2010 Population Census

Followers of Religion	Percentage among the Chinese	Percentage of the total population
Muslims	4.65	87.51
Christians	42.80	9.90
Buddhists	49.06	0.72
Hindus	0.13	1.69
Confucians	3.32	0.05
Others	0.04	0.13
Total	100.00	100.00

Source: Ananta et al. (2015), pp. 257, 271.

Conclusion

The study of state and Chinese minority religions clearly shows that the Indonesian state was strong during the Suharto era and it had a profound impact on these religions. The state decided the form of these Chinese religions and forced some contents to change in order to suit the state regulations. The most obvious was reflected in Indonesian Confucianism. The religion was Indonesianized, and the teachings were adjusted. Regardless of this transformation, due to its "Chineseness" of the religion, it was eventually de-recognized by the state which resulted in the decline of the Confucian religion. The decline was quite dramatic and the number of Confucians has continued to decrease even after the fall of Suharto. Confucianism has been struggling to survive in Indonesia.

The story of Tridharma is similar to that of Confucianism but less dramatic since the Tridharma identity is unclear. One group identified with Buddhism, therefore it did not become a problem; but the other group inclined towards Taoism and was unable to develop. The government at one time attempted to transform Tridharma *klenteng* but without much success.

As noted earlier, Buddhism has had a better experience compared to Confucianism and Tridharma as the Suharto government intended to use Buddhism to undermine Confucianism and Tridharma (Taoism). However, the intervention of the Indonesian state also resulted in the division within Buddhist organizations. Besides this, one sect wanted to adjust the Buddhist teaching to suit the state ideology, Pancasila: belief in one supreme god. But with the passing away of Ashin, this group has also been weakening. The number of Buddhists in Indonesia has increased slightly but its percentage has been declining.

In the past, when we talked about Chinese cultural pillars outside China (especially in Southeast Asia), we often identified only three of them: Chinese organizations, Chinese newspapers (press) and Chinese-medium schools. As a matter of fact, there is another pillar, namely "Chinese religions", which has been forgotten. One can argue that Chinese religions during the Suharto era had been used by the Chinese community to retain their Chinese identity as religious freedom has been included in the state ideology, Pancasila, and many Chinese Indonesians used Chinese religions quite effectively to achieve this objective.

However, after the fall of Suharto and the introduction of political democracy, Chinese religions have lost much of the function of Chinese identity as there are now many ways for Chinese Indonesians to preserve their identity. The three cultural pillars have been restored and the Chinese can now practise their customs, use their language and celebrate their festivals. The Lunar New Year or Chinese New Year, which is considered to be the symbol of Chinese culture, has also been declared as a national holiday in Indonesia since 2002. One can, therefore, argue that Chinese Indonesian identity has been re-established.

Notes

*This chapter was first published in Tan Chee Beng, ed., *After Migration and Religious Affiliation: Religions, Chinese Identities and Transnational Networks* (Singapore: World Scientific Publishing, 2014), pp. 19–42.

1. Tan Chee Beng suggests that Chinese religions can be divided into "Chinese religions" and "Chinese Buddhism" as they have two different components. In his view, Chinese religions subscribe to the multiple-deities concept. Buddhism, when it was transformed in China and became Mahayana Buddhism, also adopted the multiple-deities concept. See Tan Chee Beng, "The Study of Chinese Religions in Southeast Asia: Some Views", in *Southeast Asian Chinese: The Socio-cultural Dimension*, edited by Leo Suryadinata (Singapore: Times Academic Press, 1995), pp. 139–65. I have adopted Tan's concept of Chinese religions in this chapter.

2. According to the 2010 population census, Chinese Indonesians only constitute 1.2 per cent of the total population (*Kewarganegaraan*, 2011, p. 10). As many ethnic Chinese did not identify themselves as "Chinese" during the population census, I believe that the actual Chinese figure is slightly higher.

3. In this chapter, the term "Confucians" is used to refer to the followers of Agama Khonghucu (the Confucian religion).

4. Soeharto, *Soeharto, Pikiran, Ucapan, dan Tindakan Saya: Otobiografi seperti dipaparkan kepada G. Dwipayana dan Ramadhan K.H.* (Jakarta: Citra Lamtoro Gung Persada, 1989), p. 279.

5. In the past, when speaking of Chinese cultural pillars, "Chinese religions" was not included. This is a major shortcoming which should be corrected.

6. Pancasila has five principles. The first principle is the belief in one supreme god (*Ketuhanan yang mahaesa*). It does not indicate that one has to be a Muslim in order to be accepted as a Pancasila-ist. As long as the person

believes in one supreme god, he/she is already an Indonesian who accepted the state ideology.

7. There are a number of studies on Agama Khonghucu in Indonesia. Apart from my own works which are mentioned in this chapter, Charles A. Coppel has also published a number of papers (see Coppel 1977, 1981, 1984 and 1986). Lasiyo has also written a PhD thesis submitted to the University of London (1992). Wang Aiping has completed a PhD thesis (in Chinese) submitted to Xiamen University (2007), which was later revised and published as a book (2010).

8. Tan Chee Beng, "Confucianism", in *The Blackwell Encyclopedia of Sociology*, vol. 2, edited by George Ritzer (Oxford: Blackwell Publishing, 2007), pp. 668–72; Liao Jianyu (廖建裕, Leo Suryadinata), *Yinni Kongjiao Chutan* 印尼孔教初探 [Indonesian Confucian Religion: A Preliminary Study] (Singapore: Chinese Heritage Centre, 2010), pp. 2–4, 58–61.

9. Zhang Songzhi (张颂之), "Kongjiao Hui Simo huikao 孔教会始末汇考" [The Confucius Religious Society: Origins and Demise], in 文史哲 *Wen Shi Zhe*, no. 1 (2008): 55–72, https://www.rujiazg.com/article/5951 (accessed 22 January 2013); Yen Ching-hwang (颜清湟), "1899–1911 nian Xinjiapo he Malaiya de kongjiao fuxing yundong 1899–1911 年新加坡和马来亚的孔教复兴运动" [1899–1911 Confucian Movement in Singapore and Malaya], in *Cong Lishi jiaodu kan haiwai huaren shehui bianqe* 从历史角度看海外华人社会变革 [Social Change of Chinese Overseas: A Historical Perspective], by Yen Ching-hwang 颜清湟 (Singapore: Youth Book, 2007), p. 128.

10. Charles A. Coppel, "The Origins of Confucianism as an Organized Religion in Java, 1900–1923", *Journal of Southeast Asian Studies* 12, no. 1 (1981): 180.

11. Liao, *Yinni Kongjiao Chutan*.

12. Wang Aiping (王爱平), *Yindunixiya Kongjiao Yanjiu* 印度尼西亚孔教研究 [Confucian Religion in Indonesia: A Study] (Beijing: Zhongguo Wenjiao Chubanshe, 2010), pp. 230–23.

13. See "Pencabutan Surat Edaran Mentri Dalam Negeri No. 477/74054, tertanggal 18 November 1978".

14. Leo Suryadinata, *Prominent Indonesian Chinese: Biographical Sketches* (Singapore: Institute of Southeast Asian Studies, 1998), p. 22.

15. Ibid., p. 20.

16. Ibid., p. 205; Liao, *Yinni Kongjiao Chutan*, p. 62.

17. Interview with Ongko Pra Wiro, 17 February 2011.

18. Ibid.

19. W.D. Sukisman, "Perkembangan Budaya Cina di Indonesia Dalam Kaitannya dengan Inpres No. 14/1967" [The Development of Chinese Culture in Indonesia and its Relation to the Presidential Instruction No. 14/1967], paper presented at Rapat PokjaInterdep Pembauran di Jakarta tgl. 23-24/1-1995 [paper presented at the inter-departmental workshop meeting], Sesuai Kawat

Mendari No. T451.3/189 (identical with the telegraph of the Interior Minister, No. T451.3/189), 1995, p. 9.
20. Ibid.
21. The temple is located in the Sunter Agung Permai area.
22. Leo Suryadinata, "Buddhism and Confucianism in Contemporary Indonesia: Recent Developments", in *Chinese Indonesians: Remembering, Distorting, Forgetting*, edited by Tim Lindsey and Helen Pausacker (Singapore: Institute of Southeast Asian Studies and Monash Asia Institute, 2005), p. 85.
23. See "Instruksi Presiden no. 6, 2000, tertanggal 17 Januari 2000".
24. See "Pencabutan Surat Edaran Mentri Dalam Negeri No. 477/74054, tertanggal 18 November 1978".
25. Iis Zatnika, "1 April Khonghucu Diakui Administrasi Kependudukan", *Media Indonesia*, 26 March 2006.
26. Aris Ananta, Evi Nurvidya Arifin, and Bakhtiar, "Chinese Indonesians in Indonesia and the Province of Riau Archipelago: A Demographic Analysis", in *The Ethnic Chinese in Contemporary Indonesia*, edited by Leo Suryadinata (Singapore: Institute of Southeast Asian Studies, 2008), p. 30.
27. Liao *Yinni Kongjiao Chutan*, p. 82.
28. *Kewarganegaraan, Suku Bangsa, Agama, dan Bahasa Sehari-hari Penduduk Indonesia: Hasil Sensus Penduduk 2010* (Jakarta: Badan Pusat Statistik, 2011), p. 10.
29. See *Kunjungi dan Rasakan kedamaian Maitreya di pulau Batam* (published by Maha Vihara Duta Maitreya, n.d.), pp. 10–11. According to the story, Tianran and Yuehui are two leading figures in China's Maitreya Buddhism who were believed to have spread Maitreya Buddhism beyond China.
30. Information provided by Sutrisno Murtiyoso, a researcher on Chinese temples in Indonesia, 29 November 2012.
31. Suryadinata, "Buddhism and Confucianism in Contemporary Indonesia: Recent Developments", p. 104.
32. Liao, *Yinni Kongjiao Chutan*, p. 81.
33. *Kewarganegaraan*, 2011, p. 10.

13

PERANAKAN CHINESE POLITICS AND DECOLONIZATION IN INDONESIA*

Introduction

It is important to understand the Peranakan Chinese community during the era of decolonization as it helps us understand their post-independence position. Much of the post-independence development, in fact, had its basis during the era of decolonization. Let us first look at the colonial period, primarily from the twentieth century towards the end of colonial rule.

Pre-World War II Peranakan Politics

Peranakan Chinese got involved in politics during the Dutch colonial period. However, initially there was only a rise of Chinese cultural nationalism rather than Chinese political nationalism. The latter was symbolized by the establishment of the Tiong Hoa Hwee Koan (THHK, 中华会馆), a pan-Chinese organization that aimed at reforming Chinese Peranakan customs through the teachings of Confucius. As some Chinese are required to understand Confucianism, THHK was first established in Jakarta and later in almost every town in Java and the Outer Islands.

It was only later that Sun Yat Sen's revolutionary movement impacted the Chinese in Indonesia through the organization of Soe Poh Sia (Shu Bao She, reading clubs, 书报社). The *totoks* were ardent supporters of the revolutionary movement but it was only later that the Peranakan Chinese were also influenced. Leading this Chinese nationalism was *Sin Po*, a Peranakan Chinese newspaper in Java which was first published in 1910. It later developed into a group which symbolized Chinese nationalism. It even organized the Peranakan Chinese to go against the Dutch subjectship (Nederlandsch Onderdaanschap) and Peranakan Chinese participation in the Volksraad (the colonial parliament which had very limited power). Basically, the Sin Po group was against Dutch colonialism.

However, the increasing number of Dutch-educated Peranakans led to the formation of Chung Hwa Hui (CHH, a Chinese organization) in 1928 in Semarang, a town that was Dutch East Indies-oriented. Politically, the CHH was also oriented towards the colonial power. Semarang at that time was the headquarters of Oei Tiong Ham, the largest Chinese company in Indonesia then. Other Peranakans, many of them journalists and lawyers, disagreed with the political stand of the CHH, eventually established Partai Tionghoa Indonesia (PTI) in Surabaya in 1932 that supported Indonesia's independence. The leader of this group was Liem Koen Hian who later joined Gerakan Rakyat Indonesia (Gerindo), an indigenous Indonesian political party, when it opened its doors to the Peranakan Chinese.

Of these three political groups,[1] one (Sin Po Group) was not an organization, while CHH and PTI were political parties and participated in the Volksraad. Nevertheless, all of these groups were banned during the Japanese Occupation of Indonesia from 1942 to 1945.

The Japanese Occupation

The Japanese Occupation of Indonesia between 1942 and 1945 had a major impact on Indonesian history as well as on the Peranakan Chinese. The Japanese defeated the Dutch colonialists and replaced the Dutch as the new master. However, towards the end of the Occupation, when the Japanese were experiencing difficulties on various fronts, they began to promise Indonesians the granting of independence. The Investigative Committee for the Preparation of Indonesian Independence (BPUPKI) was established in 1944, consisting of sixty-two members, of which four were Peranakan Chinese (Liem Koen Hian 林群贤, Oei Tjong Hauw 黄宗孝, Oey Tiang Tjoei 黄长水 and Tan Eng Hoa 陈荣华) and one Peranakan Arab (A.R. Baswedan). The BPUPKI prepared the Indonesian Constitution as well as the citizenship law after Indonesia attained independence. The Chinese members unitedly supported Indonesian independence, but their views on citizenship of the Peranakan Chinese in independent Indonesia differed. Liem Koen Hian, the former leader of PTI, wanted the future Indonesian government to grant citizenship to the Peranakan Chinese. Oei Tjong Hauw, the son of tycoon Oei Tiong Ham 黄仲函, proposed that the future government should grant the Peranakan Chinese China's citizenship. Oey Tiang Tjoei, the editor of a pro-Japanese Indonesian language newspaper, also proposed Chinese citizenship for ethnic Chinese in Indonesia. There is no record about the view of lawyer Tan Eng Hoa regarding citizenship, but it was reported that he proposed that Indonesians should be granted the freedom of association.

Japan capitulated on 15 August 1945 before the BPUPKI got a chance to declare independence. It was said that the Japanese in fact were very reluctant to grant independence and purposely delayed the process. However, when the Japanese surrendered, Indonesian youth kidnapped Sukarno and Hatta and forced them to proclaim Indonesia's independence on behalf of the Indonesian people on 17 August 1945. On 18 August 1945, a twenty-six-member Preparatory Committee for Indonesian Independence (PPKI) held a meeting to formalize the Constitution of the Republic of Indonesia. It had first been prepared by the BPUPKI but with a revision regarding the "requirements for Muslims to practise Shariah Law". The phrase was dropped from the Constitution as it would have likely resulted in the disintegration of Indonesia had it been included. The twenty-six-member committee included some members of the BPUPKI and a few new members. There was only one Chinese member on the PPKI, a pharmacist named Yap Tjwan Bing who later emerged as an ardent Indonesian nationalist.

Indonesia's Independence

With the help of the British, the Dutch returned and refused to grant independence to Indonesia. But the Indonesians were intent on gaining independence from the Dutch. Indonesia was then divided into two areas: the Republican government-controlled area and the Dutch-controlled area, with the latter being much larger. Conflicts between the two continued to take place and the Chinese minorities were often caught in between. Chinese Indonesians initially supported Indonesian independence or at least did not oppose it. Yet many Chinese became victims in the conflicts: they lost not only their properties but also their lives. Some Chinese wanted to defend themselves by organizing Poh An Tui (*Bao'an dui*, 保安队) security force and it was reported that their arms were provided by the Dutch. Pro-Indonesia Chinese in Surabaya refused to form Poh An Tui as it was considered a pro-Dutch organization. It can be argued that Poh An Tui was the most controversial organization in the history of ethnic Chinese-ethnic Indonesian relations of that period. Despite this, many Peranakan Chinese continued to side with indigenous Indonesians. John Lie, for instance, smuggled weapons for the republican army and became an admiral in the Indonesian navy. Siauw Giok Tjhan sided with the Republic and was made the State Minister for Peranakan Affairs.

Between 1945 and 1949, Indonesians used both diplomacy and armed struggle against the Dutch, and in December 1949, the Dutch eventually agreed to grant independence to Indonesia. They returned the entire Dutch East Indies except Papua (or West Irian as the Indonesians called it at that time). The newly independent Indonesian government introduced a passive citizenship law, claiming all Indonesia-born Chinese citizens of the Republic of Indonesia, unless they rejected the citizenship. Some Chinese who had had a bad experience during the revolution rejected the citizenship but the majority appeared to accept it. In Java, Thio Thiam Tjong (张添聪) established the Persatuan Tionghoa in 1948 but by early 1950 it changed its name to Partai Demokrat Tionghoa Indonesia (PDTI). A few months earlier, Liem Koen Hian, the former founder of the pre-war Partai Tionghoa Indonesia (PTI), set up a multi-ethnic party called Pusat Tenaga Indonesia (abbreviated as PTI, known as the new PTI) but it failed to develop.[2]

The issue of citizenship became important as the new Indonesian government was preparing a new Indonesian citizenship law which aimed to change the passive system into an active system. It was feared that this might result in the number of Peranakan Chinese losing their Indonesian citizenship. This is because all non-indigenous Indonesians were required to choose their citizenship again. Peranakan Chinese who were well-educated were concerned with the draft of the citizenship law—they were afraid that the draft would become law without revisions. Those in the Indonesian Parliament and Peranakan Chinese associations were eager to express their views on the issue. The 1955 election was also scheduled to be held and Chinese Indonesians, especially the Peranakans, were interested to be represented. How to participate in Indonesian politics became an issue, especially within the PDTI.

After World War II, many Indonesian parties opened their doors to the Chinese minority. Some Peranakan Chinese argued that the Chinese should not form their own party but join the existing Indonesian parties in order to avoid being isolated. But others maintained that the Chinese minority group was a reality and their interests should also be protected, as indigenous Indonesian parties would not look after Chinese interests. There was a split and quite a few members eventually left the PDTI. Yap Tjwan Bing (叶全明) joined the PNI, Tan Po Goan (陈宝源) and Tan Boen An (陈文安) joined the Partai Sosialis Indonesia, and Tjoeng Tin Jan (钟鼎远) joined the Catholic party. By 1953 Thio Thiam Tjong, president of the PDTI, complained that the party existed only in name.[3] Facing the new urgent issues and the 1955 elections, the PDTI began to think of reform.

Baperki and Siauw Giok Tjhan

The initiative for reform of the PDTI occurred under the leadership of Thio Thiam Tjong. A few smaller Chinese organizations such as Perwit, Peratuan Tionghoa Surabaya etc. were invited to join the discussion; eventually they proposed the formation of the Badan Permusyawaratan Kewarganegaraan Turunan Tionghoa or abbreviated as Baperwat. Oei Tjoe Tat (黄自达), a Peranakan lawyer from a Chinese social organization Sin Ming Hui (新明会) drafted the constitution of the new organization. Before the launching of the new organization, Peranakan Chinese personalities, regardless of their ideology and party affiliation, were invited to discuss the constitution and the objectives of the new party. The meeting was chaired by Thio Thiam Tjong who referred to past mistakes of the PDTI: one such mistake was that the PDTI did not allow its members to hold dual party membership. He also argued that the party was exclusively for Chinese Indonesians and this in itself was a form of racial discrimination. He hoped that the new organization would not repeat past mistakes.

Initially, the name of the new organization became an issue. One group represented by a Christian lawyer Yap Thiam Hien favoured the retention of the word "Tionghoa" (Chinese) while the other represented by Siauw Giok Tjhan (蕭玉灿), a left-wing nationalist/socialist, preferred a non-Chinese organization. Yap argued that the purpose of the new organization was to fight for Chinese Indonesian citizenship rights and therefore it should be clearly stated that discrimination against the Chinese minority was a fact and should be challenged; but Siauw argued that it was not wise to fight racial discrimination alone, and that non-Chinese Indonesians should be welcome to join the organization if they agreed with the objectives of the new organization. After the debate, Siauw's view gained the majority support and the new organization was named "Badan Permusjawaratan Kewarganegaraan Indonesia" abbreviated as Baperki.

On 13 March 1954, Baperki was officially established. The new organization stated that it "aims particularly to study and resolve citizenship problems and only engage in the field of citizenship".[4] There were three major objectives:

1. To strive for the accomplishment of a national ideal (*tjita-tjita bangsa*), that is, to make every Indonesian citizen a genuine citizen of the Republic of Indonesia (*Warganegara Republik Indonesia Sedjati*);
2. To strive for the realization of Democratic Principles and Basic Human Rights;
3. To strive for the same rights and obligations of every citizen, regardless of his/her descent, culture, customs and religion.

The focus was on citizenship. It said that after Indonesia declared independence, the government decided to have Indonesian citizenship for all groups of its people (*semua golongan rakyatnya*) without differentiating their origin (*keturunan*), to be genuine Indonesian democrats (*democrat Indonesia sedjati*). Indonesian political parties also agreed with this—but in daily life, there was still differentiation between citizens based on their ethnic descent.

Due to its concentration on eradicating ethnic/racial discrimination among Indonesian citizens, Baperki asserted that it did not compete with other organizations and political parties. Baperki, therefore, was an organization of Indonesian citizens regardless of their political ideology.[5] The purpose was to get the citizens of Indonesia to understand citizenship, to know their rights and obligations as Indonesian citizens and to be loyal to their fatherland Indonesia (*loyaliteit dan rasa tjinta yang besar terhadap tanahairnya Indonesia*).[6] In order to realize the objective, Baperki would be active in the general elections as this was related to the formulation of the national laws and regulations in order to establish a just and equal society of Indonesia.[7]

Many Peranakan Chinese were enthusiastic about the new organization. The Peranakan elites, regardless of their ideological persuasions, agreed to participate in the forthcoming 1955 General Election under the Baperki umbrella. However, the solidarity of the Peranakan Chinese was short lived as there was ideological conflict within the organization. There was a tussle between the left-wing and right-wing Peranakans. As a result, the right-wing Peranakans withdrew from Baperki even before the election. Those who had already joined the other Indonesian parties contested the election under their respective party banner. Even non-party men such as leading journalists Awyong Peng Koen (Ojong P.K. 欧阳炳昆) and Khoe Woen Sioe (丘文秀) left Baperki because of their disagreement with Siauw. During the 1955 election, Baperki only gained one seat by Siauw Giok Tjhan. Baperki, although claiming to be an Indonesian party, was actually still regarded as a Chinese organization. It is also worthwhile to note that the leadership of Siauw Giok Tjhan was quite dominant initially but it completely controlled the organization after 1959.

Baperki, Siauw Giok Tjhan and Indonesian Citizenship

Some background information on the Peranakan Chinese left-wing intellectuals is in order. Unlike in Malaya/Singapore where the left-wing movement was led by Chinese-educated *singkeh* (*totok*), the Peranakan Chinese in Indonesia were exposed to left-wing ideology as early as the 1920s. There were a significant number of Peranakan Chinese who participated in the 1926–27 Communist Uprisings in Java which were eventually crushed by the colonial government. The left-wing *totok* Chinese, who were Chinese-educated, were often members of the left-wing Kuomintang (KMT) or Chinese Communist Party (CCP); they were interested in China's politics. It is also worth noting that quite a few Peranakan Chinese students in the Netherlands joined the Dutch Communist Party before returning to Indonesia; those who were well known include Tan Ling Djie (陈舜如), Tjoa Siek Ien (蔡锡胤), Tio Oen Bik (张温毕) amongst others. Tan Ling Djie, who became a close friend of Siauw Giok Tjhan, later joined Partai Sosialis Indonesia (PSI). Siauw also joined the same party. Tan later left PSI and joined the Partai Komunis Indonesia (PKI) and emerged as its secretary-general until he was defeated by D.N. Aidit in 1951 and ousted from the central committee in 1953. Siauw was the director of *Harian Rakjat*, a PKI newspaper between 1951 and 1953[8] but he did not admit to his membership in the PKI. Siauw stepped down around the same time that Tan Ling Djie was ousted from the central committee. It is worth noting that Siauw, who used to work as a journalist for a few Peranakan newspapers before World War II, was close to indigenous Indonesian nationalists. He supported the nationalist struggle for independence and was acquainted with leaders like Sukarno, Syahril and Amir Sjarifuddin. In fact during the second cabinet of Sjarifuddin (1947), Siauw was appointed as the State Minister for Peranakan Affairs.

It should also be pointed out that Siauw who was Dutch-educated did not read Chinese. Initially Baperki's/his ideas were not known by the *totok* Chinese community. In order to reach that community he published *Juexing Zhoukan* (觉醒周刊), 1954–59, also known as *Chiao Shing*, or *Mingguan Sadar*) and served as the director. Its editor-in-chief was Wu Xiaoyi (吴孝义), a Peranakan Chinese, but the real chief editor was Ie Chu Yip (余柱业), a Malayan Communist Party (MCP) leader who had fled to Indonesia. After Ie Chu Yip the editorship was mainly taken over by other MCP members namely Zhang Tai Quan (张泰泉) assisted by Chen Mengzhou (陈蒙洲) and other *totok* Chinese writers.[9] This was the only locally-oriented Chinese language weekly as others were China-oriented. Only after 1959 did all Chinese language newspapers become Indonesia-oriented as they were required to be associated with the existing Indonesian political parties.

As stated earlier, Siauw became the chairman of Baperki and fought for equal rights for the minority groups in Indonesia, including Indonesian citizens of Chinese descent. He was also very outspoken about racial discrimination which existed in post-independent Indonesia. The most important concept for the Peranakan Chinese leaders was citizenship, not nationhood. The focus on citizenship during that period was linked to the Indonesian government's intention to issue a new citizenship law designed to change the original passive system to an active system.

After Indonesia declared independence, Chinese who were born in Indonesia were automatically Indonesian citizens if he/she did not reject Indonesian citizenship. This was due to the fact that Indonesian nationalists required the support of the Indonesian Chinese to gain independence and to develop Indonesia. However, after the transfer of power some indigenous Indonesian nationalists wanted to change the passive system into an active one. All Chinese Indonesians, the so-called *bukan asli* (non-indigenous group) were supposed to choose Indonesian citizenship again. If this system became law, many Chinese Indonesians would have lost their Indonesian citizenship if they did not proactively choose their citizenship. Also, the Chinese in the villages might not have known how to do it and they too would become foreigners again. Siauw Giok Tjhan and Baperki worked hard for the citizenship of the Chinese in Indonesia and had contributed greatly to making many Chinese Indonesians remain as Indonesian citizens.

The concept of "nation" was, in fact, new and Western. In Indonesia "nation" has often been translated as *bangsa*, but since pre-World War II, the term *bangsa* had already had a racial connotation. It is not surprising, when the leader of Baperki, Siauw Giok Tjhan, talked about nation in 1957, he used the English term "nation" as well as *bangsa*. In his view, the Indonesian nation was not yet harmonious because there was still racial discrimination against the minority groups, especially Indonesian citizens of Chinese descent. A harmonious Indonesian nation could only be achieved if racial discrimination against Indonesians of foreign descent was eliminated.[10]

In Siauw Giok Tjhan's view, to build a fair and just Indonesia, citizenship was the most important for building a prosperous society. It appears that Siauw and his Baperki equated citizenship (*kewarganegaraan*) with nationhood (*bangsa*). Siauw Giok Tjhan argued that Indonesia consists of many *sukus* and *keturunan* (Indonesians of foreign descent). He mentioned three types of *keturunan*, i.e. Chinese, Arabs and Eurasians. These Indonesians of foreign descent are comparable to Indonesian *suku*.[11] This concept was never accepted by indigenous Indonesians nor developed by Siauw at the beginning because he was mainly concerned with citizenship, which, for him, was the most concrete and crucial. He only addressed the nationhood issue when a rival group appeared to challenge Baperki. This group wanted the Chinese Indonesians to abandon their ethnic identity and be absorbed into the indigenous population.

Baperki and the Indonesian Revolution

It should be noted that the parliamentary democracy in Indonesia was unstable. There was discontent and rebellions. The rebellions were eventually crushed giving rise to the extra-parliamentary actors, namely the Indonesian military and President Sukarno. Sukarno was invited to form the government and with the support of the army and PKI, he eventually re-introduced the 1945 Constitution which gives tremendous power to the president. Indonesia entered the so-called Guided Democracy period (1959–65). Sukarno played the balance of power game: when the PKI was strong, he sided with the military and when the military was strong he sided with the PKI. Gradually Sukarno moved closer to the PKI.

Baperki under the leadership of Siauw Giok Tjhan moved towards the left. It was perhaps forced by the situation—most political parties and groups did not accept Siauw and Baperki's position whereas only President Sukarno and the PKI supported them. Increasingly, Baperki's survival depended on the protection of President Sukarno. There was also a split within Baperki. Yap Thiam Hien, a Christian lawyer who was anti-communist, was eventually ousted from the Baperki leadership, but he stayed on as a member.

A group of ten Peranakan Chinese intellectuals led by Awyong Peng Koen (who had left Baperki) then proposed another solution to Indonesian Chinese problem—assimilation, i.e. through name-changing and intermarriage. This group also advocated the dissolution of Chinese parties such as Baperki in order to build a harmonious nation. Yap Thiam Hien of Baperki wrote three articles in the *Star Weekly*, commenting on the unrealistic view of these ten intellectuals. Yap considered that every ethnic group had the right to exist in accordance with Pancasila Indonesia (the Five Principles of the State), and name-changing and intermarriage would not resolve the so-called Chinese problem.

Yap also alluded to the Siauw Giok Tjhan "therapy". Yap had analysed Siauw's writings and speeches since mid-1957 up to early 1960 and came to the conclusion that Siauw wanted to change the structure of Indonesian society which was feudalistic, colonial and capitalistic, and therefore not harmonious. Society had to be changed to communism to achieve racial/ethnic harmony. The living example was the Soviet Union and the People's Republic of China (PRC). Before the realization of such a society, Chinese Indonesians should be allowed to remain as an ethnic group through integration. But Yap said that Siauw did not explain its concept of integration. Yap noted that 94 per cent of the Indonesian population were either Muslims or Christians and they were against communism. It was unlikely that the communists were to be in power soon. Even if the communists eventually came to power, it would take a long time and it would not help solve the current problems. Yap concluded by saying that Siauw's "therapy" was a communist "therapy" as where racial discrimination could only be abolished in a communist society.

Siauw replied. He explained that the society he advocated was a "just and prosperous society" as proposed by President Sukarno. This society was called "Indonesian style socialism" (*sosialisme ala Indonesia*) as described by President Sukarno in his 1959 national day speech. He advocated the eradication of exploitation within a society. The speech was endorsed by the Supreme People's Assembly and was made into a national guidance called "The Indonesian Political Manifesto", accepted both by the communists and non-communists. Siauw noted that this just and prosperous society might come much sooner than Yap anticipated. Siauw also said that "until today, no sociologists can deny that the measures used to solve the minority issues in the Soviet Union and People's Republic of China are the most ideal. Many anti-communist sociologists also admitted this point."[12] Siauw finally noted that to accept his solution to the minority problem means: "to struggle for the realization of a society mentioned in the Indonesian Political Manifesto".[13]

Siauw denied that he proposed a "communist society", but Sukarno's "Indonesian style socialism". He did not elaborate the differences between these two societies. He admitted that he used the Soviet Union and PRC as the models for the solution to the minority problem but did not elaborate the differences between "socialism" practised by the communists in the Soviets and the PRC and "Indonesian style socialism". Nevertheless, he rejected to call his solution a communist solution. At the same time, Siauw also felt that the revolutionary force supporting Sukarno had been growing rapidly, and "Indonesian style socialism" would be realized much sooner than what Yap Thiam Hien predicted.

Yap Thiam Hien was obviously against assimilation and favoured pluralism, but he also opposed Siauw Giok Tjhan's "communist therapy". He advocated "heart cleansing" as a solution to the minority problem. As all men are God's creations, therefore they have to be respected and should not be forced to assume a different racial identity. He disagreed with the changing structure of society but advocated soul searching and follow the golden rule of Jesus Christ. The elite should change their attitude so that they become an elite who served society. He also argued the importance of laws against racial discrimination, advocating that those who violated the laws should be punished. After the fall of Sukarno, Yap continued to advocate his "heart cleansing" concept, protection of human rights and anti-discrimination laws and regulations. He came into direct conflict with Siauw over Baperki's support of the 1945 Constitution in which there was a clause that only "indigenous Indonesian" (Indonesia *asli*) could become the President of Indonesia". Siauw had strongly supported Sukarno as the survival of Baperki required a strong president, whereas Yap opposed the 1945 law because the clause was a reflection of racial discrimination. Equally important was that Yap was basically anti-communist and did not agree with Siauw's leaning towards the left. It was in the 1960 congress that Yap was eventually ousted from the Baperki leadership group.

Siauw and the left-wing group firmly controlled Baperki and fully supported Sukarno's policy, especially his Indonesian style of socialism. Siauw interpreted "integration" as the full participation of the Chinese Indonesian community in the Indonesian revolution. The purpose was to realize an Indonesian socialist society where there would be no oppressive class. This society did not happen. Instead, the 30 September 1965 coup brought an end to Sukarno's rule. Siauw had underestimated the anti-Sukarno groups—the army and the Islamic forces. He never expected that Sukarno would be overthrown soon. The PKI was demolished in the 1965 coup which saw the rise of an anti-communist military represented by General Suharto.

Baperki and the Indonesian Nation

In fact, as early as 1957, President Sukarno talked about nation building and considered the Chinese Indonesians as people with skills that were needed for the economic development of Indonesia.[14] He was sympathetic to the Baperki movement as it brought the Chinese towards Indonesian society, although one can argue that in the 1945 Pancasila Speech, Sukarno vaguely defined an Indonesian nation by using the concept of Ernest Renan. Sukarno stated that "the Indonesian nation (*Bangsa Indonesia*) was based on the desire to be together of all the people who live from the northern part of Sumatra to Irian".[15] Nevertheless, Sukarno never explicitly put forward a concept of Indonesian nation and its components. Only in March 1963, when he addressed the Baperki Congress, did Sukarno talk about nation-building in Indonesia. He defined the Indonesian nation in terms of Indonesian *suku* (ethnic group). His message was that:

> There are many *sukus* in Indonesia. In Indonesia, *suku* means foot. [In fact, *suku* in Indonesian also means ethnic group—author.] Indonesia has many feet, just like a stampede: it has Javanese foot, Sunda foot, Sumatran foot, Irian foot, Dayak foot, Bali foot, Sumba foot, peranakan Chinese foot (*kaki peranakan Tionghoa*). Yes, peranakan foot. They all come from one body, the body of Indonesian nation (*tubuh bangsa Indonesia*).[16]

It is crucial to note here that Sukarno considered only Peranakan Chinese, not all Chinese, as *suku*. In other words those who are not born in Indonesia and culturally not "assimilated" into Indonesian culture are not members of the Indonesian nation.

Siauw Giok Tjhan who was a Peranakan, interestingly, did not develop Sukarno's concept. He continued to address the problem of citizenship, and later the Indonesian revolution. In the Baperki's documents, there was no differentiation between Peranakan and *totok* Chinese. In fact, the term Peranakan did not even appear in the Constitution of Baperki. It only mentioned the "Indonesian citizens of foreign descent"—there was no reference to suku Tionghoa or suku Peranakan Tionghoa.

Siauw Giok Tjhan did not pursue the concept of "suku Peranakan Tionghoa" as he would not want to contradict Sukarno. He kept it ambiguous. He only wanted to talk about citizenship, as if "citizenship" equalled "nationhood"—to obtain Indonesian citizenship meant to be a member of the Indonesian nation.

Why was Siauw not interested in separating the Peranakans from the *totoks*? There are three possible explanations: firstly, *totoks* were better off economically than the Peranakans, and Baperki needed the support of the *totoks* in promoting education; secondly, Siauw Giok Tjhan was an admirer of the People's Republic of China and believed that the Chinese language was important for the Peranakans if they wanted to understand China; thirdly, he believed that the children of *totok* would eventually become Peranakan.

Nevertheless, from the argument put forward by Baperki, the Chinese (Tionghoa) are a minority group and should be allowed to preserve their culture and identity in accordance with the Indonesian motto of *Bhinneka Tunggal Ika* (Unity in Diversity). There was no need for assimilation. One can, therefore, maintain that Baperki saw the Chinese minority as an Indonesian *suku*. It was also the case with Arab Indonesians and Eurasian Indonesians—two other Indonesian *sukus* that do not have their own geographical region in the Republic of Indonesia.

Conclusion

Prior to World War II, Peranakan Chinese were first influenced by Chinese nationalism (Sin Po Group) but in the late 1920s, the Dutch East Indies-oriented group (Chung Hwa Hui) emerged followed in the early 1930s by the Indonesia-oriented group (PTI). Peranakan politics were divided but the Dutch East Indies-oriented group was more influential than the Indonesia-oriented group. However, during the Japanese Occupation, the Chinese minority became involved in the preparation committee for Indonesian independence. Soon after independence, Peranakan Chinese were still divided in their orientation but gradually the Indonesia-oriented group became dominant (Persatuan Tionghoa/PDTI).

Peranakan Chinese who identified themselves with Indonesian nationalists replaced the old leaders who were pro-Dutch East Indies. As the Indonesian revolution was a left-wing revolution, it is not surprising that left-wing leaders became leaders of the Peranakan Chinese community. Nevertheless, Indonesia's independence also gave rise to Indonesian indigenism, not only in the economic sector but also in the political arena. The Peranakan Chinese community tended to be united in opposing racial discrimination as reflected in the establishment of Baperki, a large Peranakan Chinese socio-political organization.

Baperki fought for equal citizenship for all Indonesian citizens regardless of race. Siauw Giok Tjhan, a Peranakan socialist, became the leader of the new organization and eventually brought Baperki to the left, coinciding with the country's overall situation where Sukarno, who was also influenced by Marxism and Socialism, brought Indonesia closer to the left-wing camp. Baperki fully supported President Sukarno and allied with the PKI in order to survive. However, during the 1965 coup the PKI was banned, Sukarno was overthrown and the right-wing army represented by General Suharto emerged as the new leader of Indonesia. He abandoned the pluralism policy towards Peranakan Chinese introduced by Sukarno and initiated a total assimilation policy. Sukarno's concept of Peranakan Chinese as an Indonesian *suku* was also rejected by the Suharto government.

It should be noted that Sukarno's concept of Peranakan Chinese as an Indonesian *suku* was in fact quite different from the concept of Siauw Giok Tjhan/Baperki. The latter wanted to have Tionghoa as a *suku*, not only Peranakan Chinese. However, there was no debate between these two concepts as Baperki used the two terms—Tionghoa and Peranakan Tionghoa—interchangeably. This concept of suku Tionghoa was still alive during the post-Suharto Indonesia.

Notes

*This chapter was first published in Leo Suryadinata, ed., *Peranakan Communities in the Era of Decolonization and Globalization* (Singapore: Chinese Heritage Centre and NUS Baba House, 2015). This is a slightly revised version.

1. For a detailed discussion on pre-World War II Peranakan politics, see Leo Suryadinata, *Peranakan Chinese Politics in Java, 1917–1942* (Singapore: Marshall Cavendish, 2005).

2. Leo Suryadinata, *Pribumi Indonesians, the Chinese Minority and China: A Study of Perceptions and Policies* (Kuala Lumpur and London: Heinemann Publishers, 1978).

3. Leo Suryadinata, *Peranakan's Search for National Identity: Biographical Studies of Seven Indonesian Chinese* (Singapore: Marshall Cavendish, 2004), p. 129.

4. "chusus bertudjuan mempeladjari dan menjelesaikan masalah2 kewarganegaraan dan berdjuang se-mata2 dilapangan kewarganegaraa". (See "Mukadimah", *Anggaran Dasar dan Anggaran Rumah Tangga Baperki*, no page number).

5. *Anggaran Dasar*, pp. 7–8.

6. Ibid., p. 7.

7. Ibid., p. 9.

8. Regarding whether or not *Harian Rakjat* between 1951 and 1953 was already the PKI newspaper, there are two views. One view argues that *Harian Rakjat*

was a PKI newspaper from the beginning as Nyoto was the person in charge in the newspaper; the other maintains that it became the PKI newspaper only after Siauw Giok Tjhan stepped down as its director. But if we examine the editorial and announcement made on the day when Siauw stepped down, it tended to support the first view. The editorial called the newspaper during Siauw's directorship as "our newspaper". It stated that "our newspaper has served the people and their struggle for over two years. When people's interests came into conflict with the colonialist interests, our newspaper stood on the side of people's interests. When the people came into conflict with the people's enemy, our newspaper stood with the people." It further noted that "from today onward our newspaper begins to have a reform. The leadership of the publishing company has been changed, and the editorial section has also been adjusted. These changes were meant to improve them so that they would be more perfect." Siauw in his announcement also said that he hoped the writers and readers of the newspaper would continue to support the new leadership, so that *Harian Rakjat* would continue to be the tool of people's struggle, so that genuine democracy can be achieved". In fact, during Siauw's directorship, many PKI leaders (including Nyoto) were already on the editorial committee. For a detailed discussion on Siauw's relationship with *Harian Rakjat* and the PKI, see Liao Jianyu (廖建裕), "Youguan Xiao yucan de Yinni minzu guan yu 'huaren buzu' de yixie fansi" (有关萧玉灿的印尼民族观与 '华人部族' 的一些反思, "Some reflections on Siauw Giok Tjhan's concept of the Indonesian Nation and 'Suku Tionghoa'"), in *Xiao yucan bainian danchen jinian wenji* (萧玉灿百年诞辰纪念文集) (Hong Kong: Shenghuo Wenhua jijinhui (生活文化基金会), 2014), pp. 41–63.

9. In fact, Zhang Tai Quan was a Chinese from Siantar, Sumatra, who went to Singapore/Malaya to study and became a member of the MCP. Chen Mengzhou was from Singapore. A few other writers who helped in the editorial board were Chinese left-wing journalists and writers from Indonesia. See Zhang Tai Quan, "Xiao Yucan yu 'Jue Xing'" (萧玉灿与'觉醒' Siauw Giok Tjhan and Mingguan Juexing), in *Xiao yucan bainian danchen jinian wenji* (萧玉灿百年诞辰纪念文集) (Hong Kong: Shenghuo Wenhua jijinhui (生活文化基金会), 2014), pp. 134–70 (especially pp. 137–41). Also *Shen mai xin zhong de mimi* (深埋心中的秘密, The secret deeply buried in the heart) (Kuala Lumpur: 21st Century Publisher, 2008), pp. 74–81.

10. "Debat Siauw Giok Tjhan", in *Simposium Baperki tentang Sumbangsih apakah yang dapat diberikan oleh warganegara2 Indonesia keturunan asing kepada pembangunan dan perkembangan kebudayaan nasional Indonesia 1957*, pp. 25–31.

11. Ibid.

12. Siauw, "Terapi Manifesto Politik RI", *Star Weekly*, 23 April 1960.

13. Ibid.

14. "Wedjangan Presiden Sukarno kepada Delegasi Baperki", in *Simposium Baperki tentang Sumbangsih*, n.p.

15. *Risalah Sidang Badan Penyelidik Usaha-Usaha Persiapan Kemerdekaan Indonesia (BPUPKI) Panitia Persiapan Kemerdekaan Indonesia (PPKI), 29 Mei 1945–19 Agustus 1945* (Jakarta: Sekretariat Negara Republik Indonesia, 1992), pp. 62–63.

16. Siauw Giok Tjhan, "Amanat P.J.M. Presiden Soekarno Pada Kongres Nasional ke-VIII Baperki", in *Gotong Rojong Nasakom untuk Melaksanakan Ampera*, edited by Siauw Giok Tjhan (Djakarta: Baperki, 1963), p. 14.

14

THE INTEGRATION OF INDONESIAN CHINESE INTO MAINSTREAM SOCIETY: A REFLECTION

To discuss the integration of Indonesian Chinese into mainstream society is not as simple as it looks. It involves many aspects which have to be clarified prior to the discussion: What is "mainstream society"? Are Indonesian Chinese not yet integrated? In what ways are Indonesian Chinese considered to have been integrated?

Mainstream Society

In fact, "mainstream society" is not an academic term; it is often used in the mass media and in conversations. Some have interpreted it as the main ideology in a given society at a given time; others have used the term to mean "the majority group within a society". The latter is used in conjunction with "a minority group within a society". Even when the "mainstream society" is to mean "the majority group within a society", there is no consensus on the composition of this group. Is this group ethnically homogeneous or heterogeneous? Does this majority group share a common culture? There is no generally agreed concept on the above-mentioned issues.

Nonetheless, in a multi-ethnic society, people believe that there is a "mainstream society". When referring to this society, people usually mean the ethnic group/groups which is/are the majority group. The non-mainstream society consists of an ethnic minority (or minorities).

Speaking of Indonesian society, it consists of many ethnic groups: ethnic Javanese form 42 per cent of the Indonesian population and is the largest ethnic group in the country; the rest are ethnic minorities such as Bugis, Sundanese, Madurese, Malays, and others. According to the 2000 population census, there were more than 100 ethnic minorities, many did not even make up one per cent of the Indonesian total population.[1] Nevertheless, these minority groups occupy their own region, therefore they are considered as "regional minorities" or "homeland minorities". As a matter of fact, there are a few "non-regional minorities" in Indonesia; ethnic Chinese is one of these minorities.

Indonesia is a young "nation-state" and it is still in the process of nation-building. "Unity in Diversity" (*Bhinneka Tunggal Ika*) has become the motto of nation-building. The Javanese have not regarded their ethnic group as the basis for the Indonesian nation; on the contrary, the Indonesian "nation" is based on the Indonesian language (formerly called Malay) which was a linga franca, and all ethnic minorities are allowed to preserve their own cultural identity.

During the Suharto era, the Indonesian government's policy towards ethnic minorities was not always consistent. "Unity in Diversity" was only applied to the regional minorities (or homeland minorities); but towards ethnic Chinese, the policy of "total assimilation" was adopted. The reasons for such difference are as follows: the Chinese are migrants or descendants of the migrants and hence they do not identify with any region in Indonesia. In other words, the Chinese are "non-indigenous" (non-*pribumi*) people, which is different from the "indigenous" (*pribumi*) people.[2]

Indigenism or *pribumi-isme* was the nation-building principle during the Suharto era (1965–98). Indonesia was a country of indigenous people—this view was shared not only by the Javanese, but also the ethnic minorities. According to the concept of an indigenous state (*Negara pribumi*), the mainstream in Indonesian society refers to the "indigenous society". This society is not homogeneous but heterogeneous, comprising both Javanese and non-Javanese. The integration of Indonesian Chinese into the "mainstream society" means to be integrated into the "*pribumi* society", and not a newly emerged society.

Integration of Indonesian Chinese

"Nation-building" in Indonesia has gradually become a movement, and reached its peak during the Sukarno era (1959–65). When Suharto came to power, he did not abandon this "nation-building" project towards the ethnic Chinese. On the contrary, he implemented the assimilationist policy by eradicating the three Chinese cultural pillars—Chinese organizations, Chinese mass media and Chinese schools. The impact on the ethnic Chinese community was tremendous; Indonesian Chinese intensified their identity with the "Indonesian nation", so that they would be able to live in Indonesia and attained development. Indonesian Chinese realized that they would be able to live in Indonesia in peace and prosperity provided that they formed national unity with the "indigenous" population. If they refused to do so, they might become the scapegoats. In general, Indonesian Chinese felt that only through integrating themselves into the "indigenous society", their life and property would be safe. This kind of national solidarity with the indigenous population was temporarily destroyed during the anti-Chinese riots in May 1998. But not long after the fall of the Suharto regime, this belief in "national belonging" re-emerges among the Chinese in Indonesia.

In what way could the "integration of the Chinese Indonesians" into Indonesian mainstream society be measured? From the theoretical perspective, one can see it from two aspects: firstly, it means that the Chinese Indonesians identify themselves with the "Indonesian nation", accept Indonesia as their country, get actively involved in the development of the country and share happiness and sorrow with the Indonesian population; secondly, Chinese Indonesians actively participate in Indonesian politics, safeguard the country's prosperity and security, and strive for the legitimate rights of the Chinese Indonesians. Nevertheless, the process of the integration of Chinese Indonesians into "mainstream society" has not been smooth. This is due to many reasons: the Chinese in Indonesia are not a homogeneous group, and in Indonesia, anti-Chinese forces have been strong, ideological struggle in Indonesia has been fierce and the Chinese were often caught in between, and the international situation sometimes also serves as a hindrance for ethnic Chinese integration into Indonesian society.

Indonesian Nation and the Ethnic Chinese

Indigenism or *pribumi-isme* reached its peak during the Suharto New Order. It became the foundation of the Indonesian nation (*bangsa*). What is an Indonesian nation? According to this indigenous concept, it constitutes the ethnic groups of the indigenous people. The Indonesian national culture is based on the indigenous people's cultures, and the ethnic Chinese culture is not part of this culture.

In fact, the Indonesian nation is not always defined this way. When Sukarno and Hatta declared Indonesia's independence, Sukarno used the definition based on Ernst Renan's concept of nation, which is the politico-cultural definition of nation.[3] Those who regarded Indonesia as their country and were born and lived in the territories of the Republic of Indonesia were members of the Indonesian nation.

However, Sukarno did not explain what is meant by members of the Indonesian nation in detail. It was only in 1963, when nation-building became a political movement, did Sukarno present a rather concrete argument. According to Sukarno, "Suku means leg, Indonesian nation has many legs, just like a centipede, which possesses Javanese leg, Sundanese leg, Sumatran leg, Irian leg, Dayak leg, Bali leg, Sumba leg, Peranakan Chinese leg, Peranakan Chinese leg is one of the Indonesian national legs."[4]

This was the first time that the President of the Republic of Indonesia clearly stated that "Peranakan Chinese" are a member of the Indonesian nation. In other words, Peranakan Chinese are already members of the Indonesian nation and therefore do not need to be assimilated into the "indigenous Indonesian nation". Nevertheless, Sukarno did not clarify who Peranakan Chinese are. Are they Indonesia-born Chinese who use Bahasa Indonesia as their home language, or all Indonesian Chinese who have obtained Indonesian citizenship?

Heterogeneous Chinese Indonesians

In reality, Indonesian Chinese do not constitute a homogeneous group. Prior to World War II, Indonesian Chinese were divided into "Peranakan Chinese" and "*totok* Chinese" (or migrant Chinese). The former refers to those Chinese born in Indonesia; they came before the *totok* Chinese, and have been influenced by the local (Malay) culture. Peranakan Chinese usually lost their command of the Chinese language and used a local dialect or Malay (Indonesian) as a home language and the language of communication. Those Chinese who came to Indonesia during the twentieth century usually still retained the Chinese language and culture. They use a Chinese dialect or Mandarin as their home language and the language of communication. Therefore, they are not classified as "Peranakan Chinese". Their children who were born in Indonesia before World War II or soon after the war, i.e. the second-generation migrant Chinese, linguistically and culturally are still closer to the "*totok* Chinese", therefore they are often considered as "*totok*", and not "Peranakan".

However, after Suharto assumed power, he eliminated three cultural pillars of the Chinese, and the descendants of the *totok* Chinese were rapidly "peranakanized" and were transformed into a new type of Peranakan Chinese: they used Bahasa Indonesia and Indonesian dialect and strengthened the Peranakan Chinese community.

In fact, if the concept of "Peranakan Chinese" as a member of the Indonesian nation could be accepted and developed, Chinese Indonesian's national identity could have been resolved. However, when Suharto came to power in October 1965, he immediately abandoned Sukarno's concept. He not only refused to acknowledge "Peranakan Chinese" as an Indonesian *suku* (ethnic group), but also advocated total assimilation of the Chinese Indonesians. He closed down all Chinese language schools, dissolved ethnic Chinese organizations, banned Chinese mass media, and prohibited use of the Chinese language.

Moreover, he promulgated the "name-changing" regulation, "appealing" to Chinese Indonesians to change their names to Indonesian names.[5] He also restricted the development of the Confucian religion (Agama Khonghucu), an Indonesian Chinese religion, by derecognizing it as a non-religion in 1979 and denied the Confucian organization to hold a congress. Nevertheless, since Indonesia is based on Pancasila (Five Principles), and according to the Pancasila principle, Indonesians have the right to religious freedom and therefore he was unable to dissolve the Confucian religion.

However, Suharto's assimilationist policy has a profound impact on the Indonesian Chinese community; Indonesian Chinese in the thirty-two years of Suharto's rule have become "more Indonesianized". But it does not mean that Chinese Indonesians have been homogenized. The division between "Peranakan" and "*totok*" continues to exist, but the number of *totok* Chinese have rapidly declined. However, the *totoks* are more dynamic in the cultural and economic fields, and their presence has been strongly felt. It is also worth noting that during the Suharto rule, almost all *totok* Chinese have obtained Indonesian citizenship and became the new masters of the country.

Indonesian Chinese in the Post-Suharto Period

In the era of globalization and democratization, Suharto was eventually forced to step down, the military power has been undermined, reform was introduced and political participation has also increased.

During this new era, the government policy also underwent changes. The three pillars of the Chinese culture, to a largest extent, have been restored. The concept of an Indonesian nation has been affected. Chinese Indonesians started to regard themselves as a suku Tionghoa of Indonesia. Some Indonesian intellectuals have also begun to accept this concept. However, the concept of "suku Tionghoa" is unclear. Does it refer to the suku Peranakan Tionghoa as in the Sukarno era, or is it used to refer to all Indonesian citizens of Chinese descent (both peranakan and *totok*)? In fact, "nationhood" is different from "citizenship", the former is a cultural and historical concept while the latter is a legal concept.

As a matter of fact, prior to becoming the President of Indonesia, Abdurrahman Wahid (Gus Dur) proposed an idea that the Indonesian nation comprised of three races (*ras*): Malay race, Chinese race and Austro-Melanesian race.[6] It seems that no one has supported his view;

even his own Partai Kebangkitan Bangsa (National Awakening Party) has never mentioned this concept.

Nevertheless, it is clear that during the era of *reformasi*, the government appears to have accepted multi-culturalism rather than mono-culturalism as the basis of the Indonesian nation. But the thirty-two-year rule of the New Order, during which "indigenism" was the basis of the state policy, has been deeply rooted in the minds of Indonesians. The social distance between Indonesian ethnic groups became wide. According to a survey conducted by *Tempo* in 2001, 52 per cent of the respondents indicated that they did not want to have their relatives marry an ethnic Chinese; 78 per cent could not accept Indonesian citizens of Chinese descent speaking their own Chinese dialect or Mandarin.[7]

Political Participation of the Ethnic Chinese

To be a member of the Indonesian nation (as a *suku bangsa*) is one indicator of "integrating into Indonesian mainstream society"; to actively participate in Indonesian politics is another indicator.

As soon as Suharto stepped down, Indonesian indigenous and ethnic Chinese immediately established new political parties. Apart from the three old parties, there were more than 100 new parties formed. During that period, Chinese Indonesians set up three political parties: Partai Reformasi Tionghoa Indonesia (Parti), Partai Pembauran and Partai Bhinneka Tunggal Ika Indonesia (PBI). Partai Pembauran was transformed into a social organization soon after its formation as total assimilation was no longer popular, Parti did not develop and only the PBI contested in the 1999 election, but it performed poorly: it only gained a seat in the national parliament (by Susanto T.L. from West Kalimantan),[8] and failed to contest in the 2004 election. It did not contest the 2009 election either.

Chinese Indonesians forming their own ethnic political parties is a result of Chinese political consciousness. But the number of Chinese Indonesians is small and they are divided in their political ideology. It is unlikely that ethnic Chinese would be able to win parliamentary seats through ethnic Chinese parties. It is therefore not surprising that those Chinese who were interested in politics joined "indigenous-based" political parties. In the 1999 and 2004 elections, many Chinese Indonesians were elected as members of parliaments (MPs) at national and provincial levels on the "indigenous-based" parties' tickets.[9] For instance, in 1999, there were eight Chinese Indonesians in the parliament: five from Partai Demokrasi Indonesia-Perjuangan (PDI-P), one from Golkar, one from Partai Amanat Nasional (PAN), and one from PBI. In 2009, there were nine Chinese Indonesian MPs, three from Partai Demokrasi Indonesia-Perjuangan (PDI-P), three from Golkar, and three from the Partai Demokrat (PD). There were also Chinese Indonesians who were elected as mayor or regent (*bupati*). For instance, Basuki Tjahaja Purnama (Zhong Wanxue, 钟万学 alias A Hok) who was the regent of East Belitung, and Hasan Karman (Huang Shaofan, 黄少凡) who was mayor of Singkawang (West Kalimantan). This is a new development in the Indonesian political history.

Nevertheless, to participate in politics does not necessarily have to go through official channels (i.e., joining political parties); joining non-governmental organizations (NGOs) also allow one to participate in informal politics. After the fall of Suharto, many Chinese Indonesians established socio-cultural organizations. The Paguyuban Sosial Marga Tionghoa Indonesia (PSMTI) and Perhimpunan INTI are two examples of Chinese NGOs. Seen from the perspective of the mainstream society, participating in Chinese NGOs is less significant compared to that of Indonesian NGOs.

It should be noted that the long suppression towards ethnic Chinese in Indonesia and the violence against the Chinese have a long-term impact on the Chinese political participation. Some Chinese Indonesians still fear participating in formal politics as they were afraid this may jeopardize their personal safety.

While political participation is a way to integrate the Chinese into Indonesian "mainstream society", the process is not always smooth. Racial discriminations have not gone away easily and racial attacks have been used in order to defeat political opponents. This has happened during many national, provincial, and municipal elections. One of the examples is the Jakarta gubernatorial election in 11 July 2012.

Six pairs of candidates contested in this election, among which two were the strongest. They were, firstly, the incumbent governor Fauzi

Bowo with his partner Nachrowi Ramli who were supported by President Susilo Bambang Yudhoyono's party, Partai Demokrat (PD). Next was the pair comprised of Joko Widodo (known as Jokowi) and Basuki Tjahaja Purnama (A Hok). Jokowi was the mayor of Surakarta (Central Java), a Muslim, and portrayed by the media as a clean and able administrator. He was supported by the PDI-P. Jokowi's deputy, Basuki, the former regent of East Belitung, is a Christian Chinese Indonesian. Basuki was supported by the Gerindra Party.[10]

During the first round of the election, the government-backed candidates only gained 34 per cent while the Jokowi-Basuki pair obtained 43 per cent of the votes. As no candidates exceeded 50 per cent of the votes, there was a second round of election between these two pairs on 20 September.

Soon after the unexpected results of the first round were announced, a smear campaign against Jokowi-Basuki began. A YouTube video entitled "Chinese Cowboy Leads Jakarta" attempted to incite racial hatred, attacking Basuki (A Hok) as a representative of an ethnic group which could not be trusted. One popular indigenous singer and preacher Rhoma Irama also urged the people not to vote for the pair of non-Muslim leaders.

In fact, Jokowi is a Muslim and only Basuki is a Christian. The authorities eventually moved in and removed the racist video.[11] It is worth noting that ethnicity is still used and will continue to be used as a political weapon, but not against Indonesians of Arab and Pakistani descent where the issue of ethnicity was never raised. It seems that Indonesians of Arab and Pakistani descent are "automatically" accepted as "Indonesians", primarily due to their Islamic religion.

Chinese Indonesian Identity and the Rise of China

With globalization and democratization, the Indonesian government changed its policy towards the ethnic Chinese, the three pillars of Chinese culture have been restored, and many Chinese Indonesians began to re-identify themselves with "Chinese culture".

In fact, during the Suharto era, Chinese Indonesians' identification with Chinese culture was suppressed; complete assimilation was the state policy. Under this situation, Chinese Indonesians changed their names to Indonesian-sounding names, received "pure" Indonesian education, and strived to become "Indonesian" rather than "ethnic Chinese". However, in reality, many Chinese Indonesians remained unassimilated in the sense that they were not transformed into the "indigenous population".

The democratization of Indonesia caused ethnic minorities, including the Chinese minority, to regain their freedom to have their own identity. They began to feel "Chinese" again and felt proud of the rise of China. The resurgence of Chinese economic and soft power made an impact in the world. Many Chinese Indonesians, including those who have been peranakanized, started to learn Mandarin, and to study Chinese culture.

However, it does not mean that they are re-sinicized, as the situation in Indonesia is different from that of China and it is impossible for Chinese Indonesians to be transformed back into mainland Chinese. Nevertheless, it cannot be denied that the rise of China provided an impetus to Chinese Indonesians to be re-oriented toward Chinese culture, resulting in the greater difference between ethnic Chinese and "indigenous" Indonesians.

Many "indigenous" Indonesians were unable to differentiate "cultural identity" from "political identity"; they thought that Chinese Indonesians have shifted their political orientation towards China because they re-oriented towards Chinese culture. As a result, frictions between Chinese and non-Chinese may recur. It is also very unfortunate that they are Chinese Indonesians who are Indonesian citizens yet continue to claim themselves as "Zhongguo ren" (中国人, China's nationals) and not "Yinni Ren" (印尼人, Indonesians) and this resulted in discontent among the "indigenous" Indonesians.

It should be noted that since the 1980s, some Mainland Chinese have migrated to the developed countries in North America, Europe, Australia and New Zealand, while others have taken up local citizenship. These new migrants would like China to re-introduce the dual nationality status so that they will be able to retain Chinese citizenship. Towards the end of the 1990s, the question of dual citizenship was debated again in China's political assembly, but China still adopts the single citizenship policy. If the dual citizenship policy is re-introduced, the

Chinese in Southeast Asia are likely to be victimized again when there is political or economic instability in the region.

Although in principle, China continues to divide Chinese citizens from non-Chinese citizens among the Chinese overseas, however, the implementation of the policy towards ethnic Chinese has undergone some changes: it tends to regard foreign citizens of Chinese descent as "Chinese citizens"; this makes the national status of the ethnic Chinese in Southeast Asia problematic.[12] Many Peranakan Chinese elites in Indonesia have complained that the Chinese embassy has been too close to Chinese Indonesian associations/organizations. For instance, during the celebration of Indonesian Independence Day, Chinese Indonesian associations only invited Chinese embassy officials but not Indonesian officials. This would jeopardize the interests of the Chinese Indonesians in the long run.[13] The Peranakan Chinese elites appealed to the Chinese embassy to implement the Zhou Enlai's "Overseas Chinese Policy", i.e., to educate Chinese Indonesians to be "loyal to their adopted country".[14]

The rise of China and Indonesian democratization provided an opportunity to the Chinese in Indonesia to identify with "Chinese culture". Some Chinese Indonesians, especially members of the older generation, have very weak Indonesian identity. Under this circumstance, those Chinese who have not integrated into Indonesia's "mainstream society" will find identifying with "Indonesian nation" "less attractive" as they have not been part of the Indonesian culture to begin with.

As stated earlier, the ethnic Chinese in Indonesia are not a homogeneous group. However, it cannot be denied that they play a significant role in the commercial sector. Globalization has enabled Chinese Indonesians to have more freedom and opportunities to expand their economic activities. As a result, the economic position of the ethnic Chinese in Indonesia has become stronger. However, many indigenous Indonesians still encounter a lot of economic difficulties and many still live below the poverty line. Hence, the gap between the rich and the poor is quite obvious. If the division between the rich and the poor is along the ethnic line, or is perceived along ethnic lines, and if the general economic condition of Indonesia declines bringing hardship to the people, then there will be no guarantee that anti-Chinese riots will not recur. Many Chinese Indonesian leaders recently appealed to the local Chinese community that with the indigenous population still living in poverty, the Chinese should not indulge themselves in having big celebrations and parties.[15]

China has now become "the world's factory". Chinese products are cheaper than those of the developing countries. These cheap products have a major impact on the Small and Medium-sized Enterprises (SMEs) in Southeast Asia (including Indonesia). Many of the owners/proprietors of these SMEs happen to be ethnic Chinese. In order to cope with globalization, especially the challenge of China, they have begun to reorganize their businesses. Many SME manufacturers are unable to compete with cheap Chinese goods; their factories were forced to close down, although some have managed to transform themselves into commercial firms and survived. This resulted in an increase in the number of Chinese businessmen, strengthening the impression that Chinese Indonesians are mainly businessmen. This is quite worrying.

Conclusion

Chinese Indonesians are a heterogeneous group. Some have been integrated and even assimilated into Indonesian mainstream society, while others have yet to be fully integrated.

For Chinese Indonesians to integrate into "mainstream society" is complex. To be integrated into the "mainstream society" means that Chinese Indonesians have to be members of the "Indonesian nation": they not only need to have Indonesian citizenship, but also actively participate in both formal and informal politics; they need to fulfill the obligations of a citizen and to contribute to the prosperity and security of the Indonesian nation-state.

However, to be members of the Indonesian nation is not easy. The concept of the "Indonesian nation" has been changing in accordance with the regime. The "indigenous-based Indonesian nation" is no longer suitable. The Peranakan Chinese as an Indonesian *suku* (ethnic group) may be acceptable but is not without problem, as the definition of a Peranakan has not been well defined. In the past, only "Peranakan Chinese" participated in politics, while today, Chinese Indonesians of *totok* background also took part. These *totoks* have been peranakanized and can be considered as Peranakans. In the 2004 general elections and provincial heads elections, many Chinese Indonesians had been actively involved.

As a matter of fact, if Chinese Indonesians want to integrate into "mainstream society", the indigenous Indonesians should also change their attitude towards the ethnic Chinese; they need to sincerely accept the Chinese Indonesians. However, the thirty-two years of Suharto's "anti-Chinese" policy has been deeply rooted in the hearts and minds of the indigenous population. It is difficult to eradicate the deep prejudice of the population overnight. At the same time, the strengthening position of the Chinese Indonesians in the economic field and the poverty of many "indigenous Indonesians" will pose a hindrance to Chinese Indonesian's integration into "mainstream society". Last but not least, Beijing's policy towards the Chinese overseas will also determine whether Chinese Indonesians will genuinely become members of the Indonesian nation.

Notes

*This is a revised/updated keynote speech that I delivered at the international conference organized by the Hong Kong Society for Indonesian Studies and the Hong Kong City University on 24–25 May 2008. It was first published in *Asian Culture* 36 (August 2012).

1. Leo Suryadinata, Evi Nurvidya Arifin, and Aris Ananta, *Indonesia's Population: Ethnicity and Religion in a Changing Political Landscape* (Singapore: Institute of Southeast Asian Studies, 2003), p. 12.
2. Leo Suryadinata, "Government Policy and National Integration in Indonesia", in *Chinese and Nation-Building in Southeast Asia* (Singapore: Marshall Cavendish, 2005), pp. 81–100.
3. Sukarno's well-known Pancasila speech was reproduced in *Risalah Sidang Badan Penyelidik Usaha-Usaha Persiapan Kemerdekaan Indonesia (BPUPKI) Panitia Persiapan Kemerdekaan Indonesia (PPKI), 29 Mei 1945–19 Agustus 1945* (Jakarta: Sekretariat Negara Republik Indonesia, 1992). His argument on the concept of nation is found on pp. 62–63. Lahirnja Pantjasila, pp. 55–72.
4. "Amanat P.J.M. Presiden Soekarno Pada Kongres Nasional ke-VIII Baperki", in *Gotong Rojong Nasakom untuk Melaksanakan Ampera*, edited by Siauw Giok Tjhan (Djakarta: Baperki, 1963), p. 14.

5. Name-changing regulation was promulgated in 1966. It is interesting to note that the so-called Indonesian name is difficult to define, many argued that as long as it is not a "Chinese name", it can be accepted as an Indonesian name.

6. Abdurahaman Wahid, "Prolog: PKB Didirikan oleh PBNU", in *Pro-Kontra Partai Kebangkitan Bangsa*, edited by Munib Huda Muhammad (Jakarta: Fatma Pers, 1998), pp. 7–8.

7. "Tionghoa belum diterima apa adanya", *Tempo*, 4 February 2001, pp. 12–13. I do not have more recent surveys by *Tempo*.

8. His Chinese name is Lin Guanyu (林冠玉).

9. For a list of Chinese Indonesian MPs in the 1999 election, see Liao Jianyu (廖建裕), *Dongnanya yu Huaren Zuqun yanjiu* 东南亚与华人族群研究 (Singapore: Singapore Qingnian Shuju 新加坡青年书局, 2008), pp. 159–60; for the 2009 list, see "Xinjie guohui tese yu huarenyiyuanjingyan jiaoxun 新届国会特色与华人议员经验教训", *Guoji Ribao* (国际日报), 30 May 2009.

10. Andreas D. Arditya, "It's Fauzi vs Jokowi on Sept. 20", *Jakarta Post*, 12 September 2012.

11. Zakir Hussain, "Jakarta Removes Racist Video, Hunts for Culprits", *Straits Times*, 26 August 2012.

12. Yang Ping (杨平), "Yange qufen Huaqiao huaren de jiexian 严格区分华侨华人的界限", *Kumpulan Makalah Masalah Tionghoa Indonesia* 印尼华人专题论文集, 24–25 May 2008, pp. 43–46.

13. Benny G. Setiono, "Beberapa catatan mengenai perkembangan Organisasi-Organisasi Tionghoa di Indonesia", *Kumpulan makalah masalah Tionghoa di Indonesia*, 24–25 May 2008, pp. 16–22.

14. Ibid.

15. Ibid.

APPENDIX 1

The Prospects of the Peranakan Community at the Age of Globalization

Tan Ta Sen*

Ladies and Gentlemen, I felt extremely honoured to be here today to share with you my thoughts on the prospects of the Peranakan community at the age of globalization. Being a Baba and Nyonya yourself, I am sure you are very concerned about the future of the Peranakan community. The word "Peranakan" is more commonly used in Bahasa Indonesia than in Bahasa Melayu. In the past, the terms "Baba and Nyonya" were commonly used to refer to the localized Chinese. However, Peranakan in fact includes all localized foreigners or their descendants. Thus, we have the Chinese Peranakans (Baba and Nyonya), Indian Peranakans (Chitty or Mamak-Indian Muslim), Portuguese Peranakans, and European Peranakans (Eurasian or Serani). Melaka is the home of the Peranakans in both Malaysia and Singapore and so it is not only appropriate and relevant but also historically significant for me to deal with this topic here. Although I am a Singaporean, and not a Baba myself, in the past decades I have business concerns in Melaka and frequently visited Melaka. Thus, I am virtually a local Melakan, living at the centre of the old town and have witnessed the change that has taken place in the past two decades.

I would like to begin by giving you a few significant glimpses into the history of the Chinese diaspora as well as the eventual development of the Peranakan community in Melaka so as to set the tone of proper historical perspective. The Chinese have been migrating southward from China to Southeast Asia for centuries, driven from their homeland by economic necessity, political disturbance, flood and drought. Chinese diaspora outside China are generally addressed as Tang Ren (Teng Lang, 唐人) because since the seventh century in the Tang dynasty, Chinese mariners and traders were engaging in considerable international maritime trade, travelling as far afield as East Africa through the Straits of Melaka. They actually went to mainland Southeast Asia as early as the Qin dynasty and were addressed as Qin Ren (秦人). However, they were merely sojourners before the fourteenth century.

Cheng Ho's (Zheng He, 郑和) historic seven voyages to the western ocean in the early fifteenth century marked the first wave of Chinese migration to Southeast Asia. Cheng Ho discovered the presence of Chinese settlements in Island Southeast Asia. Three crew members of Cheng Ho's fleet, Ma Huan, Fei Xin and Gong Zhen have recorded their eye-witness accounts of Cheng Ho's voyages to the western ocean in their books. They witnessed the existence of Chinese settlements in Sumatra's Palembang and Java's Majapahit, Tuban, Gresik and Surabaya. This first wave of Chinese emigration was characterized by indigenization (localization) as these pioneers were quick to interact and even intermarried with the natives and as a result were gradually assimilated into the local population. However, Ma Huan and Gong Zhen made no mention of Chinese settlement in Melaka but Fei Xin casually referred to some pale-looking people among the Melaka residents as the "Tang" people. "Tang", like "Han", is commonly used to refer to the Chinese. Therefore, we could safely conclude that there was a handful of Chinese in Melaka during Cheng Ho's era, but they were too few in number to form any so-called Chinese settlement. As Cheng Ho built an outpost in Melaka and all ships coming from China and going to other ports were required to assemble in Melaka awaiting fair wind to make the homeward journey, there were certainly sizable crew members of Cheng Ho's fleet temporarily putting up in the *guanchang* (government warehouse complex). Ma Huan, Gong Zhen and Fei Xin were quite clear about these itinerant Chinese and so it was unlikely that they would be confused between the itinerant Chinese crew members who were sojourners and the few Chinese residents.

The legend of Hang Li Poh has hinted the existence of Melaka's earliest Chinese settlement at Bukit Cina during the Cheng Ho era. Princess Hang Li Poh has long been conveniently dismissed by historians as a myth. But I would like to review the Hang Li Poh story in a fresh historical perspective. On the subject of Hang Li Poh, in my opinion, it was a historical event which might have possibly taken place. When we survey the legends of Southeast Asia, especially of Indonesia and Malaya, we often find stories of Chinese princesses marrying native rulers. It can be attributed to the fact that China, throughout history, was a great power and a cultural centre surrounded by undeveloped native states. These native rulers would feel extremely honoured to marry a Chinese princess as it could enhance the prestige of the native rulers and win the trust of the Chinese emperors. During the colonial period, it would be a great honour for a native to marry a white girl. In history, there were many examples of Chinese princesses marrying native rulers such as Princess Wencheng who was married to a Tibetan king and Wang Zhaojun to a Xiongnu ruler. Hang Li Poh could have been another Wang Zhaojun who was not a princess but a maid in the imperial palace. In fact, the Malay Annals' story of Hang Li Poh marrying Sultan Mansor Shah was an error. The sultan who married Hang Li Poh should have been Megat Iskandar Shah (Parameswara's son). Western scholars were also agreeable to this version but mistakenly regarded her as the daughter of a local Chinese Kapitan. The Kapitan system was only introduced by the Portuguese in the sixteenth century but the Hang Li Poh story took place in the early fifteenth century. In my view, Hang Li Poh was very likely one of the maids in the palace of the Ming dynasty's Yongle Emperor. In addition, "Puteri" in Malay and Indonesian languages may not necessarily mean "princess". It is widely used as a pet name for girls, like what the Chinese would call their daughters as *qianjin* (千金, or a thousand *jin* of gold). Historian's suggestion about the story of Hang Li Poh as a legend simply because there was no record on her in the Ming dynastic history may not be totally correct. The Malay and Indonesian historiographies are fairly similar to the Chinese historiography as literature and history are inseparable. Literature, biography, or even mythology are in complete harmony with historical facts. Moreover, Hang Li Poh was not a princess, why should Chinese officials record this event?

Cheng Ho's historic seven voyages to the western ocean in the fifteenth century opened the door for the Chinese living in the coastal provinces in China such as Guangdong and Fujian to migrate abroad. The second wave of Chinese emigration took place between 1644 and the 1840s and was characterized by Westernization. The overthrow of the Ming dynasty by the Manchus in 1644 led to an exodus of Ming royalists to Southeast Asia. A group of these Ming royalists, like Melaka's second Chinese Kapitan Li Wei King (李为经) also known as Li Jun Chang (李君常) or Li Kap, took refuge in Melaka and was later given the Kapitan post by the Dutch ruler.

These cultured Ming royalists soon made fortunes from trade and were picked by the Portuguese (Dutch colonial government) as community leaders, who appointed them as Kapitans to be in charge of the Chinese affairs from the seventeenth to nineteenth centuries. The British colonists accepted these Chinese community leaders and called them Teng Chu (*tingzhu*, 亭主). The office of the Teng Chu was located in the Cheng Hoon Teng Temple (Qing Yun Ting, 青云亭), the oldest Chinese temple in Melaka and Malaysia. Hence, Cheng Hoon Teng was the most important power base of the Chinese in Melaka. Cheng Hoon Teng Temple was jointly established by the first two Chinese Kapitans, Tay Hong Yoe (Zheng Fang Yang, 郑芳扬), also known as Tay Kap and Li Wei King in 1673. Then, the Chinese population in Melaka was small (about 100 plus). But it had increased to 160 in 1675, two years after the foundation of the Cheng Hoon Teng Temple. In 1678, the Chinese population increased significantly to 426. Since they were entrusted to be in charge of the Chinese affairs, they took the first step to organize the Chinese community by forming the Cheng Hoon Teng Temple.

Li Kap, a native of Xiamen (厦门), was one of the Ming royalists who fled from Manchu rule after the downfall of the Ming dynasty in 1644. Together with other like-minded Ming royalists, he took refuge in Melaka. These Ming royalists being learned Confucian scholars, brought Chinese culture to Melaka. Li Kap went into business and made his fortunes. He then collaborated with Tay Kap to establish the Cheng Hoon Teng Temple. Later, he bought and donated a piece of land for use by the Chinese community in Melaka as a burial ground in Bukit China or Sam Po Hill (San Bao Shan, 三宝山). It is not surprising that Tay Kap and Li Kap had targeted temple and burial ground as urgent services for the Chinese in Melaka. For the Chinese immigrants, the temple is constantly the first refuge to seek salvation of inner peace and spiritual attachment and to link up with fellow clansmen in a foreign land, and the cemetery is to ensure the wanderers a last resting place. In any early Chinese settlement abroad, temple, clan associations and burial ground are always the first forms of social organizations as they bond the immigrant community into a cohesive society.

In 1698, a French business delegation on its way to China made a brief stopover in Melaka and visited Cheng Hoon Teng. One of the delegation members, Francois Froger paid a visit to the Cheng Hoon Teng and he wrote about the temple with a temple layout plan. He described that the temple consisted of four major sections, namely, the main hall, front hall, inner hall and the women's prayer quarter. On the day of his visit, the temple priests were performing religious ritual. He was so engrossed that he stayed in the temple for two hours and jotted down his impressions of the happenings. Froger made one important remark of very historical significance. He called the Cheng Hoon Teng Temple: "The Pagoda of the Chinese Refugees in Melaka". It testified the existence of a considerable group of Ming royalists taking refuge in Melaka after the Manchus overthrew the Ming dynasty in 1644. After half a century, this "refugee" impression of Melaka was still distinctively noticeable.

These refugees or Ming royalists were the pioneers of Melaka Chinese society. They brought Chinese culture to Melaka shaping the development of the Chinese society in Melaka and eventually nurtured the birth of a Peranakan Chinese culture showing the fusion of the cultural traits of both Chinese, English and Malay cultures.

The Kapitan system was a legacy of the Portuguese, Dutch and British colonial governments from the sixteenth to early nineteenth centuries. The Kapitans were acknowledged as Chinese leaders by virtue of their enormous wealth and high social status. Their descendants attended Portuguese, Dutch and English schools. Many of them worked in foreign firms while others started their own companies engaging in imports and exports of spices and China trade. They were the forefathers of the Westernized prosperous Peranakans. For instance, Kapitan Chua Soo Chong in the eighteenth century was the father of prominent Baba Chua Chong Long and the grandfather of Baba Chua Yan Ling.

The British abolished the Kapitan system in 1825. Thereafter Cheng Hoon Teng Temple introduced an appointment of temple president, i.e. the Teng Chu, to be the leader of the Chinese community in Melaka in place of Kapitan. The temple presidential system was later abolished in 1915. From 1825 to 1915, there were a total of six temple presidents: Liang Mei Ji (梁美吉), Si Hoo Keh (薛佛记), Tan Kim Seng (陈金声), Tan Beng Swee (陈明水), Tan Beng Jiak (陈明岩) and Tan Jiak Wai (陈若准). Si Hoo Keh, Tan Kim Seng, Tan Beng Swee, Tan Beng Jiak and so on were prominent Babas and dominant Chinese leaders in Singapore and Melaka. It shows that the Peranakans were the backbone of the Chinese in Singapore and Melaka in the nineteenth century through the first half of the twentieth century.

In the eighteenth and nineteenth centuries, the Babas were involved in opium, sireh, nutmeg, pepper and gambier cultivation, tin mining, commodity trading and property. In the early twentieth century, many Babas invested in rubber. Baba and Nyonya were financially better off than China-born Chinese. Their family wealth and connections with the Malay royalties and the British and Dutch colonialists enabled them to form a Straits-Chinese elite class, whose loyalty was strictly to Britain or the Netherlands. Most Peranakans were English or Dutch-educated, as a result of the Western colonization of Malaya and Indonesia. The Peranakans readily embraced English and Dutch culture and education as a means to advance economically. Thus, administrative and civil service posts were often filled by prominent Straits Chinese. Many in the community also worked as compradores (Chinese middlemen) for big Western companies and banks. The Peranakan community thereby became very influential in Malaya, Singapore and Indonesia, and was known also as the King's Chinese due to their loyalty to the British Crown.

The third wave of Chinese migration to Southeast Asia in the nineteenth century coincided with political turmoil in China and economic exploitation of Southeast Asia by the Dutch and British colonial powers. The Taiping Rebellion in China was a widespread civil war in southern China from 1850 to 1864. The First Opium War (1839 to 1842) and the Second Opium War (1856 to 1860) fought between Qing Dynasty China and the British Empire, were events which had caused great hardships and economic dislodgements to the farmers in the Fujian and Guangdong provinces. In the meantime, the Dutch and British colonial governments were earnestly engaged in developing labour-intensive sugar and tin-mining industries in the Dutch Indies (present-day Indonesia) and British Malaya. As a consequence, the job opportunities in Indonesia and Malaya led to the mass exodus of the dislodged farmers in Fujian and Guangdong to the region. These new arrivals, mostly illiterate, worked as cheap labourers in plantations and tin mines. As a result of the massive influx of the Chinese immigrants, the China-born Chinese outnumbered Peranakan Chinese. The demographic change coupled with the rise of a good number of adventurous new rich who made their fortunes from tin mines, gambier and rubber plantations as well as trade, ushered in a new phase in the history of the Chinese diaspora. The rising China-born Chinese merchants overtook Peranakans as community leaders. They actively built temples, clan associations and Chinese schools to educate the immigrants' children. As a result, it signified a phase of re-Sinicization as a dominant feature of this third wave of Chinese migration, and the Chinese-educated Chinese became the mainstream of the Chinese communities.

This re-Sinicization process remained predominant during the fourth wave of Chinese migration which was triggered by the outbreak of the Sino-Japanese War in 1937. Soon after the war, a great number of Chinese literates and intelligentsia such as teachers, journalists and so on migrated to Southeast Asia and they reinforced the dissemination of Chinese culture in these overseas Chinese communities.

The post-war political developments in Indonesia, Malaysia and Singapore had great impact on the history of Chinese diaspora. The end of the Pacific War in 1945 saw a rise of multi-racial nationalist movements in Southeast Asia and people of all ethnic groups of former colonies were united to fight for independence. Changing Chinese communities entered a phase of commitment to national identity after World War II. We saw two noticeable features in this process. Firstly, the rise of a local pan-Chinese identity signified the decline of the Chinese dialect or sub-ethnic groups including the Peranakan Chinese when the Chinese joined hands with the Malays and Indians in the struggle for independence. Secondly, after independence, the Chinese moved to adopt citizenship and develop a sense of national identity and actively engaged in nation-building.

Now we come back to review how these postwar changes had affected the Peranakan community. As a community that always considered Malaya home, many Peranakans were involved in civic projects and local government. Due to their strict loyalty, they did not support Malaysian independence. Things started to change in the latter half of the twentieth century, with some leading Melakan Peranakans, for example Tan Cheng Lock (陈祯禄) and Tan Siew Sin (陈修信), starting to support Malaysian independence.

Peranakan culture has started to decline in Malaysia and Singapore after independence. Without British colonial support for their perceived racial neutrality, they have been faced with a cultural identity crisis. The Japanese Occupation and the government policies in both countries following independence from the British have resulted in the assimilation of Peranakans back into mainstream Chinese culture. Singapore classifies the Peranakans as ethnically Chinese, so they receive formal instruction in Mandarin Chinese as a second language instead of Malay. In Malaysia, the standardization of Malay as Bahasa Melayu (required for all ethnic groups) has led to a disappearance of the unique characteristics of Baba Malay. The Peranakan culture is losing popularity to modern Western culture, but to some degree, Peranakans try to retain their language, cuisines and customs. Young Peranakans still speak their creole language, although many young women no longer wear the *kebaya*. Marriages normally follow the Western culture because the traditional Peranakan customs are losing popularity.

The situation has been aggravated in the present age of globalization in which we see the fifth and latest wave of Chinese emigration into Southeast Asia in the last thirty years since the Chinese government relaxed the policy on overseas emigration. The rapid economic integration and the improved political relations between ASEAN and China resulted in new Chinese migration to Southeast Asia being possible and acceptable. Following the rise of China as a world's powerful political and economic nation, China's export, Chinese investment and contracted project constructions in Southeast Asia, have risen dramatically with massive new Chinese immigrants coming into Southeast Asia.

This new wave of Chinese migrants to Southeast Asia and beyond is unprecedented in Chinese history not only because these new migrants originate from northern and central Chinese provinces, but also because travel has become easier due to better transportation links both inside and outside of China. That results in potentially larger numbers than previous waves of Chinese migration throughout the globe. These new immigrants are a breed apart from their forebears, who spoke regional dialects and exhibited little nationalism, identifying more with the localities in China from which they hailed. The recent arrivals are not only better educated, speak Mandarin, but also tend to identify with China as a whole. They are patriotic and loyal to the motherland. They are currently rising up as an important force within overseas Chinese and ethnic Chinese communities. However, the new immigrants have to move along with time to develop a sense of national identity and integrate into the mainstream local Chinese society.

The Peranakans were therefore squeezed on the one hand by the governments' nation-building policies and on the other hand by the influx of the Chinese new immigrants. Despite the national overtone of nation-building policies, it consciously draws Peranakans into the mainstream Chinese society politically and culturally. The Chinese immigrant phenomenon also puts pressure on the Peranakans to be re-Sinicized.

Hence, in the twenty-first century, the Peranakans face the same dilemmas and problems as the other Chinese communities in Singapore and Malaysia: the decline of traditions, the inability to speak the dialect, and the growing number of mixed marriages. All these factors lead to the great changes in the culture and uncertainty about the future. The frenzied activities revolving around Peranakan life and language in this decade could perhaps be seen as the frantic last throes of a declining community. But the Peranakan community seems determined to re-assert its identity in the face of encroaching modernity and loss of traditional culture and within the context of language shift and re-acculturation.

In short, the Peranakan community was born during the Cheng Ho and Western colonial eras. Their main characteristic was at first being localized (indigenized-Malay or Indonesian); Westernized during the colonial era, and re-Sinicized at the present national stage.

Thank you.

Note

*This is a transcript of the speech that Dr Tan Ta Sen (TS Tan), President of the International Zheng He Society (Singapore), presented to the Peranakan Chinese Association in Melaka in 2013. It was first published in *Asian Culture* 40 (December 2016).

APPENDIX 2

Some Books on the Peranakan Chinese Published between 2007 and 2021

Ang Yan Goan. 2009. *Memoar Ang Yan Goan*. Jakarta: Yayasan Nabil and Hasta Mitra.

Anggraeni, Dewi. 2010. *Mereka Bilang Aku China: Jalan Mendaki Menjadi Bagian Bangsa*. Yogyakarta: Bentang Pustaka.

Chia, Ruth, Linda Kow and Soh Tiang Keng. 2019. *Chia Ann Siang and Family: The Tides of Fortune*. Singapore: Marshall Cavendish International (Asia).

Dawis, Aimee. 2009. *The Chinese of Indonesia and Their Search for Identity: The Relationship between Collective Memory and the Media*. New York: Cambria Press.

Go Tik Swan. 2008. *Jawa Sejati: Otobiografi Go Tik Swan Hardjonagoro, Seperti yang dituturkan kepada Rustopo*. Jakarta: Yayasan Nabil.

Jahja, Junus. 2009. *Catatan Orang Indonesia*. Jakarta: Kumunitas Bambu.

Julianto, Irwan (Penggagas). 2009. *Peranakan Tionghoa di Indonesia: Sebuah Perjalanan Budaya*. Jakarta: Lintas Budaya Indonesia and Intisari.

Jusuf, Tedy. 2015. *Kacang Mencari Kulitnya: Seorang Tionghoa Anak Bangsa yang Menempuh Perjalanan Hidup sebagai Prajurit TNI*. Jakarta: Privately published.

———. 2021. *Menggapai Kesetaraan: Kisah Terbentuknya PSMTI*. Jakarta: No publisher.

Kee Ming-Yuet; Low Hock Seng. 2009. *Peranakan Chinese Porcelain: Vibrant Festive Ware of the Straits Chinese*. Singapore: Tuttle Publishing.

Knapp, Ronald. G. 2013. *The Peranakan Chinese Home: Art Culture in Daily Life.* Singapore: Tuttle Publishing.

Kusno, Abidin. 2016. *Visual Cultures of the Ethnic Chinese in Indonesia.* London and New York: Rowman and Littlefield.

Lee, Peter H. 2014. *Sarong Kebaya: Peranakan Fashion in an Interconnected World 1500–1950.* Singapore: Asian Civilisations Museum. (The electronic version was published by the Cambridge University Press, 2017).

Lev, Daniel S. 2011. *No Concessions: The Life of Yap Thiam Hien, Indonesian human rights lawyer.* Seattle: University of Washington Press.

Ong Kiat Neo, Christine. 2019. *Nyonya Kebaya Peranakan Heritage Fashion.* London: Transnational Press.

Ooi Kee Beng. 2010. *In Lieu of Ideology: An Intellectual Biography of Goh Keng Swee.* Singapore: Institute of Southeast Asian Studies.

———. 2020. *As Empires Fell: The Life and Times of Lee Hau-Shik.* Singapore: ISEAS – Yusof Ishak Institute.

Pearson, Stuart. 2008. *Bitter Sweet: The Memoir of a Chinese Indonesian Family in the Twentieth Century.* Singapore: NUS Press

Post, Peter. 2018. *The Kwee Family of Ciledug: Family, Status and the Modernity in Colonial Java.* Edam, Netherlands: LM Publishers.

Salmon, Claudine. 2010. *Sastra Indonesia Awal: Kontribusi Orang Tionghoa.* Jakarta: Kepustakaan Populer Gramedia.

Santosa, Iwan. 2012. *Peranakan Tionghoa Di Nusantara.* Jakarta: ASPERTINA and Penerbit Buku Kompas.

Suryadinata, Leo, ed. 2010. *Peranakan Chinese in a Globalizing Southeast Asia.* Singapore: Chinese Heritage Centre and NUS Baba House.

———, ed. 2015. *Peranakan Communities in the Era of Decolonization and Globalization.* Singapore: Chinese Heritage Centre and NUS Baba House.

———. Chief Editor. 2016. *Tionghoa Dalam KeIndonesiaan: Peran dan Kontribusi bagi Pembangunan Bangsa.* 3 Jilid (Three volumes). Jakarta: Yayasan Nabil.

Tan, Vivienne. 2019. *Tan Kim Seng: A Biography.* Singapore: Landmark Books.

Tempo. 2013. *Yap Thiam Hien: Sang Pendekar Keadilan.* Seri Buku Tempo. Jakarta: Kepustakaan Populer Gramedia.

———. 2016. *Gie: Dan Surat-surat yang Tersembunyi.* Seri Buku Tempo. Jakarta: Kepustakaan Populer Gramedia.

———. 2020. *Aktivis Cina Diawal Republik.* Seri Buku Tempo. Jakarta: Kepustakaan Populer Gramedia.

Tjahaja Purnama, Basuki (Ahok). 2008. *Merubah Indonesia: The Story of Basuki Tjahaja Purnama.* Jakarta: Center for Democracy and Transparency.

Tong, Lillian. 2014. *Straits Chinese Gold Jewellery.* Penang: Penang Peranakan Mansion.

Triyana, Bonnie. 2011. *Eddie Lembong: Mencintai Tanah Air Sepenuh Hati.* Jakarta: Penerbit Buku Kompas.

Wibisono, Lily, ed. 2009. *Indonesian Chinese Peranakan: A Cultural Journey.* Jakarta: Intisari Mediatama.

Wirawan, Yerry. 2014. *Sejarah Masyarakat Tionghoa Makassar.* Jakarta: Kepustakaan Populer Gramedia.

Wong Tet Phin, Peter. 2014. *Unsung Patriot: Wong Pow Nee.* Georgetown, Penang: Bumblogger Connexion Marketers.

Zhuang Wubin. 2011. *Chinese Muslims in Indonesia.* Singapore: Select Books.

BIBLIOGRAPHY

Abdullah bin Abdul Kadir. 1970. *The Hikayat Abdullah*. An Annotated Translation by A.H. Hill. Kuala Lumpur: Oxford University Press.

———. 1975. *The Voyages of Mohamed Ibrahim Munshi*. Translated with an introduction and notes by Amin Sweeney and Nigel Philips. Kuala Lumpur: Oxford University Press.

Ahmat B. Adam. 1994. *Isu Bahasa dan Pembentukan Bangsa*. Kuala Lumpur: Dewan Bahasa dan Pustaka.

———. 1995. *The Vernacular Press and the Emergence of Modern Indonesian Consciousness (1855–1913)*. Ithaca, New York: Southeast Asia Program, Cornell University.

Ai Qing. 1981. *Pemberitahuan Subuh* 黎明的通知. Kuala Lumpur: Universiti Malaya.

Ananta, Aris, Evi Nurvidya Arifin, and Bakhtiar. 2008. "Chinese Indonesians in Indonesia and the Province of Riau Archipelago: A Demographic Analysis". In *The Ethnic Chinese in Contemporary Indonesia*, edited by Leo Suryadinata, pp. 17–47. Singapore: Institute of Southeast Asian Studies.

Ananta, Aris, Evi Nurvidya Arifin, M. Sairi Hasbullah, Nur Budi Handayani, and Wahyu Pramono. 2015. *Demography of Indonesia's Ethnicity*. Singapore: Institute of Southeast Asian Studies.

Anderson, Benedict. 1991. *Imagined Communities: Reflections on Origin and Spread of Nationalism*. Revised ed. London and New York: Verso.

Anggaran Dasar dan Anggaran Rumah Tangga Baperki, 1954.

Arditya, Andreas D. 2012. "It's Fauzi vs Jokowi on Sept. 20". *Jakarta Post*, 12 September 2012.

A.S., Marcus and Pax Benedanto, eds. 2000. *Kesastraan Melayu Tionghoa dan Kebangsaan Indonesia*, Jilid 1. Jakarta: Kepustakaan Populer Gramedia.

Asosiasi Peranakan Tionghoa Indonesia (ASPERTINA). N.d. https://www.facebook. com/Aspertina/ (accessed 22 June 2020).

Budiman, Amen. 1979. *Masyarakat Islam Tionghoa di Indonesia*. Semarang: Tanjung Sari.

Budyatna, Muh. 1982. "Harapan Baru Bagi Keturunan Tionghoa". *Merdeka*, 15 January 1982.

"Bukan Sebuah Pecinan + Masjid". *Tempo*, 23 August 1980, p. 52.

Carey, Peter. 1984. "Changing Javanese Perceptions of the Chinese Communities in Central Java, 1755–1825". *Indonesia*, no. 37 (April): 1–47.

Chang, Queeny. 1981. *Memoirs of a Nonya*. Singapore: Eastern Universities Press.

Chen Dasheng (陈达生, Tan Ta Sen). 2008. *Zheng He yu Dongnanya Yisilan* 郑和与东南亚伊斯兰. Beijing: Haiyang Chubanshe.

Chen Jinghe (陈荆和) and Chen Yusong (陈育崧). 1972. *Xinjiapo huawen beimingjilu* 新加坡华文碑铭集录. Hong Kong: Chinese University of Hong Kong.

Chia, Felix. 1980. *The Babas*. Singapore: Times Book International.

———. 1994. *The Babas Revisited*. Singapore: Heinemann Asia.

Chiung Yao. 1997. *Enam Mimpi*. Jakarta: Gramedia.

Chong, Alan, eds. 2015. "Lee Kuan Yew 李光耀". In *Great Peranakans: Fifty Remarkable Lives*. Singapore: Asian Civilisations Museum. https://www. nhb.gov.sg/peranakanmuseum/~/media/tpm/document/exhibitions/english%20 gallery%20guide.pdf (accessed 25 April 2021).

Clammer, John. 1980. *Straits Chinese Society: Studies in the Sociology of the Baba Communities of Malaysia and Singapore*. Singapore: Singapore University Press.

Coppel, Charles A. 1977. "Contemporary Confucianism in Indonesia". Proceedings of the Seventh IAHA Conference, Bangkok, 22–26 August 1977, pp. 739–57. Bangkok: Chulalongkorn University Press.

———. 1981. "The Origins of Confucianism as an Organized Religion in Java, 1900–1923". *Journal of Southeast Asian Studies* 12, no. 1: 179–96.

———. 1984. "Yoe Tjay Siang: Portrait of a Syncretist". Paper presented at the Asian Association Studies of Australia Fifth Annual Conference, 13–19 May 1984 at Adelaide University. Published in *Studying Ethnic Chinese in Indonesia*, by Charles A. Coppel, pp. 279–90. Singapore: Singapore Society of Asian Studies, 2002.

———. 1986. "From Christian Mission to Confucian Religion: The Nederlandsche Zendingsvereeniging and the Chinese of West Java, 1870–1910". In *Nineteenth and Twentieth Centuries Indonesia: Essays in Honour of Professor J.D. Legge*, edited by D.P. Chandler and M.C. Ricklefs, pp. 15–39. Monash Papers on Southeast Asia, no. 14. Clayton: Monash University.

———. 2002a. "Khong Kauw: Confucian Religion in Indonesia". In *Studying Ethnic Chinese in Indonesia*, by Charles A. Coppel, pp. 228–42. Singapore: Singapore Society of Asian Studies.

————. 2002b. "Mapping the Peranakan Chinese in Java". In *Studying Ethnic Chinese in Indonesia*, by Charles A. Coppel. Singapore: Singapore Society of Asian Studies.

De Haan, F. 1935. *Oud Batavia*, vol II. Bandoeng.

Departemen Penerangan Republik Indonesia. 1963. *Baperki Supaja Mendjadi Sumbangan Besar Terhadap Revolusi Indonesia*. Djakarta.

Fatmawati. 1983. *Catatan Kecil Bersama Bung Karno* (Part 1). Jakarta: Sinar Harapan.

Geertz, Clifford. 1960. *The Religion of Java*. New York: Free Press.

Giles, Herbert A. 1900. *A Glossary of Reference on Subjects Connected with the Far East*. Originally published in Shanghai in 1900. Reprinted in 1974.

Guo Moruo (郭沫若). 1981. *Ibuku Sang Bumi* 地球, 我的母亲. Kuala Lumpur: Universiti Malaya.

Gwee Thiam Hock. 1985. *My Mother's Childhood*. Singapore: Times Book International.

"H. Abdul Karim Oey: Pengabdi Agama, Bangsa dan tanah Air". *Kiblat*, No. 2/XXX (1982): 11–13.

Heidhues, Mary Somers. 2003. *Golddiggers, Farmers, and Traders in the "Chinese Districts" of West Kalimantan, Indonesia*. Ithaca: Southeast Asia Program Publications, Cornell University.

————. 2012. "Kan Hok Hoei". In *Southeast Asian Personalities of Chinese Descent: A Biographical Dictionary*, Vol. 1, edited by Leo Suryadinata, pp. 393–95. Singapore: Institute of Southeast Asian Studies.

Heryanto, Ariel, ed. 1985. *Perdebatan Sastra Konstekstual*. Jakarta: Rajawali.

Ho Eng Seng. 1986. "Problems of Identity among the Overseas Chinese: A Historical Examination of the Baba Chinese in Penang". Honours essay for the major in social sciences, Stanford University, Department of Anthropology, June 1986.

Ishwara, Helen. 2001. *P.K. Ojong: Hidup Sederhana, Berpikir Mulia*. Jakarta: Penerbit Buku Kompas.

Jahja, Junus. [1983]. *Garis Rasial Garis Usang*. Jakarta: Badan Komunikasi Penghayatan Kesatuan Bangsa.

————. 1984. *Zaman Harapan Bagi Keturunan Tionghoa: Rekaman Dakwah Islamiyah 1979–1984*. Jakarta: Yayasan Ukhuwah Islamiyah.

————. 1985. *Muslim Tionghoa: Kumpulan Karangan*. Jakarta: Yayasan Ukhuwah Islamiyah.

————. [1988]. *Kisah-kisah Saudara Baru*. Jakarta: Yayasan Ukhuwah Islamiyah.

Jusuf, Tedy. 2015. *Kacang Mencari Kulitnya*. 2nd ed., privately published.

Kamus Besar Bahasa Indonesia. 3rd ed. Jakarta: Balai Pustaka, 2005.

Kamus Dewan. Kuala Lumpur: Dewan Bahasa, 1970.

Kewarganegaraan, Suku Bangsa, Agama, dan Bahasa Sehari-hari Penduduk Indonesia: Hasil Sensus Penduduk 2010. Jakarta: Badan Pusat Statistik, 2011.

Khoo Joo Ee. 1993. "The Straits Chinese Today". *Suara Baba: The Voice of the Peranakan Associations in Malaysia and Singapore*, no. 2 (November).

————. 1996. *The Straits Chinese: A Cultural History*. Kuala Lumpur: Pepin Press.

Khoo Kay Kim. 2007. "The Making of Malaya, 1946–1955: The Fruits of Ethnic Cooperation". In *Malaysian Chinese and Nation-Building: Before Merdeka and Fifty Years After*, edited by Voon Phin Keong. Kuala Lumpur: Centre for Chinese Studies.

Kisah Lelaki Tua dan Seekor Anjing: Kumpulan Cerita Pendek Cina Kontemporer. Jakarta: Yayasan Obor Indonesia, 1991.

Koesoemaningrat, D. 1935. "Sin Po dan Bangsa serta Pergerakan Bangsa Kita". *Sin Po Jubileum Nummer 1910-1935*. Batavia: Sin Po.

Kunjungi dan rasakan kedamaian Maitreya di pulau Batam (Pulau Batam, Maha Vihara Duta Maitreya). N.d. The text is in three languages: Indonesian, Chinese and English.

Kuok, Kenson. 2015. "Museum of the Peranakan Culture: Local and Global Impetus". In *Peranakan Communities in the Era of Decolonization and Globalization*, edited by Leo Suryadinata, pp. 115–25. Singapore: Chinese Heritage Centre and NUS Baba House.

Kwa Chong Guan. 2015. "Political Dilemma and Transformation of the Straits-born Chinese Community: The Era of Decolonization". In *Peranakan Communities in the Era of Decolonization and Globalization*, edited by Leo Suryadinata. Singapore: Chinese Heritage Centre and NUS Baba House.

Kwartanada, Didi. 2016. "Tokoh Tionghoa dalam Lembaga BPUPK dan PPK". In *Tionghoa dalam Keindonesiaan: Peran dan Kontribusi Bagi Pembangunan Bangsa*, vol. 3, edited by Leo Suryadinata and Didi Kwartanada. Jakarta: Yayasan Nabil.

Kwee Hing Tjiat. 1934. "Baba Dewasa". *Mata Hari*, 1 August 1934.

Kwee Tek Hoay. 1928. "Almarhoem Toean Gouw Peng Liang". *Panorama*, 3 November 1928, pp. 11683–85.

————. 2001. "Atsal Mulahnya Pergerakan Tionghoa yang Modern di Indonesia" (1933). Republished in *Kesastraan Melayu Tionghoa dan kebangsaan Indonesia: Empat Karya Kwee Tek Hoay*, Jilid 4, pp. 395–534. Jakarta: Kepustakaan Populer Gramedia.

Lasiyo. 1992. "Agama Khonghucu: An Emerging Form of Religious Life among the Indonesian Chinese". Unpublished PhD thesis submitted to the University of London.

Lee Kuan Yew. 2012. *My Lifelong Challenge: Singapore Bilingual Journey*. Singapore: Straits Times Press.

Lee, Peter H. 2014. *Sarong Kebaya: Peranakan Fashion in an Interconnected World, 1500–1950*. Singapore: Asian Civilisations Museum.

Leong, Trinna. 2017. "Who are Malaysia's Bumiputera?" *Straits Times*, 3 August 2017. https://www.straitstimes.com/asia/se-asia/who-are-malaysias-bumiputera (accessed 5 March 2019).

Li Chih-chu, trans. 1960. "Kalau Nasib Malang Menimpa". *Budaya* (December): 34–44.

Li Minghuan. 2000. "Batavia's Chinese Society in Transition: Indications based upon the Tandjoeng Cemetery Archives 1881–1896". *Asian Culture* 24 (June): 90–107.

Li Yuan Jin (李元瑾, Lee Guan Kin). 2001. *Dongxi wenhua de zhuangji yu Xinhua zhishifenzhi de sanzhong huiying* 东西文化的撞击与新华知识份子的三种回应. Singapore: Department of Chinese Studies, NUS and Global Publishing Co.

Liao Jianyu (廖建裕, Leo Suryadinata). 1993. "Yinni wuxia xiaoshuo gailun 印尼武侠小说概论". In *Yinni huaren wenhua yu shehui* 印尼华人文化与社会. Singapore: Singapore Society of Asian Studies.

———. 2008. *Dongnanya yu Huaren Zuqun yanjiu* 东南亚与华人族群研究. Singapore: Singapore Qingnian Shuju 新加坡青年书局.

———. 2010. *Yinni Kongjiao Chutan* 印尼孔教初探 [Indonesian Confucian Religion: A Preliminary Study]. Singapore: Chinese Heritage Centre.

———. 2014. "Youguan Xiao yucan de Yinni minzu guan yu 'huaren buzu' de yixie fansi" (有关萧玉灿的印尼民族观与 '华人部族' 的一些反思, "Some reflections on Siauw Giok Tjhan's concept of the Indonesian Nation and 'Suku Tionghoa'"). In *Xiao yucan bainian danchen jinian wenji* (萧玉灿百年诞辰纪念文集), pp. 41–63. Hong Kong: Shenghuo Wenhua jijinhui (生活文化基金会).

Liaw Yock Fang. 1995. "Lie Kimhok and the First Modern Malay/Indonesian Grammar Book". In *Southeast Asian Chinese: The Socio-cultural Dimension*, edited by Leo Suryadinata. Singapore: Times Academic Press.

Lie Kim Hok. 1884. *Malajoe Batawi*. Batawi: W. Bruining & Co.

Liem Koen Hian. 1919. "Oedang Oendang Kerakyatan Olanda". *Sinar Sumatra*, 5 February 1919.

———. 1930a. "Ka-Indonesierschap". *Sin Tit Po*, 2 April 1930.

———. 1930b. "Haloean Kita II". *Sin Tit Po*, 10 April 1930.

———. 1930c. "Haloean Kita IV". *Sin Tit Po*, 12 April 1930.

———. 1930d. "Haloean Kita V". *Sin Tit Po*, 13 April 1930.

———. 1932a. "Tiga Aliran Politiek dalam Doenia Tionghoa Peranakan". *Sin Tit Po*, 26 August 1932.

———. 1932b. "Causerie Pikiran Indonesia dan Peranakan Tionghoa". *Djawa Tengah*, 11–12 October 1932.

———. 1936. "Sekali Lagi boeat Toean Soedarjo Tjokrosisworo". *Sin Tit Po*, 25 August 1936.

Lim, Shirley. 1996. *Among the White Moonfaces: Memoirs of a Nyonya Feminist*. Singapore: Times Books International.

Lin Xiaosheng (林孝胜, Lim How Seng). 1995. *Xinjiapo huashe yu huashang* 新加坡华社与华商. Singapore: Singapore Society of Asian Studies.

Lohanda, Mona. 1996. *The Kapitan Cina of Batavia, 1837–1942*. Jakarta: Penerbit Djambatan.

———. 2009. "Menjadi Peranakan Tionghoa". In *Peranakan Tionghoa Indonesia: Sebuah Perjalanan Budaya*, edited by Lily Wibisono and Rusdi Tjahyadi. Jakarta: Intisari dan Komunitas Lintas Budaya.

Lu Hsun. 1963. *Ah So Hsiang Lin dan Cerpen-Cerpen Lain*. Singapore: Dewan Bahasa dan Kebudayaan Singapura.

———. 1984. *Lampu yang tak kunjung Padam*. Kuala Lumpur: Dewan Bahasa dan Pustaka.

———. 1989. *Catatan Harian Seorang Gila dan Cerita Pendek Lainnya*, translated by Nur Rachmi and Rasti Suryandani, edited by Sapardi Djoko Damono. Jakarta: Yayasan Obor Indonesia.

Lun Yu: Pembicaraan Confucius. Kuala Lumpur: Dewan Bahasa dan Pustaka, 1994.

Maier, Hendrik M.J. 1991. "Forms of Censorship in the Dutch Indies: The Marginalization of Chinese-Malay Literature". *Indonesia* (Special Issue: The Role of the Indonesian Chinese in Shaping Modern Indonesian Life): 67–81.

Marsden, William. 1973. *A Dictionary of the Malayan Language*. New York: Cox and Baylis. Reprinted, originally published in 1812.

"Masjid Cheng Hoo Mengapa di Surabaya?". *Komunitas*, no. 35 (October 2007): 3–4.

Meng Zi. Kuala Lumpur: Dewan Bahasa dan Pustaka, 1994.

Minzu Cidian 民族词典. Si Chuan 四川: Si Chuan Minzu Chubanshe 四川民族出版社, 1984.

Mundingsari. 1949. *Himpunan Sadjak Tionghoa*. Jakarta: Balai Pustaka.

Murali, R.S.N. 2017. "Nazri: Peranakan Chinese have the Right to pursue Bumiputera Status". *The Star*, 25 August 2017. https://www.thestar.com.my/metro/community/2017/08/25/seeking-recognition-nazri-peranakan-chinese-has-the-right-to-pursue-bumiputra-status/ (accessed 26 February 2019).

Oetomo, Dede. 1991. "The Chinese of Indonesia and the Development of the Indonesian Language". *Indonesia* (Special Issue: The Role of the Indonesian Chinese in Shaping Modern Indonesian Life): 53–66.

———. 2016. "Tionghoa dalam Perkembangan Bahasa Indonesia". In *Tionghoa dalam Keindonesiaan: Peran dan Kontribusi Bagi Pembangunan Bangsa*, vol. 1, edited by Leo Suryadinata and Didi Kwartanada, pp. 157–68. Jakarta: Yayasan Nabil.

Oey Kim Tiang, trans. 1990. *San Pek Eng Tay: Romantika Emansipasi Seorang Perempuan*. Jakarta: Yayasan Obor Indonesia.

Oey Tjeng Hien (Abdul Karim). 1982. *Mengabdi Agama, Nusa dan Bangsa: Sahabat Karib Bung Karno*. Jakarta: Gunung Agung.

Ooi, Diana. 1957. "The English-educated Chinese in Penang". Master's thesis, University of Malaya.

"Orang Tionghoa dalam Volksraad I". *Sin Po*, 1 November 1917.

Parera, Frans M. 1990. "P.K. Ojong: Intelektual yang Menganut Sosialisme-Fabian". In *Mencari Identitas Nasional: Dari Tjoe Bou San sampai Yap Thiam Hien*, edited by Leo Suryadinata, pp. 137–72. Jakarta: LP3ES.

Pratiknya, Ahmad W., ed. 1986. *Tak Semua Kakek Meilan Tak Semua Pak Ogah.* Yogyakarta: Laboratorium Da'wah.

"Profil Seorang Ulama Islam Tionghoa". *Pelita*, 2 January 1979 and 3 November 1980.

Rahman, Jamal D. 2014. "Arief Budiman: Sumbangan bagi Kritik dan Pemikiran Sastra". In *33 Tokoh Sastra Indonesia Paling Berpengaruh*, edited by Jamal D. Rahman et al., pp. 457–80. Jakarta: Kepustakaan Populer Gramedia.

Rieger, Thomas. 1989. "Roman 'Drama Di Boven Digul' oleh Kwee Tek Hoay: Sebuah Ulasan Ringkas". In *100 Tahun Kwee Tek Hoay: Dari Penjaja Tekstil sampai ke Pendekar Pena*, edited by Myra Sidharta, pp. 122–53. Jakarta: Sinar Harapan, 1989.

Risalah Sidang Badan Penyelidik Usaha-Usaha Persiapan Kemerdekaan Indonesia (BPUPKI) Panitia Persiapan Kemerdekaan Indonesia (PPKI), 29 Mei 1945–19 Agustus 1945. Jakarta: Sekretariat Negara Republik Indonesia, 1992.

Salmon, Claudine. 1977. "Writings in Romanized Malay by the Chinese of Malaya: A Preliminary Inquiry". *Kertas-kertas Pengajian Tionghoa: Papers on Chinese Studies* 1 (December): 69–95.

———. 1981. *Literature in Malay by the Chinese of Indonesia: A Provisional Annotated Bibliography*. Etudes Insulindies-archipel 3. Paris: Éditions de la Maison des sciences de l'Homme.

———, ed. 1987. *Literary Migrations: Traditional Chinese Fiction in Asia (17th–20th Centuries)*. Beijing: International Culture Publishing Corporation.

———. 2016. "Apakah Bahasa 'Melayu Tionghoa' bisa diterima?" In *Tionghoa dalam Keindonesiaan: Peran dan Kontribusi Bagi Pembangunan Bangsa*, vol. 1, edited by Leo Suryadinata and Didi Kwartanada, pp. 171–80. Jakarta: Yayasan Nabil.

Salmon, Claudine and Myra Sidharta. 2018. "Sino-Insulindian Private History Museums, Cultural Heritage Places, and the (Re)construction of the Past". *Asian Culture* 42 (December).

"Samboengan Verslag". *Perniagaan*, 16 November 1917.

Sekilas Tentang Masjid Muhammad Cheng Hoo Indonesia (Brochure). N.d.

Setiono, Benny G. 2008. "Beberapa catatan mengenai perkembangan Organisasi-Organisasi Tionghoa di Indonesia". *Kumpulan makalah masalah Tionghoa di Indonesia*, 24–25 May 2008, pp. 16–22.

Shen mai xin zhong de mimi (深埋心中的秘密, The secret deeply buried in the heart). Kuala Lumpur: 21st Century Publisher, 2008.

Siauw Giok Tjhan. 1960. "Terapi Manifesto Politik R.I.". *Star Weekly* (Jakarta), 23 April 1960.

———. 1963a. "Amanat P.J.M. Presiden Soekarno pada Kongres Nasional ke-VIII Baperki". In *Gotong Rojong Nasakom untuk Melaksanakan Ampera*, edited by Siauw Giok Tjhan. Djakarta: Baperki.

———. 1963b. "Pidato Siauw Giok Tjhan Ketua Umum Pusat BAPERKI, diutjapkan pada tgl. 14 Maret 1953 dihadapan PJM Presiden Soekarno, bertempat di 'Gelora Bung Karno'". In *Gotong Rojong, Nasakom untuk Melaksanakan Ampera*, pp. 72–84. Djakarta: Baperki.

———. 1981. *Lima Jaman: Perwujudan Integrasi Wajar*. Jakarta: Yayasan Teratai.

Siauw Tiong Djin. 1999. *Perjuangan seorang Patriot membangun Nasion Indonesia dan masyarakat Bhineka Tunggal Ika.* Jakarta: Hasta Mitra.

———. 2018. *Siauw Giok Tjhan: Bicultural Leader in Emerging Indonesia.* Victoria: Monash University Publishing.

Sidharta, Myra, ed. 1989. *100 Tahun Kwee Tek Hoay: Dari Penjaja Tekstil sampai ke Pendekar Pena.* Jakarta: Sinar Harapan.

Simposium Baperki tentang Sumbangsih apakah yang dapat diberikan oleh warganegara2 Indonesia keturunan asing kepada pembangunan dan perkembangan kebudayaan nasional Indonesia 1957, pp. 25–31.

Sixth Baba Convention, 26–27 November 1993.

Skinner, G. William, 1958. "The Chinese in Java". In *Colloquium on Overseas Chinese*, edited by Morton H. Fried, pp. 1–10. New York: Institute of Pacific Relations.

———. 1963. "The Chinese Minority". In *Indonesia*, edited by Ruth McVey. New Haven: Yale University Press.

Soeharto. 1989. *Soeharto, Pikiran, Ucapan, dan Tindakan Saya: Otobiografi seperti dipaparkan kepada G. Dwipayana dan Ramadhan K.H.* Jakarta: Citra Lamtoro Gung Persada.

Soekarno. N.d. *Baperki Supaja Mendjadi Sumbangan Besar terhadap Revolusi Indonesia.* Djakarta: Departemen Penerangan R.I.

Soetriyono, Eddy. 1986. *Kisah Sukses Liem Sioe Liong.* Jakarta: N.p.

Somers, Mary F.A. 1965. "Peranakan Chinese Politics in Indonesia". Unpublished PhD thesis, Cornell University.

Song Ong Siang. 1984. *One Hundred Years' History of the Chinese in Singapore* (with an introduction by Edwin Lee). Singapore: Oxford University Press.

Steenbrink, Karel A. 1984. *Beberapa Aspek tentang Islam di Indonesia Abad ke-19.* Jakarta: Bulan Bintang.

Suara Baba (Special Issue), November 2018.

Suara Baba: Exploring the Roots of PERANAKAN, 31st Peranakan Convention. Published in Tangerang, November 2018.

Sukisman, W.D. 1995. "Perkembangan Budaya Cina di Indonesia Dalam Kaitannya dengan Inpres No. 14/1967" [The Development of Chinese Culture in Indonesia and its Relation to the Presidential Instruction No. 14/1967]. Paper presented at Rapat PokjaInterdep Pembauran di Jakarta tgl. 23-24/1-1995 [Paper presented at the inter-departmental workshop meeting]. Sesuai Kawat Mendari No. T451.3/189 (identical with the telegraph of the Interior Minister, No. T451.3/189).

Sumardjo, Jakob. 2016. "Meninjau Kembali Sastra Melaju Tionghoa". In *Tionghoa dalam Keindonesiaan: Peran dan Kontribusi Bagi Pembangunan Bangsa*, vol. 1, edited by Leo Suryadinata and Didi Kwartanada, pp. 259–69. Jakarta: Yayasan Nabil.

Suryadinata, Leo. 1966. "Dari Sastra Peranakan ke Sastra Indonesia". In *Sastra Peranakan Tionghoa Indonesia*, edited by Leo Suryadinata, pp. 20–21. Jakarta: Grasindo.

————. 1971. *The Pre-World War II Peranakan Chinese Press of Java: A Preliminary Survey*. Papers in International Studies, Southeast Asia Series, No. 18. Athens, Ohio: Ohio University, Center for International Studies.

————. 1978. *Pribumi Indonesians, the Chinese Minority and China: A Study of Perceptions and Policies*. Kuala Lumpur and London: Heinemann Publishers.

————. 1981. *Eminent Indonesian Chinese: Biographical Sketches*. Singapore: Gunung Agung.

————. 1988. *Kebudayaan Minoritas Tionghoa di Indonesia*. Jakarta: Gramedia.

————. 1989. "Chinese Literature in Indonesia and Malay Translations: A Preliminary Study". In *Chinese Literature in Southeast Asia*, edited by Wong Yoon Wah and Horst Pastoors. Singapore: Goethe-Institut and Singapore Association of Writers.

————. 1995. "The Study of Peranakan Chinese Literature: A Preliminary Survey". In *Southeast Asian Chinese: The Socio-cultural Dimension*, edited by Leo Suryadinata. Singapore: Times Academic Press.

————. ed. 1996. *Sastra Peranakan Tionghoa Indonesia*. Jakarta: Grasindo.

————. 1998a. *Prominent Indonesian Chinese: Biographical Sketches*. Singapore: Institute of Southeast Asian Studies.

————. 1998b. "State and Minority Religion in Contemporary Indonesia: Recent Government Policy towards Confucianism, Tridharma and Buddhism". In *Nation-State, Identity and Religion in Southeast Asia*, edited by Tsuneo Ayabe, pp. 5–24. Singapore: Singapore Society of Asian Studies.

————. 2001. "Pers Melayu-Tionghoa". In *Beberapa Segi Perkembangan Sejarah Pers di Indonesia*, edited by Abdurrachman Surjomihardjo, pp. 41–75. Jakarta: Penerbit Buku Kompas. Originally published by LIPI, 1980.

————. 2002. "Peranakan Chinese Identities in Singapore and Malaysia: A Re-examination". In *Ethnic Chinese in Singapore and Malaysia: A Dialogue between Tradition and Modernity*, edited by Leo Suryadinata. Singapore: Times Academic Press.

————. 2004. *Peranakan's Search for National Identity: Biographical Studies of Seven Indonesian Chinese*. Singapore: Marshall Cavendish.

————. 2005a. "Buddhism and Confucianism in Contemporary Indonesia: Recent Developments". In *Chinese Indonesians: Remembering, Distorting, Forgetting*, edited by Tim Lindsey and Helen Pausacker, pp. 77–94. Singapore: Institute of Southeast Asian Studies and Monash Asia Institute.

————. 2005b. "Government Policy and National Integration in Indonesia". In *Chinese and Nation-Building in Southeast Asia*, pp. 81–100. Singapore: Marshall Cavendish.

————. 2005c. *Peranakan Chinese Politics in Java, 1917–1942*. Singapore: Marshall Cavendish.

————, ed. 2012. *Southeast Asian Personalities of Chinese Descent: A Biographical Dictionary*. Singapore: Institute of Southeast Asian Studies.

————, ed. 2015a. *Peranakan Communities in the Era of Decolonization and Globalization*. Singapore: Chinese Heritage Centre and NUS Baba House.

————. 2015b. *Prominent Chinese Indonesian: Biographical Sketches*. 4th ed. Singapore: Institute of Southeast Asian Studies.

————. 2016. "Lie Kim Hok: Bapak Bahasa 'Melayu Tionghoa'". In *Tionghoa dalam Keindonesiaan: Peran dan Kontribusi Bagi Pembangunan Bangsa*, vol. 1, edited by Leo Suryadinata and Didi Kwartanada, pp. 181–83. Jakarta: Yayasan Nabil.

Suryadinata, Leo, Evi Nurvidya Arifin, and Aris Ananta. 2003. *Indonesia's Population: Ethnicity and Religion in a Changing Political Landscape*. Singapore: Institute of Southeast Asian Studies.

Suryatmoko, Hari. 1984. "Prof. Dr. Tjan Tjoe Siem". *Intisari*, April 1979. Reproduced in *Zaman Harapan Bagi Keturunan Tionghoa: Rekaman Dakwah Islamiyah, 1979–1984*, edited by Junus Jahja, pp. 9–13. Jakarta: Yayasan Ukhuwah Islamiyah.

"Taman Budaya Tionghoa TMII Rampung 2010". *Kompas*, 7 February 2008. https://nasional.kompas.com/read/2008/02/07/15075732/Taman.Budaya.Tionghoa. TMII.Rampung.2010 (accessed 30 March 2021).

Tan, Bonny. N.d. "The Straits Chinese Magazine". https://eresources.nlb.gov.sg/ infopedia/articles/SIP_2015-10-19_160335.html (accessed 21 April 2021).

Tan Chee Beng. 1981. "Baba Chinese Publication in Romanized Malay". *Journal of African and Asian Studies* 22: 158–93.

————. 1988. *The Baba of Melaka: Culture and Identity of a Chinese Peranakan Community in Malaysia*. Petaling Jaya: Pelanduk Publications.

————. 1993. *Chinese Peranakan Heritage in Malaysia and Singapore*. Kuala Lumpur: Fajar Bakti.

————. 1995. "The Study of Chinese Religions in Southeast Asia: Some Views". In *Southeast Asian Chinese: The Socio-cultural Dimension*, edited by Leo Suryadinata, pp. 139–65. Singapore: Times Academic Press.

————. 1996. *Chinese Peranakan Heritage in Malaysia and Singapore*. Kuala Lumpur: Fajar Bakti.

————. 2002. *Chinese Minority in a Malay State: The Case of Terengganu in Malaysia*. Singapore: Eastern Universities Press.

————. 2004. *Chinese Overseas: Comparative Cultural Issues*. Hong Kong: Hong Kong University Press.

————. 2007. "Confucianism". In *The Blackwell Encyclopedia of Sociology*, vol. 2, edited by George Ritzer, pp. 668–72. Oxford: Blackwell Publishing.

————. 2010. "Intermarriage and the Chinese Peranakan in Southeast Asia". In *Peranakan Chinese in a Globalizing Southeast Asia*, edited by Leo Suryadinata, pp. 27–40. Singapore: Chinese Heritage Centre and NUS Baba House.

Tan, Kevin Y.L. 2020. "The King's Chinese: The Life of Sir Song Ong Siang". *BiblioAsia*, 1 April 2020. https://biblioasia.nlb.gov.sg/vol-16/issue-1/apr-jun-2020/ king (accessed 22 April 2021).

Tan Liok Ee. 1988. "Chinese Independent Schools in West Malaysia: Varying Responses to Changing Demands". In *Changing Identities of the Southeast Asia Chinese since World War II*, edited by Jennifer Cushman and Wang Gungwu, pp. 61–74. Hong Kong: Hong Kong University Press.

———. 1997. *The Politics of Chinese Education in Malaya, 1945–1961*. Kuala Lumpur: Oxford University Press.

———. 2000. "Chinese Schools in Malaysia: A Case of Cultural Resilience". In *The Chinese in Malaysia*, edited by Lee Kam Hing and Tan Chee-Beng, pp. 228–54. Shah Alam, Malaysia: Oxford University Press.

Tan Ta Sen. 1977. *Yinni wenhua lunwen ji* (Essays on Indonesian Culture). Singapore: Jiaoyu chubanshe.

———. 2014. *Cheng Ho and Malaya*. Singapore and Malacca: International Zheng He Society and Cheng Ho Cultural Museum.

Teng, Amelia. 2015. "Lee Kuan Yew Fund for Bilingualism supports another nine proposals". *Straits Times*, 20 August 2015. https://www.straitstimes.com/singapore/education/lee-kuan-yew-fund-for-bilingualism-supports-another-nine-proposals (accessed 28 April 2021).

Teo Kok Seong. 2003. *The Peranakan Chinese of Kelantan: A Study of the Culture, Language and Communication of an Assimilated Group in Malaysia*. London: ASEAN Academic Press.

Thung Ju Lan. 2015. "Peranakan Chinese Community in Indonesia and Globalization". In *Peranakan Communities in the Era of Decolonization and Globalization*, edited by Leo Suryadinata. Singapore: Chinese Heritage Centre and NUS Baba House.

Tio Ie Soei. 1951. "Pers, Melaju-Betawi dan Wartawan". *Istimewa* (Surabaja, 1 August 1951).

———. 1958. *Lie Kim Hok (1853–1912)*. Bandung: Good Luck.

Tjokrosisworo, Sudarjo. 1958. "Pertumbuhan Pers Nasional di Djawa Timur". In *Kenangan Sekilas Perdjuangan Suratkabar*, edited by Sudarjo Tjokrosisworo, pp. 214–32. Djakarta: Serikat Perusahaan Surat Kabar.

Toer, Pramoedya Ananta (1961?). *Sedjarah Modern Indonesia* (stensilan). Jakarta: Fakultas Sastra, Universitas Republika.

Tsao Hsueh Chin. 1989. *Impian di Bilik Merah* (Hung Lou Meng). Jakarta: Bhuana Ilmu Populer.

Tu Fu. Jakarta: Komite Perdamaian Indonesia, n.d. (c.1963).

"Tun Tan Cheng Lock". N.d. https://img.mca.org.my/MCA/article/bd571db3-6bb3-4483-904e-0fcd46e6edb0.pdf (accessed 22 April 2021).

Vaughan, J.D. 1879. *The Manners and Customs of the Chinese in the Straits Settlements*. Originally published in 1879. Reprinted by the Oxford University Press in 1974.

Volkstelling 1930, vol. VII. Batavia: Department van Economische Zaken, 1935.

Wahid, Abdurahaman. 1998. "Prolog: PKB Didirikan oleh PBNU". In *Pro-Kontra Partai Kebangkitan Bangsa*, edited by Munib Huda Muhammad. Jakarta: Fatma Pers.

Wahono, Riyanto D. 1997. *70 Tahun Junus Jahja: Pribumi Kuat Kunci Pembauran.* Jakarta: PT Bina Rena Pariwara. (First published in 1994.)

Wang Aiping (王爱平). 2007. "Zongjiao yishi yu wenhua chuancheng—yindunixiya Kongjiao yanjiu 宗教仪式与文化传承—印度尼西亚孔教研究" [Religious Rituals and the Inheriting of Culture: A Study of Indonesian Confucianism (*Kongjiao*)]. PhD thesis submitted to Xiamen University, Amoy, China.

———. 2010. *Yindunixiya Kongjiao Yanjiu* 印度尼西亚孔教研究 [Confucian Religion in Indonesia: A Study]. Beijing: Zhongguo Wenjiao Chubanshe.

Wang Chen Fa (王琛发). 2007. *Wei wanshi kai taiping: Chen Zhen Lu sixiang guoji yantaohui lunwenji* 为万世开太平: 陈祯禄思想国际研讨会论文集. Kuala Lumpur: MCA School of Political Studies.

Wei Yueping (魏月萍). 2004. "Huayi zuojia de malaiwen chuangzuo: kuayue bianjie de huama wenxue 华裔作家的马来文创作: 跨越边界的华马文学". *Sin Chew Jit Poh* 星洲日报, 24 December 2004.

"Wet Kerahajatan Olanda". *Djawa Tengah*, 2 January 1917.

Willmott, Donald E. 1960. *The Chinese of Semarang: A Changing Community in Indonesia*. Ithaca, New York: Cornell University Press.

———. 1961. *The National Status of the Chinese in Indonesia, 1900–1958.* Monograph Series, Modern Indonesian Project, Cornell University.

"Xinjie guohui tese yu huarenyiyuanjingyan jiaoxun 新届国会特色与华人议员经验教训". *Guoji Ribao* 国际日报, 30 May 2009.

Yang Guiyi (杨贵谊, Yang Quee Yee). 1995. "Xinma tusheng huaren wenxue de xingshuai 新马土生华人文学的兴衰". In *Dongnanya huaren fanyi wenxue yu wenhua* 东南亚华人翻译文学与文化, edited by Yang Songnian 杨松年 and Wang Kangding, pp. 32–55. Singapore: Singapore Society of Asian Studies.

Yang Ping (杨平). 2008. "Yange qufen Huaqiao huaren de jiexian 严格区分华侨华人的界限". *Kumpulan Makalah Masalah Tionghoa Indonesia* 印尼华人专题论文集, 24–25 May 2008, pp. 43–46.

Yap Sin Tian, trans. 1994a. *Kitab Klasik Confucianisme: Pelajaran Agung dan Prinsip Kesederhanaan.* Kuala Lumpur: Yap Sin Tian.

———, trans. 1994b. *Tao Te Ching: Kitab Falsafah dan Moral Taoisme.* Kuala Lumpur: Yap Sin Tian.

Ye Zhongling (叶钟铃, Yeap Chong Leng). 1994. *Chen Shengtang wenji* 陈省堂文集. Singapore: Singapore Society of Asian Studies.

Yen Ching-hwang (颜清湟). 1995. "Ch'ing China and the Singapore Chinese Chamber of Commerce, 1906–1911". In *Southeast Asian Chinese and China: The Politico-Economic Dimension*, edited by Leo Suryadinata, pp. 133–60. Singapore: Times Academic Press.

———. 2007. "1899–1911 nian Xinjiapo he Malaiya de kongjiao fuxing yundong 1899–1911年新加坡和马来亚的孔教复兴运动" [1899–1911 Confucian Movement in Singapore and Malaya]. In *Cong Lishi jiaodu kan haiwai huaren shehui bianqe* 从历史角度看海外华人社会变革 [Social Change of Chinese Overseas: A Historical Perspective], by Yen Ching-hwang 颜清湟. Singapore: Youth Book.

Yeo Kim Wah and Albert Lau. 1991. "From Colonialism to Independence 1945–1965". In *A History of Singapore*, edited by Ernest C.T. Chew and Edwin Lee. Singapore: Oxford University Press.

Yeo Siew Siang. 1990. *Tan Cheng Lock: The Straits Legislator and Chinese Leader*. Petaling Jaya: Pelanduk Publications.

Yong, C.F. 1992. *Chinese Leadership and Power in Colonial Singapore*. Singapore: Times Academic Press.

Yuen Li Fung (云里风). c.1980. *Anakku, Harapanku* (Wangzi chenglong 望子成龙). Petaling Jaya: Syarikat Penerbit Universal.

———. 1986. *Pertemuan yang dikesalkan* (Xiang feng yuan 相逢怨). Kuala Lumpur: Pelanduk Publications.

Zakir Hussain. 2012a. "Chinese Indonesians Come Full Circle". *Straits Times*, 8 June 2012, p. A22.

———. 2012b. "Jakarta Removes Racist Video, Hunts for Culprits". *Straits Times*, 26 August 2012.

Zhang Songzhi (张颂之). 2008. "Kongjiao Hui Simo huikao 孔教会始末汇考" [The Confucius Religious Society: Origins and Demise]. 文史哲 *Wen Shi Zhe*, no. 1: 55–72. https://www.rujiazg.com/article/5951 (accessed 22 January 2013).

Zhang Tai Quan. 2014. "Xiao Yucan yu 'Jue Xing'" (萧玉灿与'觉醒' Siauw Giok Tjhan and Mingguan Juexing). In *Xiao yucan bainian danchen jinian wenji* (萧玉灿百年诞辰纪念文集), pp. 134–70 (especially pp. 137–41) Hong Kong: Shenghuo Wenhua jijinhui 生活文化基金会.

Zhong Cheng Bao 忠诚报 (Jakarta), 16 August 1964.

Zhuang Huaxing (庄华兴). 2000. "Lim Swee Tin 诗歌初论". In *Nyanyian Sepi* 寂寞求音: *Lim Swee Tin* 诗选 *(1973–1998)*, by Zhuang Huaxing, pp. 119–25. Kuala Lumpur: University Malaya Chinese Studies Department Graduates Association 中文系毕业生协会.

Zhuang Qinyong (庄钦永, David Chng Khin Yong). 1998. *Maliujia, Xinjiapo huawen beiwen jilu* 马六甲, 新加坡华文碑文辑录. Taipei: Institute of Ethnology, Academia Sinica.

———. 2001. "1819–1844 nian Xinjiapo de huawen xuetang 1819–1844 年新加坡的华文学堂". Unpublished manuscript, Taipei, May 2001.

INDEX

Note: Page number followed by 'n' refers to endnote.

ABOUT THE AUTHOR

Leo Suryadinata, PhD, is currently Visiting Senior Fellow, ISEAS – Yusof Ishak Institute (Singapore). He served as Director, the Chinese Heritage Centre (NTU, Singapore, 2006–13) and was a Professor in the Department of Political Science, National University of Singapore (NUS). He was also President of the International Society for the Study of Chinese Overseas (ISSCO, 2007–13). He has published extensively on ethnic Chinese in Southeast Asia and China-ASEAN relations. His latest book is *The Rise of China and the Chinese Overseas: A Study of Beijing's Changing Policy in Southeast Asia and Beyond* (2017). In September 2018 he received a Cultural Award from Indonesia for his contribution to the study of Chinese Indonesians.